Nei Jia Quan

Nei Jia Quan

Internal Martial Arts

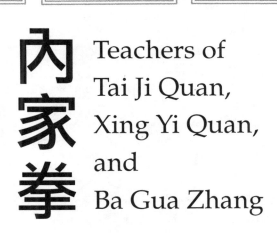

Teachers of
Tai Ji Quan,
Xing Yi Quan,
and
Ba Gua Zhang

Edited by Jess O'Brien

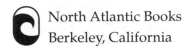
North Atlantic Books
Berkeley, California

Published by
North Atlantic Books
P.O. Box 12327
Berkeley, California 94712

Cover illustration "Guan Gong" by Eddy Deutsche
Cover and book design by Paula Morrison

This is issue number 64 in the *Io* series.
Printed in the United States of America.
Distributed to the book trade by Publishers Group West.

Nei Jia Quan: Internal Martial Arts is sponsored by the Society for the Study of Native Arts and Sciences, a nonprofit educational corporation whose goals are to develop an educational and crosscultural perspective linking various scientific, social, and artistic fields; to nurture a holistic view of arts, sciences, humanities, and healing; and to publish and distribute literature on the relationship of mind, body, and nature.

North Atlantic Books' publications are available through most bookstores. For further information, call 800-337-2665 or visit our website at www.northatlanticbooks.com.

Substantial discounts on bulk quantities are available to corporations, professional associations, and other organizations. For details and discount information, contact our special sales department.

Library of Congress Cataloging-in-Publication Data

Nei jia quan : internal martial arts teachers of tai ji quan, xing yi quan, and ba gua zhang / edited by Jess O'Brien.
    p. cm.— (Io series ; no. 64)
  ISBN 1-55643-506-1 (pbk.)
  1. Hand-to-hand fighting, Oriental—Philosophy. 2. Tai chi—Philosophy. 3. Martial arts—Philosophy. I. O'Brien, Jess, 1973– II. Io ; 64.
  GV1112.N45 2004
  796.815—dc22

2004011511

1 2 3 4 5 6 7 8 9 DATA 09 08 07 06 05 04

I dedicate this collection to all of the teachers throughout history who have made the many sacrifices necessary to develop and disseminate the treasured skills of the Chinese martial arts.

Acknowledgments

ALL OF THE FOLLOWING PEOPLE gave much time and effort to help get this book together. My heartfelt thanks goes to them and all the others who went out of their way to assist me. Thank you.

Nicole George, Kathy Glass, Stein Coriell, Jed Mefford, Matt O'Brien, Helen Rene Gale, Mike Stengl, Julio Harvey, Jason Wilson, Jason Henry, Owen Tipps, Jinn, Chad Eisner, Janet Chin, Phillip Sholtes, Joaquin Perez, Isaac Kamins, Caroline Frantzis, Beth Snowberger, Bernard Langan, Joe Davis, Eric Nomburg, Eddy Deutsche, Maija Söderholm, John Groschwitz, Hal Moser, Bob Figler, Andy Lianto, Paula Morrison, and Bryant Fong.

Table of Contents

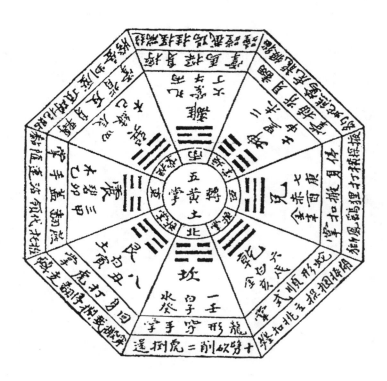

Ba Gua diagram.

Introduction

IN MY CAPACITY as the Martial Arts Editor at North Atlantic Books, I have had the opportunity to meet and train with exceptional practitioners of the Chinese Nei Jia Quan, or internal martial arts. Some of these teachers have demonstrated fascinating and unusual types of movement, as well as very persuasive and painful fighting techniques. Because my brother and I have trained in martial arts since our teenage years, I've always discussed and debated with him the value of whatever new insight or teaching that I've run across. However, I've often found it frustrating that so many aspects of the internal martial arts are difficult to convey in words. Because my level of understanding wasn't high enough, I couldn't communicate the epiphanies I was experiencing. So I decided that I would ask teachers with decades of experience to supply the answers to the questions I had. Over a two-year period I interviewed all the most seasoned practitioners and teachers that I could find. I sought out teachers during my travels, instructors with schools in my area, and visiting masters who were teaching seminars. In most cases these interviews came about as a matter of luck; I simply happened to be in the right place at the right time. In the end I gathered the best of these discussions into this book in the hopes that the explanations I couldn't give myself might be found in these selections.

The centuries-old martial arts styles of China known as "internal" have exploded in popularity in the last few decades, going from the obscure practice of a small group of dedicated practitioners to a leisure time activity enjoyed by millions. People the world over are drawn to these practices for a number of different reasons. Some seek the calmness of mind that the physical postures and sets of forms can provide; others find the unique movement exercises beneficial to their physical well-being; and still others seek out the arts' extensive repertoire of fighting techniques.

The most well-known system is Tai Ji Quan (T'ai Chi Ch'uan), which is the slow-motion series of movements practiced worldwide for its health benefits. Although its use as a fighting art is less well known, its origin is martial. Tai Ji Quan earned its place in the pantheon of Chinese styles due to the fighting abilities of early practitioners. Alongside Tai Ji, two other internal styles are usually listed: Xing Yi Quan (Hsing-I Ch'uan) and Ba Gua Zhang (Pa Kua Chang). Xing Yi is best known for its straightforward emphasis on practical fighting skills along with its physical and mental conditioning. Ba Gua is unique in its emphasis on circle walking and evasive movement drills. All three of these styles, as well as other more obscure methods such as Liu He Ba Fa, share an emphasis on training for a smooth, supple quality of movement that allows the expert to defend against powerful attacks with very little overt effort. They depend on clarity of mind and focus above and beyond reliance on muscular force. Apart from this very general commonality, the internal styles are endlessly varied and include a huge spectrum of different approaches. Some teachers demand an extremely high level of physical strength, while others use incredibly focused meditation techniques to harness the body's inherent power and reactive ability. Most fall somewhere in between, seeking a combination of mind and body to achieve health and practical self-defense skills.

No matter what aspects of the internal martial arts intrigue us, it is always fruitful to cross-train and learn from as many different perspectives as possible. With this in mind, I took the opportunity to speak with a number of different teachers across a spectrum of styles in order to view, compare, and contrast the internal martial arts from a multitude of angles. *Nei Jia Quan: Internal Martial Arts* is a collection of essays distilled from my interviews with thirteen teachers of the Chinese internal martial arts. Though presented in first-person voice, the essays have been edited for conciseness and readability. I asked roughly the same questions of each instructor, although in many cases the conversation steered into areas of my interlocutor's particular interest or expertise. Each essay is of course only a miniscule slice of a given teacher's knowledge. Regretfully, in the flow of the conversation and the limits of time, many important topics were left unexplored. Nonetheless, through these seasoned practitioners' reminiscences, observations, and hard-won training wisdom, we can see the value of a diversity of teaching styles and approaches.

This collection of casual but pointed conversations carries an undercurrent of passion for Chinese martial arts. It serves as a wide-ranging and occasionally contradictory overview of different approaches to practicing these arts, rather than a thorough and comprehensive study. There is no one way to practice "internal martial arts," and as most of these instructors will tell you, there is ultimately no difference between internal and external martial art. There are, however, some common themes and outcomes of dedicated practice. Achieving mind-body unity and fluidity of function is one. Cultivation of internal energy or power is another. And, as martial practices, self-defense is always a primary concern.

The instructors that I interviewed offer divergent opinions on the nature of *qi*; the purpose of forms training; the value of competitive tournaments; the roots of the three major internal martial arts of Tai Ji, Xing Yi, and Ba Gua; the reality or fallacy of "Death Touch"; and fascinating memories of their own training, often in Taiwan, Hong Kong, or mainland China. Many maintain the teaching as it was passed to them, honoring the traditional systems they have inherited.

The subjects of my interviews were all very gracious in sharing their teaching methods with me. I usually began by asking about the place of traditional martial arts in the modern world, followed by questions about the differences between the internal and external styles of training. I wanted to know some of their advice for beginning and intermediate levels of practice. I inquired after their teachers and their favorite fighting techniques. I asked about their understanding of the term "qi." I did my best to uncover something of what makes them practice and teach these arts, and in so doing reveal a bit about them as people.

I was reminded through conducting these interviews that the Chinese martial arts are a vast and varied study, encompassing long historical tradition, deeply rooted in Chinese culture and containing endless variation in training and application. Although self-defense is always the focus of authentic Chinese martial arts, the internal styles often utilize a more wide-ranging approach to training, including elements of meditation, medicine and spirituality that contribute to many aspect of the practitioner's life beyond fighting skill. What "internal" practitioners seek is ultimately a set of principles for achieving efficient movement and improving health and longevity.

As some of those interviewed in this book note, the people who pursue internal martial arts are often more interested in gaining knowledge about themselves than in looking for a fight. They want to learn about their body and its potential, and to get in touch with their spirit in some way. Different people have different objectives. And while the various forms of internal and external martial arts today cater to these varied goals (sometimes in a shamelessly commercial way), there is ultimately only "martial art" encompassing both inner awareness and effective fighting application. Regardless of your starting point, if you practice long enough, you learn to see both sides.

All the instructors in this book were open and generous when I met with them, and if approached with the sincere desire to learn, they will also welcome you. Even if you find something that you don't agree with in this book, you can always directly ask the source for a more detailed answer. I've found that things often appear differently in print than in person.

My intention for gathering the information in this book was to illustrate a small sample of the great variety of approaches to be found in the internal Chinese martial arts. I hope that glimpsing styles outside their own will inspire readers to double their efforts and train harder in order to achieve the deepest level of skill they can. I also hope that others are moved to publish interviews with their own teachers and grand-teachers so that we can all learn from their experiences. It is my sincere wish that other books follow to document and describe each internal style in more detail.

Most of all, I wrote this book for all my friends in the arts to enjoy, and to inspire them to head out for yet another training session. Ultimately our own practice is what matters more than the disagreements of history and theory. The joy of doing something that we love greatly is what draws us again and again to the training of the internal martial arts.

—Jess O'Brien
Berkeley, California, July 2004

Tim Cartmell

After spending more than ten years studying the internal martial arts in Taiwan and China, Tim Cartmell returned to the United States to open the successful Shen Wu Academy in southern California. His experiences fighting full-contact in Taiwan and his success in the realm of submission grappling have made him well known among a wide cross-section of the martial arts world. As well as winning in Asian full-contact competition, Mr. Cartmell has won the Pan American Brazilian Jiu Jitsu Tournament at both Brown and Black Belt levels. His books on throwing and grappling, as well as his translations from the Chinese, are very popular. Although relatively young, his dedication and long-term training set a new standard for Westerners in the internal styles.

Mr. Cartmell is well-versed in the classical martial arts of China, and although he teaches the traditional way, he trains his students as athletes, with an eye to the conditioning and strength-building practices required for competitive fighting. This sets him apart from many contemporary teachers and has helped him earn respect in numerous different venues outside the Chinese internal martial arts.

I arrived during an open mat sparring session at his school in Garden Grove. After I introduction to grappling with one of his very skilled Brazilian Jujitsu blue belt students, I asked Mr. Cartmell to show me some of his throwing techniques. Using his knowledge of timing, sensitivity, and body structure, he was able to swiftly and decisively throw me at will. Mr. Cartmell insists that training every technique in an unrehearsed fashion against a resisting opponent is the key to building skill in the martial arts. That way the body's own intuitive abilities combine with the knowledge gained through trial and error to create spontaneous combative techniques, independent of rote memorization.

Tim Cartmell
JANUARY 12, 2002

The Need for Martial Arts

AMONG PEOPLE WHO PRACTICE martial arts there's going to be a few basic groups. First there are the ones who practice self-defense. They aren't really interested in sport fighting or combat sports—they want to learn how to defend themselves. Then you get people that want to do some kind of martial art to fight in the ring. They want to compete in San Shou or kickboxing or whatever. And for a third group, it's more of a self-cultivation thing.

A lot of hobbies are just mental and you have to get exercise by some other means. But if you study a martial art, not only is it mental, it's physical as well, which keeps it interesting. People also like the whole idea that it was invented by ancient civilizations, that there's a history to it, and that there's a whole culture involved. The idea that some old Chinese guy up in the mountains made something up, or used this on a battlefield in ancient China, is appealing.

People do it even if they don't really care whether they ever get good at it, or if they are ever really going to be able to fight. A lot of people just enjoy the art of it. The Chinese martial arts have a lot of nice forms, they are good exercise, and they're more interesting than calisthenics.

Tim Cartmell practices Ba Gua.

Photo by Eric Nomburg

Tim Cartnell practices with San Soo expert Ted Sias in 1980.

You could just do jumping jacks and toe touches, but there is a whole artistry to the form, like a dance. So, there's a lot of different reasons why people practice.

I started primarily because of my background: I really only cared about fighting because I was tired of getting beat up. When I was a little kid I had heard of Karate, and right about that time the "Kung Fu" television series began. I started with Tae Kwon Do originally and did some Hapkido for a while, then I really switched over to Kung Fu. It was the beginning of the surge of Kung Fu in America. That's when I went into San Soo—it's really technique-oriented, and I wanted to learn how to fight. In all honesty, at the time I would have done any martial art that was effective; I just wanted to learn to fight better.

I went from there, and as I practiced longer and got a little older, I got more into the self-discipline of the thing. There are forms and movements that you can't do yet, and you want to work up to where you can do them—it's a sense of achievement. Or you want to improve your physical strength and endurance. Then you spar with people and, especially when you're young, when you get hit it's a blow to your ego so you want to get better. I think it teaches you toughness and self-control over time.

There's something about martial arts that I really like. It's hard to explain why people are attracted to it—why is one guy really into cars, instead of something else? You know, maybe it's better that you don't analyze it. It's just something that you gravitate toward and you really like.

The special thing about the martial arts is the idea of mind-body unity. It's not way toward the pole of being only mental or way toward the other pole of being intellectually inert and purely physical. Sports aren't generally set up like that overtly, whereas martial arts are.

If you look at the sparring part or the technique part of it, you have to be here now and pay attention or you are going to get hit. You can do forms and visualize and all that kind of stuff—that's really good when you train on your own. But when you are with other people practicing the techniques, it gives a "live" quality to the training.

Tim Cartmell teaching a seminar in 1994.

Photo courtesy of Tim Cartmell

One of my first teachers told me something that I didn't really understand until I got a little older—that there's a human need to have contact with other humans. It's a human bonding type of thing. Guys like to box around with each other, kids like to wrestle around—you don't get that with a lot of other activities. Even if you found something that was mentally challenging and physically challenging, would it involve another person, or any contact with another person? Even if you're playing tennis there's not that physical contact. A lot of people, boys especially, like contact sports. It's a primal urge. Martial arts give you an outlet where you get that kind of contact without actually having to hurt anybody.

I've heard thousands of people say this over the years: They come in to work out, they train hard and they spar and even if they've been banged up a little bit, when they leave they always say, "I feel better than I did when I came in." Whereas a person who didn't understand that would go, "You just got your ass kicked, what do you mean you feel better?" You've gotten that contact and it's a good outlet. Martial arts always has that.

Origin of the Internal Martial Arts

THE TERM NEI JIA QUAN, "internal martial arts," only came into vogue in the early twentieth century. Before that it was all just martial arts. Sun Lu Tang, Zhang Zhao Dong, Cheng Ting Hua, and some of those guys at the time got together and they came up with this idea. We can trace this back mostly to Sun Lu Tang, who did Xing Yi and Ba Gua before he learned Tai Ji. Since those were the three that he did, and that term was coming into vogue, those became the trinity of internal martial arts. If you go to China they always include Tong Bei Quan (White Ape), Liu He Ba Fa (Six Harmonies, Eight Methods), and a number of others along with the three main internal styles.

Sun Lu Tang. From *A Study of Tai Ji Quan* by Sun Lu Tang.

Because Sun Lu Tang wrote about the biggest, most popular three, they say those are the three internal styles. I talk about it like that too because everybody else does, but it's not strictly true. The reason that they coined that term—what Sun Lu Tang recognized—was that certain martial arts are based on certain principles of body use and application. What he called "internal" was a convenient label for one kind of martial arts, not only those three martial arts in particular.

You could theoretically take any martial art, modify it along the lines of those principles, and then it would have to be internal. Many people that you see doing Xing Yi, for example, are not really internal, in terms of the way it was designed. So there's really no such thing as an internal or external martial art. There's only this set of principles; we'll call them internal. There really is no internal style. There's only people doing martial arts internally or not. It's not really what style you do, it's how you do it. Now, granted, the styles that we call internal were based on those principles. But that doesn't mean that people are all going to do them that way. Just like what we call external—using force against force, a bit more tension, or whatever—if you modify those styles they would be as internal as Tai Ji. I really don't like those terms, but it's unavoidable now, you have to use them because everybody does.

It's like anything based on theory and principle, it's open to interpretation to a certain extent. I can say that one thing is correct body use, but somebody else who does Tai Ji might say, "No, that's incorrect." There's no ultimate authority that's going to come out and say that one or the other is right. Even the famous masters had different ideas.

Internal martial arts have a certain kind of body use, a certain kind of alignment, specific ways you develop power and use it in application. In a nutshell, what we call "internal" here means that you don't use force against force directly. The idea is to use your whole body power against the opponent's more vulnerable angles and weaknesses. In addition, there's always a mind-body unity component. Things like that are going

Photo by Eric Nomburg

Tim Cartmell practices Xing Yi's San Ti.

to define what we do. I can take any technique in the world and if it fits those parameters, I'll use it.

Styles and Labels

I'M NOT BOUND BY A STYLE—remember, there's no such thing as a style. If I said to you, "Show me Tai Ji," you'll start moving your arms around, but that's just you moving your arms around. Tai Ji is not a thing you can see. It's a set of principles that you apply to your own body use.

People always get caught up in the style thing, and whether they are true to their style or not. They want to kill each other over the name of something. It's just you moving around! Not that you don't have any respect for it—people put a lot of time into creating it—but remember that the names are just labels. You don't have to make a big deal out of it if somebody does something a little bit differently.

In this way people resist learning ground fighting because it's not part of their style. If you're ever in an alley and you've got somebody

Photo by Eric Nomburg

Tim Cartmell teaches grappling.

on your chest punching you in the head, the last regret you'll ever have is, "Gosh, I wish I had learned some of that stuff!" It's good to pay respect to your teachers and to realize where things came from, but don't be closed-minded because something doesn't fit into your personal world view.

Human beings are usually set up to operate within the parameters of their particular group. It makes them feel secure. They want to belong to a group, they want to feel like their group is insulated and safe, and in general they want to feel like their group is better than the other group. That's why you have different religions, different martial arts, different countries. Normally it just causes conflict: everybody's fragmented and they want to fight about it.

When it comes to the martial arts, you want to keep an open mind, and I'm not talking about collecting a zillion different techniques. I'm talking about figuring out for yourself what principles of body use work for you. You have to get away from the idea of these mysterious powers. If you use the body according to its natural design, it will be at one hundred percent efficiency. You don't morph into a Jujitsu body then change into a different body to do Xing Yi. There's only one best way to use your body. If you use a machine according to its design, you'll always be more efficient. If not, it's like trying to beat eggs with a chainsaw.

Principles of Application

A BODY IS A BODY. It's designed on a system of bony levers and it's taking place in a gravitational field. There are certain absolutes that always apply. Your body is always subject to gravity and momentum. And if somebody's hitting or pulling you, you are subject to other forces, so you've got to keep all of this in consideration: the way your bony levers are set up, and where your mass is.

For example, people always talk about using your *Tan Tien*, your *Hara*, your center, your pelvis. Why? Well, two things. Your center of gravity is there when you're standing upright. Secondly, every large muscle in your body has one end that attaches to your pelvis. If you look at how a human body is built, you'll see how it should be used. A human body is big in the middle and skinny on the ends. That's showing that the muscles in your arms and legs are to guide power, while the big muscles in your center and back should be generating the power. That's true for anything—it's true if you are pushing a car, hitting a baseball, or practicing martial arts.

When you come up with the principles of body use, they are going to be basically absolute. Then you can come up with principles of application. Let's start by assuming a bigger, stronger guy can always beat up a smaller, weaker guy of equal skill. That doesn't take any training. The definition of a martial art is an art designed for the smaller, weaker person to overcome, or at least defend themselves against, a bigger, stronger person. This is what I think all martial arts originally started from. Or else they wouldn't have been arts, they would have just been street fighting tricks.

So then you have to say, "How do I accomplish that?" Once again, if you use force directly against force, by definition the greater force

Tim Cartmell grappling with Liang Ke Quan in 1992.

will always win. So that cannot be one of your principles. If I'm smaller and weaker I want to use my body to maximum effect, which means correct body use. If I can get the right angle, lever, or position and I use one hundred percent of my body force against one of your weaker angles, I can overcome you because I am literally stronger than you at that point. If we go toe to toe, that's force against force, and I can never win because you are bigger than me.

Now I say, "You're bigger and stronger than me—how am I ever going to get to those angles?" Well, I'll need to be more sensitive than you. Because I'm not going to be able to force myself to that angle. If I could force myself to that angle I could've just knocked you over anyway. Now I have to bring in the sensitivity factor. I use things like push hands drills to learn how to neutralize force, and how to find the right rhythm and follow it. To be able to out-maneuver you and keep you from controlling my center until I can get a better angle or position I need sensitivity. Once I line up with your center I can apply my force.

That's why you push hands and all those types of things. This is where things get more complicated. What's the definition of force? There's all different kinds of force. If I was really, really strong I could grab you and crush your bones. That's OK. If I were that strong, I wouldn't be talking about this. But we're still going back to our original definition, assuming that I'm not as powerful as you. So what's correct body use to overcome a stronger person?

Zheng Ti Jing, Whole Body Power

WHEN I THINK OF BODY USE, I'm going to be potentially more successful if I use my entire body's power at all times. Every time I make any kind of a movement, defensive or offensive or otherwise, if I use my entire body force, I'm going to have a greater chance of success. So you have to figure out, what's whole body power? There are a couple of ways to think about it. I'm not going to use what the Chinese call *Jyu Bu Li*, "sectional power." That means I just use one part, like I just use my triceps to punch or I just use my forearms to grip. I'm going to use what's called *Zheng Ti Jing*, "whole body power." That implies using my entire body mass, my entire weight in every movement. That's one definition of it.

Say you're lying on the ground and I want to pin you. If I laid my arm across you, how much is that going to do? To get a better pin I add my arm and my shoulder, and pretty soon I've got my entire body lying on you. It's simple if you think about it that way. It would be harder to push me off if you had to lift my entire body weight like a bench press than if you just had to lift my arm off. So, I'm going to use my entire weight.

In Xing Yi Quan you step every time you hit to bring your entire mass into play. Where's your center of mass? In your hips with all the big muscles. Not only is the force driven by the big muscles, but you need to move the mass forward with it so you get whole body mass be-

Photo by Eric Nomburg

Tim Cartmell practices Xing Yi's Pi Quan.

hind it. Secondly, I need to align my frame correctly.

Imagine a skeleton with all its connective tissue. Connective tissue acts like rubber bands between the bones. If you line the bones up correctly and you put pressure on them, all the connective tissue is going to stretch a little bit. Just like if you compressed a spring, when you release it you get the spring's power. The better lined up you are, the more tension you can put in those springs, the more spring back you are going to get. When people talk about *peng jing* and ward-off power, that's the kind of thing they're talking about.

When pushing a car, anybody, without any training at all, will lock their arms, bend from the hips, and push with their legs. That's how you naturally push a heavy object. You don't walk up to a car in a parallel stance and push it with your triceps; you lock your arms and push from your center. You want to line up your structure correctly. You're going to use the muscles in the center of your body mostly, and you're going to try and get your whole mass into play every time. That's correct body use. It also conserves energy because I'm not exhausting individual muscles.

All these things coming into play is what I would call "internal." Really, I wouldn't want to say that's internal; I would rather say that's martial arts. It should be all martial arts! If you're not doing that, it's not really an art. Granted, in certain situations you're not going to have the perfect set-up. You have to do the best you can.

Rhythms and the Application of Force

THE NEXT THING IS, how do you apply your force correctly? My definition of coordination is correct rhythm. Everything has to be done with a correct rhythm. When you hit a baseball you have to have the correct sequence of movements through your body. You sink your weight, you put a potential base out, you drive your hips through, and the last thing to go is the bat. You get that rhythm through your body and swing that bat. If you just clubbed the ball it wouldn't go very far. In that sense, rhythm is power. Like ballet dancers, who use correct timing so they can leap while conserving energy.

If I had you walk a mile, normally you'd think it was no problem. But if I had you take a long step then a short step and shuffle along, you'd be exhausted in a hundred yards. Because there's no rhythm there, it wastes energy. If you are planning on fighting with someone, first you learn rhythm by yourself when you're doing forms. Forms are like dancing—you are teaching yourself to move in the correct rhythm with correct alignment, using the correct muscles in the correct sequence. Then you learn to apply that to someone else.

Push hands, wrestling, and sparring all teach me to keep my own body rhythm, my own alignment, my own structure, my own balance. I need to connect to you and in a way dance with you, until I can catch your rhythm. If I can become the dominant center, I can do anything I want with you. It doesn't matter how big and strong you are.

When I'm throwing you, you don't feel a lot of force, you don't feel a lot of anything; we're kind of moving around and suddenly you fall. That's internal. If you are good at Sambo, if you are good at Judo, if you are good at Western wrestling, if you are good at Ba Gua, if you are good at Tai Ji, if you are good at whatever, it's the same feeling. It's just expressed through different techniques or else within the constraints of the rules of the venue at hand. It's the same as when I box: my correct body rhythm will give me maximum power. By flowing with your rhythm I will get maximum impact because I can borrow your force.

Part of that "borrowing force" idea is that it's easier for me to spend your energy than to spend my own. Endurance becomes a huge factor. Most fights aren't over in two or three seconds with the guy lying on the ground dead or out. A lot of fights go on for minutes. Eventually you're pulled apart by third parties and you're both beat up. If the other guy is bigger and stronger than you, and you have the endurance to be evasive and outlast him, then you have a chance of at least escaping. If you blow your energy by doing non-effective things right off the bat, you'll lose. Anybody that's done a combat sport like boxing, wrestling, or Jujitsu knows that the first person who loses his wind loses the fight, regardless of the level of skill.

The correct rhythm not only gives you maximum power, it helps you conserve energy so you know when to use force and when not to. You have to be in good shape too. The stronger you are, the better—I'm not going to lie to you. All things being equal, if you ever get in a bad fight or a bad position, a little extra strength might save your life. It's important to have decent flexibility and as much strength as you think you can develop for the things you're going to do. It doesn't mean you have to be able to bench press a ton of weight, but for the kind of things you're going to do you need to have some strength. If you're going to grapple you need to build some isometric strength and some toughness in your body. You've got to get thrown and hit. You need to have wind especially—you have to have good endurance, as much as you can get.

Xing Yi Training in Taiwan

THE AMOUNT OF CONDITIONING you do depends on the school, and whether you are training to fight. If you go to some of the older masters in the park, that's one thing, but at the Xing Yi school that I was in we did about an hour of conditioning each class, including a hundred push-ups. The ground exercise set we did is called *Fu Hu Gong;* most of the exercises are taken from Judo, actually. Xu Hong Ji and his teacher Hong Yi Xiang did Kodokan Judo when they were kids. We did a lot of good conditioning on the ground, *Tien Gan* (whole body power exercises), a lot of stand-up conditioning, drills with the

pads, and we hit the bag. After that we did forms, and then sparred with protective gear on.

Everybody had to be in good shape because we fought in full-contact tournaments. Nobody has false illusions when they fight. You can wave your hands around all day and try to cultivate your *qi* and do all that, then when you get on the mat with a guy that's well trained you'll get your ass kicked. Or you'll just run out of gas. That's the reality of a real fight. Even in the schools that are a little more what you would call traditional, we'd practice in low stances— it was really hard training. There's no way around hard training if you really want to fight. All those pie-in-the-sky promises are a lot more prevalent around here than in Taiwan. You can't learn to fight unless you are regularly sparring

Tim Carmell practices Xing Yi pad training.

Photos by Eric Nomburg

with contact. You can't. At most you can learn some basic self-defense tricks. I don't know everything, but I've learned from my experiences that non-cooperative contact sparring is the key to real fighting ability.

I did a lot better in the fighting tournaments than I would have done untrained, but ring fighting was nothing like when I was training in the *dojo*. I had the mindset to fight already because I had fought since I was a little kid, and that really helped. Some of the "deadly," theoretically lethal techniques came in handy, but there were some bad fights, and I feel like I got more real ability in a year of training in Xing Yi with sparring than I got from years of doing other martial arts that were too deadly to spar. Does that mean Xing Yi is so superior to the other styles I did? No, technically it wasn't that superior. It was the training method, it was because we sparred—it's the only way you're going to find out what you can really do under pressure. It's the only way your body's going to get used to the contact, your brain's going to get used to the fear, and even then it's never going to be as intense as a real fight, I guarantee that.

I tell my students, when you fight in the ring, the goal is to win. When you fight in the street, there is only one goal in your head and that's to escape. It's not your job to punish them, that's the court's job. If a guy attacks you and you can duck, push him down, and run out of the alley or out of the bar, and get in your car and go, you can escape unharmed. They might call you names but that was smart. If you have to beat him half to death to get away, then you have to, but the goal is to escape. If the guy calls you names, you say, "Fine" and you leave, you win.

Sparring

THERE ARE FOUR BASIC THINGS that you learn from full-contact training. To begin with, you're not going to get the mindset of what it's like to be under real pressure unless you spar, and you're not going to get the experience of what it's like to hit a guy and get hit back unless you spar. You're not going to get the physical ability you need unless you train hard and spar. The fourth thing down the list is technique, and you're never going to know if your techniques work unless you spar.

In the hierarchy of things you need to survive in a real fight, number one is mindset. You could be the baddest-ass guy in the world, but without the will to fight, you're going to lose. Secondly, experience goes a long way. I've read the surveys and, statistically speaking, people that do contact sports—hockey and football—will almost always do better in their first street fight than guys that do martial arts. They are used to hard contact and getting banged up. They know that feeling, and they go right back and start swinging. They have experience with contact. So, short of getting into bar fights all the time, which is not a good idea, you'll need some experience of pain and resistance. Third is physicality. If you don't have the strength and the flexibility, and especially the endurance, you'll lose. Fourth is technique, because you can't apply technique without the first three.

Some people teach unrealistic techniques they have never applied against real resistance. They're living in dream world. And sparring is not perfect, it's not as intense as a real fight, but it's a lot closer than having a guy run at you and throw a rehearsed punch, while you pretend to strike lethal targets you've never really hit.

Again, it's not the art *per se,* it's how you do it. It's not that one art is better than another; it's the training method, whether they train realistically. I can teach anybody off the street how to throw you with no effort in about fifteen minutes. Can they do a throw right away for real? No. Why not? Because nobody will just stand there to let you throw them. Everybody in the street is giving a hundred and ten percent effort trying to mess up your techniques or do their techniques on you or hit you back or throw you or choke you. If you're not trained to set up your techniques against resistance, it's not realistic.

Grappling Arts

PEOPLE FROM CHINA know the value of grappling arts, but for some reason here in the United States many people don't seem to get this. Tai Ji is something like eighty percent wrestling, twenty percent striking. Does push hands look like boxing or wrestling? Wrestling! The reason most of the originators of internal styles gravitated toward the grappling portions of their art—like Judo did, like Shuai Jiao did, like Sambo did, like Ba Gua did, is that you can practice grappling moves ninety-nine percent the same as they will be used in a street fight.

If we are grappling on the ground and I get you in an arm bar, the only difference between that and a street fight is that I wouldn't stop when you tapped. And you are tapping because it's about to break.

Photo by Eric Nomburg

Tim Cartmell teaches grappling techniques.

Of course you can also learn to use striking styles for real. Any boxer, any Thai boxer, anybody that does kickboxing, can really hit and kick you. But you've always got to tone it down a little bit. If you go into a sensible boxing gym, even though you have head gear and a chest protector on when you're boxing, you're still not trying to hit each other as hard as you possibly can all the time.

Striking Arts

IF YOU'RE EVER IN THAILAND, go watch a Thai boxing camp. They've got a guy with Thai pads on his arms, and he's like the human punching bag—he's got guys kicking him a hundred percent, over and over. They're also working out and hitting the bag. Then when they spar it looks like play fighting; they barely touch each other. Why? Sparring without gear on is to teach you timing and set-ups. You never make any hard contact, because you can't afford to get hurt. If you're getting hurt sparring, you can never fight in the ring! You bet your ass they can fight—they can fight as well as just about anybody else in the world when it comes to stand up. How do they learn to do it? By hitting a guy with gear on for power and doing their non-cooperative stuff softly for timing.

Muay Thai.

Photo courtesy of Matt O'Brien

The point is, you can learn to fight striking, but it's never going to be as close to reality as grappling styles. Throwing and submissions are going to be closer because you can do them, then stop when they tap, and you throw the guy, who knows how to fall, on a soft surface. You need to be a little protective, like when I threw you sometimes I kind of held your head; it would be easier to just let you fall hard. You need to get hit hard sometimes, but you still have to have safety considerations, you still have to wear gloves when striking. Even then, you can get knocked out with a glove. But you've got to do those things, you've got to have contact.

Sport Fighting and Internal Principles

I F YOU READ the original Judo documents, what Jigoro Kano actually wrote, you wouldn't know that you weren't reading the Tai Ji classics—they're virtually the same. The *Ju* in Judo is *Rou* in Chinese; it's the word that people translate as "Soft." It doesn't mean soft like Jell-O. You're always halfway between hard and flaccid. Rou is like bamboo, or like grass. Rou is flexible, you have structure and strength, you yield and snap back, that's the idea of Judo. Ju means to be pliable, to use the opponent's strength against him, have a superior angle, all those things that the Chinese recognize as what we now call internal.

These principles should be present in sport fighting as well. They talk about using the lower abdomen, sinking your weight, not using force against force, and using whole body power. Read Jack Dempsey's book *Championship Fighting*—it's the best book on Xing Yi striking mechanics you could ever read and it's about Western boxing. It's about how to move your mass, how not to use force against force, so if you're talking about what I would actually call a martial art, they're all based on these principles. It just depends on how you do them.

People wonder why the internal martial artists aren't in the competitive fighting scene. Well, you don't see it because they generally don't train for that. Most of the people who call themselves internal martial artists don't condition or train realistically. They are either training for *qi* power or health or magical power, they're not really training for martial arts. These days you have to learn ground fighting as well. You can't fight a cross-trained fighter without ground skills because odds are, at one point or another, you are going to go to the ground. You can use internal principles on the ground as well, but you have to learn to grapple.

Most of these internal guys don't spar hard, they don't cross-train with other good guys, they don't know how to grapple, it's just the way it is. They can make excuses for the rest of their lives but they are living in denial. I grappled with a Brazilian black belt yesterday. I spar with kick boxers, guys that do shoot fighting. I train with all these different guys and I use the internal principles that I believe are correct. I train with all different kinds of people because I'm not bound by some style. Competent fighters from any style can teach you a great deal.

Effortless Combat Throws

Sometimes after a really clean throw I've had people get up and say, "You know, I didn't feel anything!" I'm like, "No big deal, I just got a good throw." One guy came in and said he did some Ba Gua and asked if I would do Fa Jing on him. I said, "Well, you have to hold a pad." And he's like, "No, I can take it." But I had him hold a big pad anyway. He started here and he landed there on his head. He got up and he never came back. One of my friends said, "Good job, Tim, he'll never come back." I said, "What am I supposed to do? If I didn't hit him hard he'd say I had no power, and I hit him for real and now he's scared!" People don't expect you to be able to hit that hard from such a close distance. It's just a skill, although it's something that people aren't used to seeing.

Fa Jing is a very useful skill developed in Chinese martial arts. But anyone can learn to do it; it's skill acquired over time, it's *gung fu*, not some sort of trick. It's no more mysterious than if you let a 120-pound Thai boxer kick you in the leg one time. You'll swear to God that there's no way that little guy could hit so hard!

Most of the throws in Xing Yi are called *Kao Die*, which means "knock-downs." Xing Yi doesn't usually teach big reaping throws and flips; it uses something closer to arcing throws. Your feet stay in place and your head goes down. In the Cheng Ting Hua Ba Gua styles, because Cheng Ting Hua was a wrestler, you've got more of what people think of as

Photo courtesy of Tim Cartmell

Tim Cartmell demonstrates a throwing technique.

throws, like grand amplitude or spectacular throws—big flips like when I throw you over my back, big fireman's carry type throws.

There are different focuses merely because that's how different styles develop. A lot of guys are true to their style and would never cross-train, yet their style was invented by a guy who cross-trained. You can't invent a "new" style without practicing a variety of others first. Every new style is invented by one guy who cross trained then came up with a new synthesis. It depends on your background. If your background is Aikijujitsu and Kenjitsu, you make up Aikido. If your background is walking in circles and palm changes and wrestling, you come up with Cheng Ting Hua Ba Gua. If your background is fighting with a lance on the battlefield, and you learn hand-to-hand combat, you come up with Xing Yi.

Cheng Ting Hua came up with a lot of grand amplitude throws because he was into Shuai Jiao. Yin Fu studied with the same teacher, so why does Yin Fu style look different? It's still Ba Gua, still based on the same principles, but he did Shaolin Lohan Quan. Their take is a lot more knock-downs, more striking, but it's still Ba Gua. In terms of throws, you need to understand the principle, it's like giving someone a fish or teaching them to fish. If you're always memorizing techniques and you're always trying to get your technique in faster than the other guy, it's very difficult to be spontaneous in sparring.

Yin Yu Zhang. From *Simplified Ba Gua Zhang* by Yin Yu Zhang.

Spontaneous Technique

COMBAT SPORTS, and of course real fighting, are completely spontaneous. You've got to be able to do your techniques without thinking about them constantly. When you learn to do the techniques against a cooperative partner, you go, "OK, I grab him here, I tilt him here, I sweep him here." But when you're fighting it's got to be based on feeling. You've got to practice until your own body keeps its rhythm without having to think. Principles like "Don't cross your feet!" and "Don't lean over too far, don't break your posture!" have to be a given from doing forms when there's no pressure on you.

The practice of pre-arranged forms is the *gung fu* of understanding yourself, learning to control your own body and your own rhythm when you move. That's why boxers shadowbox. They're not getting any more power—for that they'd be hitting a heavy bag. Dempsey said that, besides sparring, shadowboxing is the most important drill. Because you learn to move your own body and get rhythm. Then you've got to do drills like push hands, drills that are a little more controlled and slowed down, so you get a feeling for the opponent's body. You learn how to match his rhythm, keep him from controlling

you, learn to control him, get a better angle—that's what push hands and set drills are for. When I'm sparring, I never think of a set technique, ever. It just comes to me intuitively. I want to dance with you in a certain rhythm, I want to control the momentum of the dance, and then dominate your center and make you fall down.

There's a feeling—it's called the "ground sense" in wrestling—sort of like when you're driving a car and you

Photo by Eric Nomburg

Tim Cartmell teaching grappling.

can automatically maneuver. I get a feeling for where my dead angles are, where my weak angles are, and where yours are at all times. That's the first thing, because I'm looking at you as a body, a mass. Even if you get a better position than me, I know what you can do in those positions from experience and I keep my weight in one of your weak angles so you can't lift me. Then I wait for you to move and I sweep your foot and you go down.

One of the best things to start with is to know where your dead angles are in relationship to his. You can do any good technique according to this strategy: throw the opponent to his dead angles, know where yours are, and don't let him catch them. Learn how to flow with him and make him follow those angles, and he will fall with almost no effort if you do it correctly. If you get your momentum flow matched with his, you can dominate it, you can throw him with his own force. That's an effortless throw.

Photo courtesy of Tim Cartmell

Tim Cartmell practicing Ba Gua with Luo De Xiu in 1992.

Ba Gua Zhang Throwing

THERE AREN'T THAT MANY good Ba Gua guys anywhere, even in Beijing. Not many can fight and most don't know a whole system. I looked around for a long time and finally met Luo De Xiu. He had a lot of background in Xing Yi and other stuff, but his Ba Gua system is complete. In all honesty, is the Gao style superior to other styles of Ba Gua? No, they're all good. Luo has a complete style, and I wanted to learn it.

I like the Cheng Ting Hua method because I like to throw. Throwing is a superior way to fight when you are overpowered, as I learned when I was a kid. A fight can be over in one move basically, one hip throw. Not that a throw is your only

Tim Cartmell demonstrates a Ba Gua throw.

Photos by Eric Nomburg

option, but almost all fights will inevitably end up in the clinched position: either I'll be hitting you and you'll grab me out of pure self-preservation reflex, or vice versa. Or you just get close and you have a chance to throw. So you'll notice that most combat sports that start off as complete martial arts gravitate toward the throw. Judo has striking, Judo has ground fighting, but you win on the throw. Sambo's the same way. Shuai Jiao originally had striking and ground fighting, but they took all that out and went for the most important thing, the throw.

I got into Tai Ji because there's a lot of projecting and grappling. I learned Xing Yi first because I ran into a good teacher and I liked the striking as well, which you have to learn. When I found Ba Gua I thought it was great—there's a lot of good throwing, and a lot of principles for out-maneuvering the opponent. Over time I started to get some ideas. Not that these are secrets, a lot of people have come up with these principles. I try to be concise on those things and come up with my own way of explaining it, but I by no means invented it. I just wanted to be able to teach it to people in six months instead of five years.

You have to be well-rounded in all ranges. We do a lot of kick-boxing with gloves on. We also spend a lot of time on the take-downs, with a gi and without. We do ground fighting, and weapons defenses. You've got to have some basic ideas, or at least respect weapons enough to know that you need to run away if you can, or get another weapon.

If you have enough time to practice everything, spend any extra time you have on standing wrestling. In sport grappling we do a lot of sacrifice throws, because you want to go to the ground and wrestle with him. On the street you don't want to go to the ground, period. As much as I love to wrestle on the ground, it's the last place you really want to be in a street fight. In Judo you can't win on a sacrifice throw, because they reward what would be the best thing in a combat situation: slamming the guy really hard on the ground while staying on your feet so you are really mobile and you can get away or do whatever. I have my guys do a lot of standing wrestling. That's my take on it from my own experience and what I've seen. Ba Gua has the big theory on throws, the crossing, the angles, and how to enter with the strikes.

Wrapping, slapping, whipping, and chopping are all Ba Gua techniques that lead into the take-down. Strike him a few times and then go for the throw, this goes for Xing Yi and Tai Ji too, they've got a lot of really nice evasive entries. The entry and the set-up are the hardest part of any technique, striking or throwing.

The Entry and the Set-Up

T HE INITIAL ENTRY is very important, and then once you're in the push hands clinching position, again, you need to match their rhythms, dominate their center, and then take them down. Those are the difficult things. Once you've dominated their center, then you can throw anybody, same as if a guy just stood there and let you. In order to get to that point, you need non-cooperative partners. I got a lot out of push hands, because when we pushed hands we tried to throw and hit each other. Making the guy step back one step is probably not doing a lot. For beginners it's OK, but eventually you've got to push the limits.

When we do San Shou, or "sticky hands," we strike with a medium amount of pressure, but I don't consider anybody done until they've thrown the other guy. Most of the San Shou movements should end up with the guy on the ground. You can whack him on the

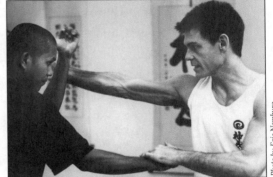

Photo by Eric Nomburg

Tim Cartmell demonstrates a Ba Gua opening technique.

way down, but I primarily want you to take him down in the flow. That's what really helps when you fight, not just slapping him a little. You have to hit, but in a lot of push hands you just shove the guy back a step. When you see real push hands in Mainland China, like the Chen Village push hands, it's done on the *lei tai*, the platform. You get points for throwing them off the *lei tai* or onto the canvas. Tai Ji is like Shuai Jiao without a jacket on. The strikes are secondary to the throws, projections and *chin na*.

Gao Style Ba Gua Zhang

THE GAO STYLE OF BA GUA has a lot of material in it. Gao Yi Sheng did Hong Quan and Xing Yi Quan first, and those martial arts are incorporated into it. In classic Ba Gua, you never close your hand, but many of the straight line forms from Gao style end up with a Beng Quan or some kind of strike. I think what Gao Yi Sheng did was take the best of all the things he learned and kept it in the style under the Ba Gua format. Sun Lu Tang mastered Xing Yi first, then learned Ba Gua Zhang from Cheng Ting Hua. He tried to keep his Ba Gua very pure and didn't incorporate so much Xing Yi. So it's a little bit more elegant in that way. There is only Single Palm Change, Double Palm Change, and eight palm changes, so there are ten forms total in Sun's system. That's it, there's no straight line forms, there's no supplementary forms, everything comes from those circular forms.

Gao Yi Sheng's straight line forms are really remedial Ba Gua, for those that can't get it from the circle forms. In the old days you practiced the circle form to learn the specific *Jing*, and using this movement as a base you could do numerous different combinations. The straight line forms are basically like the notes they took and then codified, so they could remember the applications. The essence is in the circle forms, but straight line forms help you remember the techniques and practice them.

The Gao style has a little bit bigger movements, and a lot of moves are done with more overt power. Sun Lu Tang was a hundred and forty pounds, a little guy, so his Ba Gua is a little bit tighter, a little bit quicker, a little more evasive, a little more spinning. Again, both are from the same original teacher; both are equally good as Ba Gua styles.

Forms Training

INTERNAL STYLES ARE SET UP to train you systematically, if you get a good teacher. There should be a hierarchy of training. You begin with how to stand correctly. You do basic movements over and over to build up power. You learn the footwork that makes the forms, and from those forms you go to the combined sets, or whatever forms you have to learn techniques from.

There's a certain reason you are doing a form, everybody knows that. Unfortunately, many martial artists don't know what that reason is. They're going along learning how to hit and kick a guy, but that's never the reason to practice forms. Ba Gua is a little higher-level conceptually than a lot of other martial arts, and that could work for you or against you. It depends on what you want to practice.

A palm change, for example, is not a bunch of movements that you break down into techniques. Rather, it's a flow of momentum and rhythm. Most of the sophisticated martial arts sets are generic whole-body movements that teach you to move in a certain rhythm. Then you have whole body power throughout that wave of force. If I learn the Single Palm Change correctly, I will have the right rhythm and power in a horizontal flow of momentum and I can use it in an

Tim Cartmell practices Ba Gua.

Photo by Eric Nomburg

almost infinite number of ways. I can come up with all kinds of techniques based on that principle.

Here's where the problem comes in. Although forms are not techniques, you've got to teach techniques from the forms. I have to teach you technique, so I say, "Look, this strike is from this part of the form, this is the same rhythm." But if you get caught up in the mentality of "Single Palm Change is a backhand to the face, and a head pull and a sweep," you're never going to be very good at it.

Sun Style Ba Gua Zhang

LOOK AT THE SUN STYLE for a good example. The Single and Double Palm Changes are the nuclei of the style. All eight palm changes are based on them. If you want to do Ba Gua, you ought to fix your parameters—focus on developing whole body power, good alignment, and all that stuff we talked about.

If you figure out that what you want to do is to be evasive and be able to spin, you turn to Ba Gua. Ba Gua only does two things: you orbit around a center, or you are the center and everything goes around you. When I walk around the circle I am orbiting, and when I am doing my palm change I am the center.

Along those parameters I can make up a million movements. But they have to be things that are relative to actual technique. My technique is based on out-maneuvering and spinning, so what are the two basic ways you can spin? Horizontally and vertically. Everything else is just an angle off of them. Oblique is just halfway in between. So you begin with spinning horizontally. Ba Gua is primarily a horizontal martial art, because we naturally spin that way. Single Palm Change in the Sun style is one hundred percent horizontal energy. You wrap up, then you unwrap. The Double Palm Change is vertical. You start out horizontal, then you go up and you make a vertical movement and you go out. Everything else is a variation of those two.

Sun Lu Tang
demonstrating
Ba Gua.
From *A Study
of Ba Gua Zhang*
by Sun Lu Tang.

Ba Gua *Jing*

WHEN YOU ARE PRACTICING, you are looking for the *Jing*. *Jing* is trained force, it's the flow of momentum that you're looking for. It's the correct sequence in the flow of momentum, the rhythm through your body that you can apply to something else. In Chinese terminology, you can't *Fa Jing*, or emit force, out into nothing. By definition, you can't have force without resistance. If I shoot a bullet in the air, how much force does it have? Zero! It has no force until it hits something. You can't measure force without resistance. It's one of the keys to internal movement. If I never accept any of your force, you don't have any.

Force is an interesting thing to study. *Fa* means to issue, *Jing* is trained force. People can't *Fa Jing* into the air. What they're actually doing is developing force and hitting themselves with it by tensing up and jerking back. You can practice the root of the *Jing*, you can practice the movement in the air, but you can't *Fa Jing* into nothing. You *Fa Jing* into a pad or a bag or somebody else. When you are learning these things, you're learning that the rhythm is in the form.

Although you can't measure force without resistance, it goes both ways. You can't put any force into me if I don't accept it. You can't stop my force if you don't feel it coming. That's why it's possible to throw someone and they don't feel it coming. If I catch your rhythm, you still think you're doing what you want, and then suddenly you're on your back.

Photo by Eric Nomburg

Tim Cartmell practices Ba Gua.

When my whole body is behind every individual part, that's an internal martial art. In Ba Gua I've got horizontal power, I've got vertical power, and then I've got variations of that. Within the confines of the chosen rhythms it's possible to make up all kinds of cool forms that are useless. But the old masters who already knew how to fight figured out a principle that they thought would work better, and modified what they did around it. Then within the same style it kept happening and new branches formed, like Sun Lu Tang and Gao Yi Sheng's styles.

If you want to be good at Ba Gua, you need to understand why you're doing it, what it's based on, what the principles are, and as you do it you need to be looking for the right things. I'm not doing the Single Palm Change going, "Back chop! Finger poke! Throw!" I'm concentrating on whether I'm feeling the right rhythm of momentum through my body. I'm checking my balance, I'm dealing with the two outside forces of momentum and gravity.

Mind-Body Unity

THE FORMS ARE NOT TECHNIQUES. Development of correct rhythm and whole body power are what the circle forms are for. Once you have that, you start using images of resistance, imagine you are moving through a thicker than air medium. I check my students to see that in whatever direction their force is coming out, they are immovable. The force is transiting through their bones into their feet. Which means it will come out their feet and at whatever they're aiming at, that's what forms help you to do. You begin to build mind-body unity, controlling yourself to a greater degree.

The foundation of mind-body unity is that you're paying attention. You know why most people lose fights? Because they daydream, they're in denial. You know why they are in denial? Because they are scared shitless. It's in that sequence. They're not thinking about their girlfriend or dinner when they're daydreaming—they're thinking "I hope he doesn't hit me! Damn, I hope he stops!" They're not in the moment, they're off someplace else hoping something else will happen. Most people get their ass kicked because they're in denial. This is the good thing about forms. Why did they make forms long in the old days, like the Tai Ji forms? Because the longer you can keep your intent awake and mind-body unified and focus on your movements, the stronger your mind is, the better chance you have of winning a fight.

The fighting mentality is not aggression *per se*. Mind-body unity can overcome aggression. To build that unity I pay close attention when I'm training. You can take techniques apart and do shadow boxing and visualize it, and the Ba Gua Zhang straight line forms are a good example of that. With those I can analyze where I'd be hitting someone or throwing him, or grabbing him, and so on. But if you want to practice specific strikes, the best way is to hit a heavy bag and just imagine it's a guy. Or have someone hold a pad and hit him with full force. Then when you're sparring with someone you focus in and pay attention and you say, "Within the parameters of this I'm going to be aggressive without hurting the guy." But I have to have that mindset.

You want to develop focus, whole body power and good balance, and then you develop the aggressive part in other drills. You've got to know what you're training for in each exercise. Some people like to visualize an enemy. In less sophisticated forms that are more like shadow boxing, that's OK. But Ba Gua is not going to work like that. Because there's not one move for one thing, as soon as you're thinking, "This is a hit to the head" and you're visualizing it in the form, that's all it's ever going to be. You're only getting one percent of the total you could be getting from that.

But if you feel like, "I'm moving against resistance, I'm pushing with the whole body, I feel like I'm balanced while I'm moving," that's OK. If you want to visualize an enemy, pick a technique out of it and do it a hundred times in the air or hit a bag with it. But I wouldn't be doing that in my Ba Gua forms. My Yang Tai Ji teacher, who was the best I've ever seen at Tai Ji, was dead set against that. He said, "If you always visualize an opponent, you're never going to get the flow of Tai Ji. You're only going to have a few separated techniques."

Sun Lu Tang demonstrating Tai Ji.
From *A Study of Tai Ji Quan* by Sun Lu
Tang.

Qi and Yi

L ET ME PREFACE THIS by saying that my first training was in the art of
San Soo under Jimmy H. Woo. Jimmy was Chinese, and a fluent
speaker, but he didn't mention *qi*. Jimmy talked about fighting and
body mechanics. So my entire first exposure to the idea was in reading books. I tended to believe, "Oh, maybe it's true, you can develop
some really special power." Even when I went to Taiwan, I went over
with the idea that these guys were going to have some special power.

After training for ten years with all these really good guys, I had a
complete hundred-and-eighty-degree turnaround. All my best internal teachers said basically the same thing. The more you try to think
about and develop your qi, the slower you'll get good at martial arts.
So what does qi have to do with fighting? Absolutely nothing.

I'm not a Chinese doctor, I'm not talking about giving acupuncture, I'm talking about fighting. Say you came to me and you'd never
heard of anything—*qi*, martial arts, nothing. If I taught you internal
martial arts, and I never mentioned the
word "qi," it wouldn't make a bit of difference. I'd talk about mind-body intent
and mind-body unity and moving with
your center. But no ideas of *qi* shooting
out of your fingertips, or all that stuff
about opening your meridians. You'd be
just as good, if not better.

So, do I believe it exists? That's irrelevant to the practice of martial arts. Whether
or not I believe in qi is irrelevant to me
teaching martial arts. Do I believe that
there's some kind of life force in the body?
Of course, we're alive. Does it flow through
these exact meridians? I'm not qualified

Photo by Eric Nomburg

Tim Cartmell practices Xing Yi.

to comment on that. Do I think you have to think about your qi and all that stuff to get good at martial arts? No, as a matter of fact I think it will probably slow your training down. Using your mind is plenty mysterious enough. Where you put your intent makes a huge difference on your balance— that to me is mystery enough. I don't need to complicate things with intangibles.

When it comes to things like *Ling Kong Jing* and pushing guys from a distance, across the board, I say nonsense. If you want to talk about all that stuff, I don't buy it. If you want to talk medical stuff, I'm not qualified. If you want to talk about *qi* in the martial arts, I'd say that it doesn't have anything to do with the martial arts.

Moving your mind in your body is another thing. I call that "intent," which is the word *yi*. If every time you heard the word *qi* you replaced it with *yi*, it would make much more sense. They're talking about intention mostly, and they're calling it *qi* because it sounds more mysterious. So, I don't talk about it in *qi gong* class. Qi gong is breathing exercises. *Qi* means "air." Qi gong is the same as Pranayama in Yoga. Breathing exercises. Are they good for you? Yeah, they're good for you. They'll build up your power and health. That's my stand on it, I tend to be a little bit overboard on the negative side because I hear so much nonsense.

As far as qi gong goes, relaxing and moving are good for you. Does it increase your qi flow? I don't know—it depends on what you mean by qi. My teacher Luo De Xiu explained qi as the Chinese term for when all your systems are in sync, your parasympathetic nervous system is turned on, you turn off the fight or flight system, your hormonal system is flowing, you have coherent brain waves, you're moving correctly, your circulation is going and you get this overall feeling of health. If you want to call that qi as an analogy for wellness, fine. But you could call that something else. Are you going to shoot it out of your fingertips at me? Well, maybe, but no one's done it yet.

Gabriel Chin

Gabriel Chin.

Octogenarian martial arts instructor Gabriel Chin has spent a lifetime in the internal martial arts. His study began at a young age in China, and continued in Taiwan after World War II. He eventually made his home in Ann Arbor, Michigan, where his Tai Ji and Qi Gong classes have been a permanent fixture in front of the Cube on the University of Michigan campus. Mr. Chin has seen it all over the years, and he has no shortage of opinions, no matter what the topic happens to be. Besides Qi Gong and Tai Ji he has numerous other skills, including his famed ability as a chef and his training as a professional opera singer. Most recently he has turned his attention to the use of qi in healing the human body. He has patiently instructed thousands of students, all free of charge, at the Cube over decades of dedicated teaching. Even after so many years his enthusiasm is undiminished, and he willingly shares his art with any who ask.

I arrived at the Cube to meet Mr. Chin and a group of his students one snowy morning. Although old enough to be a great-grandfather to some of them, he refuses to be anything other than "one of the boys." We retired to the student union and over the next few hours his quick wit and controversial opinions provoked constant laughter. As a source of knowledge, there is nothing secondhand about him—everything he knows comes directly out of the old Chinese culture, from a generation now mostly lost to the modern world. Mr. Chin's transmission of the teachings from that era are a valuable link with the time when these arts first emerged into public view. What today's historians write about, Gabriel Chin lived first-hand.

"Chin Jin," calligraphy by Gabriel Chin.

Gabriel Chin
DECEMBER 29, 2002

Tai Ji and Qi Gong Must Be Entwined

MY TEACHER TAUGHT ME that Tai Ji and Qi Gong must not be separated. You may learn them separately, but eventually you must get them entwined, like two fingers locked together. If you bring them together they can become very, very useful for treating any kind of pain that you feel. Healing is one of the wonderful things that can be achieved with Tai Ji and Qi Gong, up to and including the very last stages of cancer. Using Qi Gong I can heal you myself if you let me get close. In five minutes the pain will be gone. Gradually it comes back and you have to be treated again, but at least it's a good temporary release. I have had quite a few successful cases, but the doctors won't listen.

I first got interested in this thing because I ran into my teacher. Literally, I ran into my teacher, and got knocked back a long way! It was in a soccer game. We tried to see how wild we could get, especially back in the good old days. In those old days when we played soccer there was a saying, "If you've never broken someone's leg, or legs, you're no player." It was that kind of stuff. My teacher was short, skinny, and looked sickly, but I noticed he could really play soccer. Anyway, I was the center forward and he was fullback, so the two of us were always against each other.

It was very apparent that he was one of the professors, and I was a new student just getting into college, a freshman. I was quite different at the time. I was three and half inches taller, and a hundred and ninety-some pounds. I tried to test him, to see how strong he was. Soon I realized that he was faster and stronger than me, and I said to myself, "This is impossible!" So I tried a few more times. He was dribbling over here, to my left, I can still remember it was from that side

"Yang Tai Ji Quan," calligraphy by Gabriel Chin.

because I got knocked the other way. He noticed that I used strength to hit him, and so when I tried again he sent me flying. I thought, "Oh, he knows something."

After the game he said, "Come over here," and I thought, "Oh no!" Imagine, a freshman running into a professor like that! He said, "What kind of martial art do you practice?" I said government style, because in those days if you were eight and you'd never been to *chuan fang* class, you were no boy. He said, "How can you be so strong?" I said, "It must be from my grandfather, from what I know. I was born that way." So I asked him what he did and he said, "I do Tai Ji Quan." In those days we referred to Tai Ji practitioners as old people who try to catch fish empty-handed, because of the way they moved their hands in slow motion. So I joked with him and said, "Oh, like trying to catch fish empty-handed?" He laughed and I asked him if I could follow along. He said that it would be fine and told me the location and practice time.

Gabriel Chin demonstrates Tai Ji's "Shoot Tiger."

That's how I met my teacher. I got my little brother to come. I knew he would like it, so the next day I took him along with me. Unfortunately my brother has passed away now, but to my memory and knowledge, I'd say that among modern Tai Ji practitioners he was one of the best. He had gotten to the stage that he didn't seem to have the human body anymore. From a sitting position he could jump onto the table, with just a single hop! He could climb trees so easily—his hands would stick to the bark just like a monkey's.

Anyway, both my brother and I studied with him. I studied with him three years, then I had to leave, but my brother had two more years. That's how we started Tai Ji. During my life, most of the time when I arrived in a new place I practiced with people I met. It's the same form we still do today.

My teacher learned from Yang Cheng Fu's uncle, Yang Ban Hou. That is true. It's not like the books where everybody claims they were Cheng Fu's student! My teacher went to the Nanjing University, one of the very famous first five Chinese colleges. He graduated from there. In those days very few Chinese had that kind of education. He became a teacher at a girls' school to start with, and later he came to the school where I was.

Yang Ban Hou.

T'eng, the Small Country

BECAUSE IT'S SO SMALL, everybody knows the Small Country, where I am from. The Chinese system was much different from the United States. You see, the United States is divided into sections, but China became that way over many centuries, so it's much more chaotic in arrangement. Instead of calling them states, the Chinese call them countries. One of the smallest countries was T'eng, where our school was. At the school itself there were only two hundred forty-some students. T'eng is located less than twenty-five miles from Confucius's birthplace. In those days if you walked maybe an hour you were in a whole different country. Those were the days!

Protect Yourself in Good Health

PEOPLE WONDER IF traditional martial arts are still useful these days. So far I have only read about this subject in one book, the one by Sun Lu Tang. It was from the time when the Western culture of fighting with guns and all that was just about to become prominent in

China. It started by the time he was about to pass away—the gun was already being widely used. And someone asked him what use the martial arts are in modern times. He said, "This martial art is to protect your life, if necessary." It was then asked, "Who can survive if someone bayonets you—what could one do with Tai Ji?"

His answer was very reasonable. It was that since we are living in a different time, our way of protecting our life should be changed. But why do we still practice this traditional art? Of course, to buy a gun was quite an impossibility at that time but the point was that if you look at the fighting aspect why bother with martial arts? Buy a .45, that settles everything! That's what Sun Lu Tang said, but he also said that a gun does not give you good health. I think that was very reasonable. To study Tai Ji and things like that is to protect yourself in good health. For instance, if I'd never studied Tai Ji, I'd be long gone. My life was so tough, really, I'd be long gone by now. But even after all these years, if anybody wants to kill me without a gun I think it will take him a while!

Hard and Soft Strength

TAKE MY HAND. If I send qi there it turns soft yet hard at the same time. You can squeeze it any way you like, it's always that soft. Give it a try. The best way to test it is to get those weight lifters who can lift three to five hundred pounds. I've tried two. They were so shocked, One couldn't believe it, so I said for him to try it and see. He said, "No, I'll break your hand." I said, "It's OK, if you break it we can fix it!" So anyway he tried and after a few tries he stopped and I asked him what happened. He said that it hurt. I said, "I didn't do anything, you hurt yourself!"

Tai Ji training is useful if you have to protect yourself. You don't have to try and throw anybody. If they want to grab you—give it to them, they can do whatever they want until they're tired. It's not that

I'm so strong, I can lift maybe thirty pounds if I really work at it. But I don't know what you call this kind of strength. The only word I have for it is qi. The qi is there. I can't understand how it can get hard and at the same time stay soft, like a piece of rubber. While you squeeze it, it's a piece of rubber, and when you stop it's still rubber.

The terms *wai jia* and *nei jia* are merely a way to distinguish things for practice. If the person who says things like that really understands martial art, he wouldn't stress it. They are the same in the end. You can say it just to remember who does what. Nei jia, wai jia, they are the same provided you are very good at them. When you are young, you can punch hard with no problem, but at this age I can't do it like I used to—now it's a different thing.

Tai Ji and Qi Gong have to be entwined, not merely connected. When you get them entwined, the result is very strong. You ought to start off doing Tai Ji with the Qi Gong frame of mind. Here, grab my hand this way. Very light, fine, now we're only just connected. Feel how we are connected. Now, at the same time, I don't do anything, but you feel something go into your body, now go! See? It goes into you. Stronger. Stronger. And even stronger. Now I take it back gradually. Slowly it comes back. Feel something strange, like something is missing? OK, now I will draw your part out to me. Your hand will turn colder and colder. But if I suddenly shoot out, it feels different.

It feels weird because we're using what's on the inside, the so-called "qi." That's another thing I'd like to mention here. The word "qi" is wrong to start with. It is not actually qi that does this, it is my electrical current, which I have developed to be strong ever since I was born. Now grab me again. The interesting

Photo courtesy of Jinn

Gabriel Chin demonstrates Tai Ji's "Cross Arms."

part is this: I don't have to use much strength to get you to feel like I am squeezing. Now, squeeze me and see if my hand gets hard. See? It won't because it is not the strength that makes it strong, it is an electrical field from inside of me. Now try to feel as it goes into you. As soon as my head says "now do that," it gets harder, see? It's not straining, no, it is the field. The electrical field that comes with our life.

Lien Qi

To practice Tai Ji correctly is very easy and at the same time very hard. To start with, very simply, what we call qi in martial arts is not really qi. Qi actually refers to the breath. When I talk about qi, I mean a kind of electro-magnetic current inside the body. And you can learn to control the field, the practice of which is called *lien qi. Lien*

Photo courtesy of Jinn

Gabriel Chin demonstrates Tai Ji's "Cloud Hands."

qi is to practice with or train the qi.

The first step is to create a pressure within the body with your breath and seal it there. As I breathe you see my chest move. It's not a matter of holding the breath physically; it's as if your energy is compressed within you, similar to when peaches are sealed in a can. When you break the seal a pressure is released. You create this opening and closing as you practice Qi Gong and Tai Ji.

You learn to create a field and seal it. At first in the abdomen, but eventually you can put it anywhere you want to. Create a field, now get it into the arm. You practice and practice until you can create any size while keeping it steady.

In the beginning you have to use the

breathing to create the field. Take a deep breath, literally put it up here in the upper chest. Make it very comfortable, and then move it to here, lower in the chest. Then to here, in the lower abdomen, inhale and exhale. The last one is to create a field in the lower back. You practice this until it's very clear, until you can put it in the very tip of the finger. But how can you fill the finger if the arm is not full? Heaven knows. The main thing is that your mind has to control it. Practice all these things until you could almost say that using your mind you can send qi to one of your eyebrows.

The next step is to connect your body to the ground. Put a piece of paper on the ground. You want to be able to step on it without getting it dirty. If I step on it, I send qi down there so I can make myself feel lighter or heavier. In the beginning, use your mind to feel inside the body, anywhere you want it to go. Now the funny part is, you could send it to the knees only. Learn to control it to that extent. It is not as if you are straining and the qi goes. No! If one does that he doesn't know the qi at all!

Healing Others

I N ORDER TO HEAL OTHERS you first have to control your own energy so well that as soon as the idea of moving the qi starts, it's already working. In scientific analysis all energy moves as a kind of wave, no matter what form it is in. The fastest way of all is the speed of thought. It too is a kind of wave.

Imagine a pair of Siamese twins. In that manner you must practice as if you are completely connected to the creative source itself. People sometimes say, "You Qi Gong people are superstitious and crazy." They can think whatever they like. I don't intend to take sides in any religious debate. To me this is not connected to religion at all. It is a part of all humans' natural composition. When you practice Qi Gong, you have to connect yourself with the initial Big Bang of creation itself.

You can feel it very clearly when you are connected with "heaven." That is where we get the strength to heal. That's why someone can send qi from here to Egypt.

It can also be used for martial arts. Now, grab my hand. Grab really hard with the help of the other hand. It will get a lot stronger when I put the qi inside the hand. I say to it, "Don't fight." Now, go ahead and squeeze. I turn soft—there is nothing you can squeeze on, because what I did was get the help from "heaven." It came into me so you can do whatever you want. But if your strength is much, much better than mine you can squeeze, and I will be crushed. There's a limitation for everybody. But you can't beat a very good master.

Tai Ji Fa Jing

I N SENDING OUT QI when you heal people or when you heal yourself, there is only one possibility. You just intend for the qi to move

Photo courtesy of Jinn

Gabriel Chin demonstrates Tai Ji's "Single Whip."

there. Say you cut yourself, or you hammer your thumb, immediately the qi will go to that part. If you get the chance, put your hands on it directly for some time and you can heal it. But if you leave it alone for two days, it's too late. Why is the time factor so important? So far I don't have the knowledge to explain that. All I know is that it's true: the time factor is very important.

The other possibility is this—I want you to feel it. Face me, straight. Now put your hand on mine, make a connection. Now push. When we are pushing each other there are all kinds of possibilities. I can push you this way, that way, same thing you can do to me. Whatever way you want, use full strength to push me there, now push. Notice how I can guide you to go in the direction I want you to go.

When you push I can guide you. If I want to send you away, you must push full strength. Now push hard! I don't move. If I want to get you to go back it's easy—I let the qi take the lead. That's why it is very easy to push a guy who is strong and big. They may actually be in a worse position. It is the qi, the angle, and the twisting skill that makes the difference. That means we must go back to the words "the field." I can create a field, and if you push me, it goes back into you. I make you go back. I get you to your left, now to your right. It's not that I'm so strong, it's because I control the field when I am moving. In the beginning you have to study this thing from the most basic stage, breathing in and out. You have to be able to control yourself so well that, as I said, eventually you feel that a hair on your eyebrow is doing this. Because it is electrical, really, not muscular. It comes down to this: when I say "now show me" it better work! You can say anything but it is the result that counts.

Connect to Heaven

I AM NOW, based on the Chinese astronomical system, over eighty-three years old. I hope and wish that someone would have either the money or the courage so that we could establish a place to get into this study, so we could really start to find out what's going on. Because now we only know the surface. We know that the healing energy is some kind of bodily electric or magnetic current. We need a whole lot of research. How is it possible that we can actually, physically feel that we are literally connected with "heaven"? How could there be a kind of current that can literally send qi all the way to Beijing?

But regardless of the explanations for it, there's a lot of things we can do immediately. Like for instance, say you smash your finger. You can stop the pain right there, even if you break a bone. By using qi to heal it, the broken bones all find their place and in three days or so it's completely recovered. If you've seen it you can't argue with it! But I'm not concerned with arguments, I want to find out scientifically what is happening. There are obviously a lot of things going on. It shouldn't be too hard if we had the money to get the right people. We need the best electrical people and the best physicists to figure this out.

The main thing is you've got to keep training so you keep yourself in good condition, and in case you need to protect yourself it will be ready. That's all. Because nowadays it's such that no matter how smart you are or how strong you are it just takes one bullet.

This Thing Saves Lives

WE CAN DO WHAT WE CAN DO. My hope would be to find a self-supporting clinic that has a medical background. Start from there, and show people that this thing really saves lives. Start from there and go on, we can do it. The main thing that we want to do with this thing is to save life, reduce pain and suffering! That's the main thing. It really works! I have examples, a whole lot of them. Some of them seem like real miracles. That's the only word I can use. I can't perform miracles, but they sometimes happen.

There was one quite a few years ago. A woman who had arthritis for twenty-one years arrived at my door. She had to walk with two crutches. Her friend and I had to help lift her up the stairs and into the house. After about twenty-some minutes of me giving her qi, she just wiggled a little bit and stood up. She told her friend, "I am healed." With qi, just like that. She set the crutch down, stood up, picked up her stuff, grabbed her friend, walked out and disappeared, she didn't say thank you or anything. Just disappeared. I think in three days or so she sent me a large check. I sent it back with a note saying, "Not that I don't need money, who doesn't like money? But there is no such thing as less than half an hour's work with this kind of pay, it doesn't make any sense! Some day if I need money I know where you are." But she sent it back again! The note said, "Money is not what I need. After twenty-some years suddenly my arthritis disappeared, can you imagine the feeling? I am not really rich, but I have enough money to pay you, if you can do something with it, go ahead." So I took the money and gave it to some people who really needed it.

The most miraculous case was worse than that one, if I can use the word worse. Some guy got his hand sliced open with a meat cutter. When he first saw it, at that second it didn't hurt, it was numb. It was in the kitchen of a restaurant of a friend of mine. I hollered and yelled, "I know how to treat these things!" It required the emergency treatment. After about half an hour of treatment there was no bleeding, no anything. So we covered it with gauze, then ice. The next morning, can you believe it, he was there waiting to work! This thing performs miracles.

Gabriel Chin and students at the Cube.

[Mr. Chin asked that I publish the following article he wrote some time ago. Although controversial, it gives an insight into his perspective on the arts after a lifetime of practice. Edits were made for consistency and grammar, and the content was left unrevised.]

Can We Tell the Truth?

By Gabriel Chin

What is "Tai Ji Quan"?

In a way, this question has no answer. On the other hand, the answer can be very simple. That is, Tai Ji is a kind of martial art. When we say that this question has no answer, it is because Tai Ji Quan is now—how shall we put it—a kind of business, so some sharp dealers try very hard to include a whole lot of foolish Chinese stories, traditions, and mythology. In a way the purpose is to decorate it, or apply some make-up, but when the make-up is overdone, Tai Ji has lost its true form.

First let's consider to what extent the Chinese themselves are responsible for this situation. As you know, a Chinese like myself never admits there is anything they don't understand, or that they don't know. China has thousands of years of history yet is now considered by the West to be an undeveloped country. Since that is too much of an insult, some try to say, "Look, we're not undeveloped. For instance Tai Ji has several thousand years of history." They say it started with the *Yi Jing*, which is a book that, so far, nobody even knows how to punctuate. Because the term "Tai Ji" is found in that book, they say Tai Ji started with *Yi Jing*. At least the Tai Ji principle started with *Yi Jing*. That makes Tai Ji very impressive from a historical standpoint.

Following the same trend, another book, *Dao De Jing*, was chosen to back up the wonder of Tai Ji because the traditional Tai Ji people claimed that the *Dao De Jing* contained the absolute philosophy of Tai

Ji. In response, the unworthy writer must admit that he fails to see the relation between the philosophy of *Dao De Jing* and the principle of Tai Ji. I have presumed that this confusion is due to the fact that Chinese is a "tonal" language. For example, in the sentence "Mr. Baer walked out of his house bare-footed, ran into a bear, and barely escaped," all the bears in the sentence have the same sound. Similarly, whenever the term "Tai Ji" occurs, regardless of what subject it is related to, it has been falsely assumed that "Tai Ji is Tai Ji," therefore people think they must have the same meaning.

Another Chinese characteristic is the desire to attribute supernatural qualities to something by concocting for it a supernatural history. Such people want to portray Tai Ji as a mystical practice. Since Tai Ji is a "supernatural" art, a supernatural story is included. It is found in a book called *The Wandering Deities* (written at the end of the Sung Dynasty, ca. A.D. 1200–1260). One of the deities, a person named Chang Sanfeng, was picked by later generations to be the pioneer of Tai Ji, though the book only said something roughly like this: "One night while Sanfeng was sleeping, he had a dream in which a being came and taught him a set of martial art movements. The next morning when he awoke and was walking on the highway, he ran into a group of bandits. Sanfeng used the art he learned in his dream during the night and, barehanded, killed exactly one hundred of the bandits."

Well, if we believe in deities, we have to believe that deities can do anything they want to. Thus Sanfeng not only started the form, he then waited some five hundred years before he taught a disciple named Wang Tsungyueh who, if he existed at all, lived around the beginning of the Ching Dynasty (ca. A.D. 1644). Wang Tsungyueh in turn left behind the canon of Tai Ji, which is now in different books translated as the "classic" of Tai Ji. But the so-called canon, or "classic," of Tai Ji is no more than an opening consisting of about 394 characters, in one Chinese book. The entire body of literature is still less than 2,000 characters.

Chin family photograph, circa 1920s. Gabriel Chin on far right.

Gabriel Chin in the 1950s.

As to how this person, Wang Tsungyueh, got his skill to the Chenjia Village in Honan Province nobody seems to know. At least, I have not seen or heard of any book that refers to it. As a matter of fact, in the so-called Tai Ji village, Chenjiago, sixty years ago the people who lived there didn't practice Tai Ji at all. To my knowledge, that was the case, because I have been there. As a matter of fact, in those days the Chenjiago in Honan, and the Chihjia Village in Shantung, were two of the most famous martial arts villages in China. I had a classmate from the Chihjia Village and I myself have visited the Chenjia Village. During those days, they were famous for Shaolin martial arts. People believed, or the tradition said, that Tai Ji was from Chenjiago, so after the communists found out about the tradition, they said, "Since the legend says so, we will make it so." The communists literally made Chenjiago a Tai Ji practice center, for the purpose of a tourist attraction, so that whoever wants to study Tai Ji and has the interest to go can find "authentic" Tai Ji.

However, if we want to trace the story of how Chenjiago became famous as the Tai Ji village, that would involve the origin of the Yang family Tai Ji style, and the pioneer of it, Yang Luchan. One version of the story says that Yang Luchan sold himself as a page to the Chen family. While a page he stole the Tai Ji art. Afterwards, he was taken on as a student in the Chen family. That version grew out of another story that Yang Luchan, a sixteen-year-old eunuch serving at a royal banquet, was mysteriously discovered to be a martial arts master. Now the questions are: 1) Did Yang study from Chen? 2) If he did, at what age? 3) Was that before he became a eunuch or after? 4) Was he really a eunuch? 5) If so, how could he father children? The fact remains: the Yang family is historically documented and still exists. This leaves us to wonder where, when, how, and who really originated the art of Tai Ji.

We can see some of the causes for this state of affairs. First, up until World War II, missionaries were making statistics of the Chinese literacy rate. According to these studies, less than two percent of Chinese could read. Second, the Chinese tradition and common belief is, "Scholars don't lie." Well, we know how true that is. Since "Scholars don't lie," if it's in a book, it's got to be FACT and THE TRUTH. And, three, knowing politicians, they try to use anything and everything to their own advantage, so the Chinese government used this kind of belief to fool around with the people. To this day if you read Chinese history, you can still see that much of so-called history is nothing but mythology and folk stories. With Tai Ji this happened to such an extent that the liars eventually believed their own lies and so what they said turned out to be "truth."

Very unfortunately, at the time Tai Ji started to invade Western culture, it came in as a kind of commercial goods. As a Chinese saying goes, "No businessman is not a crook." The purpose of doing business is to make money. So as long as one can make money, let the end justify the means. Also, as we all know, packaging is very important to any product, so Tai Ji with mythology as packaging has more persuasive power. Thus the Western nations, especially English-speaking Americans with the business idea, changed their traditional attitude toward the scholastic research. Instead of trying to search for the facts and truth, Tai Ji merchants adopted the Chinese business principle which is, "I say so because I know it's so. If you cannot disprove me then what I said is true." The result being that Tai Ji is just like Genesis and Revelations in the Bible of Western civilization. According to the fundamentalist belief, you're not supposed to know why, and you're not supposed to express whether you understand or not, you just go ahead and believe. If you don't, you go to hell. To this extent, the English-speaking people have to take a certain responsibility.

Now, to ask again what Tai Ji really is, the answer is simple: it really is a kind of martial art. Yet it isn't a martial art. As a matter of fact, if one wants to study Tai Ji with the idea that it is a kind of martial art, he will be very much disappointed, because by definition the word Tai Ji means "the absolute and basic form of martial art." Based on this definition, you can see that it is impossible to master Tai Ji, because no one can reach an absolute state in martial art. On top of that, the common understanding of so-called martial art is that it is a kind of skill used to fight with. However, in studying Tai Ji one may learn the form but one can never know how to fight. Students of the martial arts in the West feel that they must use their art to fight, or at least to compete, to show people how good they are. In Tai Ji that is unacceptable, because if one starts to think of ways of writing rules for competition, that is against the principle of Tai Ji. In the East, anyone who accepts a challenge is putting his master's reputation in jeopardy. If the master hears of it, the student will be dismissed. The mere possession of this art should give a person confidence enough that actual conflict becomes unnecessary. Of course, there was the practice of "da lei tai," which lies outside the scope of this essay.

Now to return to the original question. A simple answer is, it is a disciplinary art which involves both the mind and the body. Also, one may say, it is a kind of *gong fu,* (which

Gabriel Chin practicing Tai Ji in the 1970s.

Photo courtesy Gabriel Chin

should be translated as "martial art") which uses the mind to conduct qi (that is, the body's energy), and uses qi to maneuver or manipulate or motivate the physical body. The practice of Tai Ji demands as the first condition a calm mind. The next step is to have absolute concentration, to attain a state where your "self" does not exist. The third step is to use your mind to conduct the qi until spirit and mind, qi or breathing system, and blood and body eventually become one harmonious unit.

As to how many steps there should be, or which school one should follow, that actually makes little difference. All the movements and the number of steps are just a means to develop qi. In terms of what school is better or which practice is right, to me that makes no difference either. Sometimes you hear, "Which is the real or fundamental or classical school?" Sometimes you hear, "Well, that is not the right stuff!" All that is like using the same alphabet to create individual language. Tai Ji is not how you move your body. The main thing is how you start with the spirit and the mind.

Since Tai Ji carries the name of "martial art," it is a martial art. Provided you find the right teacher, and you practice it diligently enough to master it, not only will you be mentally and physically healthy, Tai Ji will automatically produce as a side effect the ability to protect yourself. But self-defense is still not the primary reason for studying Tai Ji.

As to how to study, how to learn, how to practice, etc., that would take a number of books to cover. That is not the purpose of writing these few words. Seeing that the situation "on the market" is very confusing, with so many different practices and schools and especially the "theory" behind it, Tai Ji sounds so mysterious to the extent it is ridiculous. All I want to say is, Tai Ji is not that complicated, nor is it so mysterious. For example, when you see "five elements" and "eight diagrams," those two terms are nothing more than an arbitrary division of the thirteen basic movements of Tai Ji (8 + 5 = 13.) The words "elementals" and "diagrams" are nothing but decorations to the numerals. If what I said can help a little bit to solve this kind of problem, I should be satisfied.

This sounds as though I don't believe in the traditional Tai Ji at all. On the contrary, not only do I believe in the tradition, I have seen with my own eyes the wonders produced by the Tai Ji masters. The following two experiences will illustrate what I mean.

In the days of my late teens when I was strong enough to carry five hundred pounds on my back and walk up a flight of stairs, I was playing in a soccer game. In the heat of the game I was "bounced" far out of position by a short, light, middle-aged man, just by a little twist of his hip. That incident is what started me in Tai Ji. The other incident was years later, in Chungking, Szechuan. I saw an old man with one quick, easy, one-handed lift send a two-hundred-pound U.S. Navy man literally flying through the air out of a boxing ring. Later I saw an article published in a paper by Cheng Man-ching, describing the incident, and naming the old man as Chen Wei-ming. Since I was present, I did not doubt I had seen Chen Wei-ming.

Several years after this article was originally published, I had a chance to meet with Sun Chien-yuen, the daughter of Sun Lutang, in Beijing. In conversation, I mentioned this incident and the article to her. She said, "Cheng Man-ching? I never heard of such a person! Also Chen Da-gu [her relation with Chen Wei-ming made it possible for her to call him Elder Brother] was not in Chungking. He was in Shanghai at that time." Then I realized that Cheng Man-ching was telling stories. The conversation further revealed that Cheng Man-ching was not a student of Yang Cheng-fu.

I know my words will upset a whole lot of people. I have kept the tape of the conversation with master Sun. To be fair to

Photo courtesy Gabriel Chin

Gabriel Chin and Sun Chien-yuen.

Cheng Man-ching, as a fellow practitioner of tai chi, I must say, "he had gung-fu" and his style did resemble "Yang style" (whatever that means). But he was not Yang Cheng-fu's student. As to where he obtained his skill, I have no way to tell.

The final mystery is: who was that old guy in Chungking who threw the American Navy man out of the ring?

In conclusion, I would like to tell a story. The famous Tai Ji master, Sun Lutang, who was a contemporary of Yang Cheng-fu, had a daughter by the name of Sun Chien-yuen whom I met with in Beijing—herself an accomplished master by the age of nineteen. One time someone asked Miss Sun, "How true are the stories told about your father?" She answered, "One time, after a storm, my father walked on the road trying hard not to get his shoes wet, so he hopped and jumped over the puddles. Seeing what the old man did so nimbly and easily, the story started to spread. By the time it reached Shanghai, people had started to write books saying that my father traveled all over China and never took a boat because he could jump across rivers."

Gail Derin-Kellog

Long-time Xing Yi practitioner and acupuncturist Gail Derin-Kellog is based in Sacramento, California. Following the twin paths of healing and martial arts has given her a unique perspective on the relationship between Traditional Chinese Medicine and the internal fighting styles. Her ability as a healer is treasured by her students, and her expertise in the art of Xing Yi Quan has left a memorable impression on her opponents during numerous sparring sessions. As a student of Vince Black and a long-standing teacher within the North American Tang Shou Tao organization, she has had the chance to utilize both aspects of her training and to educate many fellow practitioners.

During our meeting on a blazing hot Sacramento day, Ms. Derin-Kellog shared insights gleaned from her practice and research. She emphasized that the essence of the art can only be attained by training our inner strength, not our aggressive impulses. After which she kindly subjected me to a series of very effective applications from the Twelve Animal Forms of the Xing Yi system.

Gail Derin-Kellog
MAY 17, 2003

Internal Reality

INTERNAL MARTIAL ARTS PRACTICE directly addresses the sense of imbalance that a lot of people are experiencing these days. People are being pulled away from their ability to feel into themselves in their day-to-day lives. Many of us are either reaching toward the future's promise like it is a dangling carrot, or we're stuck with our energy fixated on regrets or resentments from the past. One way we can build our internal energy in the here and now is to cultivate being fully present with the energy in our bodies.

Once we begin internal martial arts training, we start to accumulate *qi* (life force energy), which is the abundance of energy we would normally be giving out to our daily tasks. This kind of cultivation turns toward a different way of building our strength, focused on how we refine our Spirit (this is called *Shen* in Traditional Chinese Medicine). There's an internal reality going on inside, while we are operating in a seeming external reality occurring outside. If we're not mindful, we can get sucked into some external struggle, as the world's concerns are often trying to pull us away from feeling centered. So I train from the very practical point of view of wanting to feel my own bones. That's one of the reasons I think it's important to train in this day and age. The more I move within my internal reality, the more effect I can have on how I respond to my surroundings.

Chinese martial arts and Chinese Medicine often make reference to the "Three Treasures." This is the process of qi cultivation. First you refine the Jing (essence), which allows you to cultivate the Qi (life energy). When you refine your Qi you create a richer expression of Shen, which affects your intent and will-power. From there you discover the state of awareness of No Thing from which all creativity

Xing Yi's An Shen Pao. From *Xing Yi Quan Xue* by Sun Lu Tang.

arises. As I just mentioned, from a selfish point of view this cultivation gives me the resiliency to stay calm when things seem to be falling apart. It's the idea of being in the world but not of it. You then develop something precious that no one can take from you. This kind of training is a way of grounding you in your own experience, not just other people's.

Testing Yourself

AT SOME POINT in your martial arts training you will probably want to compete with others and have that experience. You need to have a time of training to try out your skills. That's why two-person drills are so important. They develop your timing and reflexes, and they force you to work with your breathing. You also need to have periods of time to refine and focus on the development of your internal connections. You have to have both. For me personally, the fighting aspect has had less importance as I get older. Initially I needed to participate in sparring tournaments. This was essential to find out what I could and couldn't do. Especially being a woman, I can't rely on sheer muscle power.

I'm always still learning because there's always going to be someone stronger or faster. Through cultivation I might be able to develop a mental edge against someone more gifted if I am able to remain calm and focused. Martial arts training works with the mind. Going into something with a bad feeling or being easily intimidated doesn't help you do well. That focus goes back to your breath. You can use your breath to calm your emotions or stay in your center despite your feelings.

Breathing

EMOTION, WHICH IS ENERGY IN MOTION, is very much affected by one's breath, and as we know, emotions will cause us to either take shallow breaths or to breathe deeply. When you work with your breath, especially if you do abdominal breathing, your emotions naturally get more centered. You can't be as scattered when you are focused on your breathing. When you focus on rooting the breath when you're training, especially when you're competing, you have a much better chance of doing well.

Our system uses a series of body conditioning drills called Fu Hu Gong. What's unique about the way we do them is that the mind's attention is initially placed on matching relaxed breathing with the motion of the body. We exhale on exertion so that we aren't at risk of putting unnecessary pressure on any of the internal organs. You're preserving and working with your qi, and at the same time you're able to work out longer without sustaining injuries. The emphasis is on strengthening the qi and the blood, which is a little different perspective from the art of pumping weights. There's nothing wrong with jumping rope, there's nothing wrong with aerobics, it's just that the emphasis is different because we are consciously combining the breath with the movements. Even if you are having a heavy workout, you're always working to build up the energy of the body. Sometimes in a hard style of martial arts if you're not relaxed, it's like taking a hose and stepping on it and then wondering why the water isn't flowing. Over the years it doesn't sustain you.

Form without Tension

QUITE EARLY IN MY TRAINING my instructor asked a man to hold two phone books in front of him and said to me, "OK, I want you to hit this guy." I was thinking that I couldn't do this, but he said,

"I just want you to try it." Being inexperienced, I *tried* to hit the guy and I hurt my hand. It really hurt! But that was falling back on the old way I used to hit, as I had trained in Korean martial arts for years before I started Xing Yi. My teacher coached me further and said, "Remember what you know from Xing Yi. I want you to be relaxed and connected, and move from your Tan Tien. When you hit, don't stop at the surface, just go right through." Next thing you know this guy is being thrown back a couple of feet. I thought, "I didn't do anything!" The third time I tried it I lost the connection and hurt my hand again. I was back into thinking that I had to hit him hard.

When I was doing everything correctly the form was still there, and I was relaxed. And everything came from the center. If I'm tense and trying to be strong, I'm actually cutting off my qi flow. It can't come out. Sometimes people mistake this tension for power. But holding tension in a punch or a kick can restrict the qi, the energy that fuels it. And when that qi is really truly expressed, it's effortless, and the strike can really penetrate. Sometimes you will notice in the tapes of the older Xing Yi practitioners, at the end of their punches there's a small vibration. That force can't come out if your body is tight. Removing tension from your movements is part of the distinction between the internal and the external arts.

You've got to allow the qi to flow. It requires relaxation, but you're not limp like seaweed—there's a difference. In the internal arts there is form without tension, yet there's force behind it. Whenever you see people locking up while doing a kick or punch, they're putting the brakes on, they're not letting the energy be fully expressed.

When you understand this the hit penetrates more. You see this principle developed in some people who train in external martial arts for many years. They end up being softer; they end up getting there just the same. I've heard it said by my teacher that if you have an internal martial artist and an external martial artist fighting, for the first three years the external practitioner often has the internal fighter beat.

This is because the internal method requires that you work on forming and developing your energy and body mechanics, and it takes time to express that power. Later as you learn to harness and work with the Tan Tien, spine, move as one unit, and work with generating force from the earth through the body, it's like night and day. And that's why they call Tai Ji the supreme ultimate art. In China it's considered one of the most powerful martial arts systems, and at the same time one of the softest.

Once I encountered a Tai Ji practitioner who had developed a technique called "sticky hands." He began by putting the back of his hand to mine in push hands. He instructed me to try to pull my hand away, and try as I might he stayed attached to me. I was quite stunned and asked myself, "What was that?" This sticky-hands technique is a very specialized development of qi. But in general we train to develop our life force, to vitalize our qi and blood, and to build our body. It seems like the longer you do internal styles correctly, the healthier you get.

There's a catch to it, though. I've heard it said that Xing Yi is designed for people over the age of thirty-five. Obviously people that are younger can do it, but what is meant by that statement is that people can come to Xing Yi with injuries and after doing it for a while, many of their injuries go away. Their back stiffness and creaky joints abate. As long as you keep training, you're fine. But if you stop for a while, those old patterns might start coming back. Xing Yi reshapes the body—it's one of the best physical therapies I know of. I often prescribe specific exercises to my patients for restoration of their health.

Beginning Xing Yi Quan

I MOVED TO SAN DIEGO IN 1984 to continue my study of acupuncture. I'd already been a private apprentice to one practitioner, but I needed to get formal training to become licensed. I went to the California Acupuncture School, and I met Vince Black. He was my supervisor there. At the time I was studying another style at his martial arts school that was taught by someone else. I would watch the end of his Xing Yi class while he taught a few students. One time I asked him, "What's that?" He said, "Don't worry about it, just keep doing what you're doing." He discouraged me from pursuing any action despite my building curiosity. I was so impressed with their relaxed manner combined with the speed of what they were practicing. When you see someone really good, there's a knowing, a sheer confidence, and a sense of precision that is so interesting, there was something really different energetically about it. There was no having to prove it, like "This is better than anything else." It was just this knowing that he had about him.

Well, I kept asking Vince and persisted for a long time. Finally he said, "Get twelve people together, pay three months in advance, then we'll start in January 1986," and we did. We began with the Fu Hu Gong training, which was quite hard for me initially. I know now that I made it more difficult on myself than it could have been because I was coming from a hard style background, so I kept training with a lot of effort and tension. He'd just look at me and laugh, and watch me exhaust myself. He let me do that for a while. And slowly as he saw me being very persistent, he'd encourage me with subtle hints, trying to help me see that what I really needed was to relax and not put all that tension into it. I was blocking my own development.

One time I injured myself. He said, "The good thing about this is that you need to practice 'old man style' for a while. You think all this exertion is making you stronger, but it's not. Keep going through the motions and allow what you do to be very precise yet soft. If you are willing to sacrifice the strength for something else that's being cultivated, you will end up being further ahead." And that was really hard. I thought I knew what I was doing but I didn't understand the internal arts, and I was forced to look at developing skill in a different way.

One of the other things that I really appreciated was that he taught persistence in your training. He said, "If you study a particular form or technique for a hundred days, you own it. If you do something for sixty days, you've just borrowed it from nature and one day you'll have to give it back." He used to challenge us to do these hundred-day training periods. I remember a few of us committed to training the Twelve Animals forms. We did ten repetitions of every animal form daily for a hundred days. That was intense. The level of where we were at the beginning compared to where we were after those three months was phenomenally different. And yet still when I go back to an old form, it's like I'm a beginner at a whole new level of discovery and development.

After Fu Hu Gong we moved on to Ba Bu Da, one of the eight step sets. It's not just about training to learn the forms, it's about what you put into them. People accumulate a lot of forms, thinking that if they know this many systems it's really special. In terms of real depth of knowledge, I think of the Xing Yi master Liang Ke Quan. When he was in prison for many years he practiced Xing Yi daily to integrate it into his being. The man had tremendous power, even to a very old age. I last saw him a few years ago. The school where we were has cinder-block walls, and he would hit the wall with his shoulder. I had my back against the wall and the whole wall was vibrating. He generated amazing power. He also shared many insights with us. One of the things he said was that every time you strike your hair should come up slightly.

I was drawn to Xing Yi when I first saw it—I knew there was something more to it

Gail Derin-Kellog practices Xing Yi's San Ti.

than what I had been doing. And my teacher Vince Black has tremendous magnetism in his being. I knew that he had something that others didn't. Which is what I alluded to in the beginning: there is a certain amount of power that accumulates around people when they do a lot of training. They carry that presence around them—it's like a magnetic energy that can be felt.

Xing Yi Details

XING YI AS A MARTIAL ART depends on correct body mechanics. For instance, at first you're constantly working with the tailbone and spine. Both have to be in the proper place, and the spine must move to generate power. You're always working with making sure that your elbows are sunk and your shoulders are relaxed. Even the

Gail Derin-Kellog demonstrates Xing Yi's Pi Quan.

stepping is different; you're often taking a little half step while your tailbone is lengthened and slightly tucked. Your stepping at first has the idea of stepping along a railroad track. It looks very linear; however, examine Zuan Quan. If you're attacking using a straight force, I counter using a corkscrew motion, making your punch go off to the side. It looks linear but in application it's circular.

Xing Yi forms have many aspects that may not be visible to the eye. The White Crane exercises are explosive but relaxed. Every animal form has a specific energy and distinct expression to it. Monkey, Snake, and Dragon, all of them are very circular, although it's not as obvious; the circles are a lot more hidden in the body and the spine, as opposed to the Ba Gua system where you're walking in a circle. Xing Yi is circular internally but it may look linear on the outside.

Maintaining the alignments is how an acrobat is able to spin plates in the circus. They start by spinning one plate, then another, then another. The idea is that as a beginner if you try to hold every possible alignment that you can think of, you will be too tight and too tense. So what you do is focus on one thing at a time, like your breathing, or lengthening your tailbone, or relaxing so your breath comes down, or relaxing your shoulders, or connecting through your lats. You just gently remind yourself of these little cues at first, and eventually everything starts to set and become integrated in your movements. It's like the idea that at first you spin one plate, remember it, and let it have its momentum. Then you can add another idea, while maintaining that initial one.

In the beginning it's enough to just relax and not force the breathing. Relax the breath, exhale on exertion, then begin to look at the basics of keeping the tailbone lengthened and tucked, the tongue on the roof of the mouth, just keeping your body mechanics somewhat correct. Don't be too picky at first and try to do it all. Just start working with the movements while being relaxed yet precise. The more work is done on focusing with intent, the more qi arrives there.

Next, use the breath to start to make the Tan Tien alive, so that everything starts to move from there. The breath comes down into that place, but you can never force it. If you force it you're going to strain your diaphragm, you're going to strain a lot of things. Make sure your pelvic floor is lifted, as if you are sealing a door.

Finding the right balance in your practice is like learning to ride a bicycle. Over time you get to know that perimeter between too much and too little, but at first you're doing all kinds of things until you find that place. You're trying too hard, or you're not trying hard enough. And then you eventually find where that right expression is. Like anything you try to get more precise with, it tends to swing like a pendulum. You work to find the correct level. It's like a car: if you have a fan belt that's too loose or too tight, it's not going to work efficiently. Remember that it's eventually driven by the qi, not necessarily the muscles. At first we use just our muscles and we think our arms are moving. Eventually we realize that we are moving from the Tan Tien and the arms are an expression of that.

The next stage is lots of practice. Vince Black used to say that the times when it seems like things are falling apart and your movements are feeling very awkward is when you're about to go to the next level. Just don't give up on it. That really helped me. There were times when I'd be going along in my training thinking everything's flowing and suddenly it's like, what's going on? Now it feels terrible! What's happening is that things are starting to get integrated in a different way. It's like a growth spurt or growing pains. You watch people go from one phase to another—it's analogous to going through puberty, feeling awkward. When that happens in your body (I'm not talking about puberty!), don't get discouraged. It's a good thing; you're growing in your training.

Gail Derin-Kellog demonstrates one of Xing Yi's animal forms.

The Power of Xing Yi Quan

THINK ABOUT WHEN a baby grabs your finger. It's always a surprise for me how strong a baby is. That baby has not learned how to disconnect its body yet; everything is moving as one force. If you watch their breathing, they're belly breathers. The key is that they're connected when they move. We get disconnected in our body movements as we get older. Xing Yi teaches body mechanics where everything moves together as one unit, just like that baby, soft but united.

This concept of being relaxed is not found only in the internal martial arts. Good distance runners are very relaxed. A good boxer, even if he's hitting hard and fast, is still relaxed with good body mechanics. People hear the word "relaxed" and they don't know what that means. They think that means no force. They think that means no tension. It's not that you're not extending your force, it's just that you're not putting the brakes on it as you put it out.

One of the things that a teacher once told me about hitting a bag showed me the different idea of power expression in the internal arts. One of his senior students said, "Watch this." He hit the bag and it flew up and away. The guy was confident in his performance and said, "Pretty good, eh?" The teacher responded, "You don't want to do that." The teacher then hit the bag and it violently shuddered but didn't move very far in space. His strike penetrated. You can imagine what it would do inside a body. That's the relaxed, explosive energy that Xing Yi can create. Yet when you look at Xing Yi it can look very forceful. It can look like an external art to the untrained eye.

Xing Yi San Shou

XING YI ALSO HAS the two-person San Shou practice, which is somewhat comparable in theory to Push Hands in the Tai Ji system. My teacher often said that we should invest in our losses. What he meant is that you can get a lot of little cheap shots in on somebody and think you're really accomplished. But if you want to relax and see the tendencies and openings of an opponent, you've got to invest initially in getting hit a few times. If you're willing to quit being so concerned with winning and start being more focused on where you're getting hit and observing your blind spots, you can learn a lot about how your mind and body work together. What occurs is that any motion initiated from your training partner is detected by your own body, unconsciously. You automatically respond to it. If you're always trying to play tag and "win," you're not likely to figure it out and develop that sensitivity.

If you're always in a hurry for that competitive edge, you won't rise above a certain level because you're not willing to explore it. That's an important strategy in training to develop fighting skills. To be able to relax in San Shou, be willing to get hit, be willing to just hang in there and watch as things are happening. Then you can be a lot calmer and more prepared when you actually do compete with another fighter.

The first step in San Shou is to stick to your opponent to build your sensitivity. Stay relaxed. Pick up the subtle hints where the other person is starting to telegraph intention in movement. If you are so

Gail Derin-Kellog demonstrates a Xing Yi technique.

invested in moving in on them, you aren't going to notice the subtle things when you really need them the most. There were times when Vince Black would do San Shou with us and we could rarely get in on him. Our intentions were too obvious; he could feel even subtle muscles moving. He already knew what we were doing, because his sensitivity is quite developed. A higher level can be established when the focus is not just on winning. Initially in training, invest in the loss to be able to see things more distinctly.

He would instruct the guys to train with the women because we tend to be sneakier and softer in our movements. They would learn so much more from us because they didn't try to overpower us for the strike.

He said women will teach you a lot if you just try to match that softness. With many of these guys, I'd be able to get in past their blocks easily. The ones who really followed his advice though, they'd get hit a lot at first, and then pretty soon, I couldn't get in on them as much. They'd start to feel my intent coming, as they had matched my sensitivity. Then I would get hit and not know where it came from; I couldn't even feel its trajectory because there was no telegraphing. When it comes out relaxed, it's faster and then hits harder. Less is more sometimes.

Power versus Force

WHEN I HAD MY SCHOOL in Cottonwood, Arizona, we were located right above a weight lifting gym. They'd hear us upstairs pounding away as we'd do body drags, rolls, and working with weapons. A couple of body builders wanted to know what we were doing, so I invited them to attend a Fu Hu Gong class. We were doing push-ups. One man said, "Oh yeah, I can do three hundred at a time." Although we just did ten repetitions each of the fourteen different push-ups, they couldn't keep up.

One problem is that when you do a lot of weight training, the ends of the muscles tend to get shortened which doesn't allow as much qi and blood to fill that area. If the muscles and tendons are not lengthened, they're just bulking up. The small muscles get weaker and the large muscles get stronger. In Xing Yi we're working all the smaller and foundational muscles as well, and we're performing the push-ups slow, with the breath. The body builders couldn't support their own weight with this distinction, yet they could bench press a lot more than that, as they were strong guys. They couldn't handle exerting slowly, either, and staying relaxed. They were flabbergasted by it. I think they could do these exercises if they allowed themselves to relax into the movements and stretch. They operated from the same paradigm I initially did, thinking that power was force.

Being a Doctor of Oriental Medicine, I look at the pains of aging as being primarily due to stagnation of qi and blood. This can be caused by a particular trauma leading to constriction—a lack of qi and blood getting to a particular area. As with an injury, too much body building can choke things up. Eventually, as people become less active with age, they aren't circulating qi and blood in the body as well as they used to. However, when you look at long-time Xing Yi practitioners in China, you'll see how healthy they are and how vital they look. And the Shen, the spirit, reflected in their eyes is very clear. At an advanced age they've got black hair; they can drop down into a Dragon posture and come right back up with an effortless yet explosive power. You don't experience this when you're using external force. There's a difference between power and force. Force is expendable—power is different, you can sustain a lot longer on power than you can on force. Force has a certain limit, and you can use it up. Power is renewable because it relies on working with the qi.

Life Force

QI IS THE LIFE FORCE that moves through the body. It is the essence derived from our parents at conception. Obviously if our parents were strong and vital we would genetically receive a greater quality and volume of qi from them, and if they weren't, we would have a weaker constitution. We would then have to work harder to maintain our health. There are some people who have a tremendous constitution: they can sleep very little, drink and eat to excess, and they don't seem to have any problems with it. For other people, indulging in any little indiscretion will cause them to end up feeling it. Basically whether you were given the equivalent of a thimble or a bucket full of qi, everyone starts with a certain amount. Once you take that first breath at birth you are working with postnatal qi. You can't add to your initial prenatal qi. But according to Chinese medical theory, you can preserve it, and that's through proper diet, lifestyle, breath, and martial arts training. It's very important.

The qi that circulates through the meridians of the body and expresses itself through the surfaces of the body is called the Wei Qi. This quality of qi protects us from external influences of wind, cold, heat, etc. There are many different types of qi in the body, and each has it's different function. The stronger your qi is cultivated, the more vibrant your health. Once you ensure your physical health, the qi is then refined toward building a stronger spirit or Shen and reflects in how you express yourself in life. Alternatively, a disturbed spirit can disrupt your qi flow and negatively affect your life.

Part of a good health practice is maintaining a balance with the seasons. For example, in the summer you should let yourself get very expressive and sweat a lot. In the winter you don't work out as heavily—work up to the edge of breaking a sweat. At that time of year you cultivate being more internal and quiet. As long as you follow the seasons diet-wise, eating cooler foods in summer and warmer in winter, while maintaining proper exercise, you'll be allowing your qi to flourish rather than be depleted. In China a lot of people practice these concepts. You see it a lot with the elderly, and you don't see as many infirm people as you see here. When I was there I saw an old man waiting for a bus. His foot was straight up, almost shoulder height, stretching against the wall while he was reading the paper. You don't see that kind of thing here.

When I visited China, what impressed me the most was the teachers—both their skill and their humility. They could train eight or ten hours a day, with endurance and stamina that were quite impressive. These men and women had learned martial arts well before the Cultural Revolution, and I suspect there's not much more than a handful around anymore. They possess a level of development of expressed Shen that is beyond most of the younger people practicing today.

That's the beauty of internal martial arts that you can see by looking at the results over time. Aging isn't the deterrent to performance that it can be in other physical activities.

Acupuncture

T HERE'S A SAYING that there are people who practice acupuncture, and then there are those that do acupuncture alongside Tai Ji— meaning that if I can move qi in my own body, then I have a better chance of understanding qi in another person's body. The more physically fit I am, the better I am at helping others. In Chinese medicine we check the body's pulses, the normal pulse being four or five beats per breath. The question is, do you follow the patient's breath or do you follow the practitioner's breath as a standard of normal? My teacher said that you should follow the practitioner's breath, because they're the ones that should be healthy and maintain a certain standard of health.

Vince Black always recommended that his assistants practice *qi gong* before his clinic opened in the morning. He said that your energy has to be full to be able to really have proper sensitivity, not only when you're feeling the pulses, but when you manipulate the needle. You have to be able to know, feel, and sense the pathways. When we first learned the acupuncture points in school, we memorized where a point was by exact measurement. The problem is that you are using something quite two-dimensional on a three-dimensional human body. With experience you feel the point. How can you do that if your qi is depleted? So it's essential that the healer's qi be healthy. It helps tremendously to keep your own practice strong.

As for martial arts, when you know medicine you know where the pressure points of the body are and what occurs when you attack them. As you practice, you also feel what's going on inside your body and its effects. This occurs as you're practicing each of the element forms of Xing Yi. When you do Pi Quan you know how that's opening up the lungs along the external and internal pathways. For many of us, medicine and the martial arts go hand in hand. One leads into the other. Awareness of the energy within often leads people into studying the effects of trauma, how to replenish energy that is depleted and damaged. From there students often go into the study of Tui Na, which is Chinese massage therapy. In doing Tui Na you learn how to work with the proper alignment of the tendons, bones, and connective tissue, and how that affects the qi and blood flow in the body.

When you train in the internal arts, the world inside yourself becomes endless. After a while, when you put your hands on another body you start to sense what's going on inside with the qi, the blood, the alignment of the bones, tendons, ligaments, and connective tissue. You begin to know when the qi feels rough, and when it feels smooth. The acupuncture needle becomes an extension of the hand. You learn to feel energy as clearly as something physical being placed in your hand.

Medicine teaches you a gentle and sensitive touch. Yet in Xing Yi there is an explosive power as well. Pi Quan has the force of an axe coming down. You wouldn't try to chop wood all day stiff and tense—you'd get wiped out. On the other hand, you have to maintain the form. I've seen people do the White Crane exercises and throw their elbows out of place because they were overly relaxed. You always have to maintain the structure and correct body mechanics.

Persistence and Patience

SOMETIMES PEOPLE IN THE WEST tend to do a little bit, think they have it, and go on to something else. What the older generation in China and long-time practitioners have in their mindset is persistence and the sense that it's not a goal to get somewhere, it's the journey. You just keep plugging away. You're always working on refining whatever you are doing. Accomplished practitioners don't try to grab as many forms as they can. They take what they have and keep working it to discover its jewels.

In the internal martial arts if you want something to come out you don't force it. Just like you don't rip a flower open to find out what it looks like—you have to let the flower bloom. Just keep coming back to it, keep polishing that stone, keep running those neuro-pathways in your brain, and eventually something shifts. Each time you come back to your practice it's a little different because your experience keeps deepening it. Yet you're not rigid about it either; you're always open to how it's changing you. The thing is, you can't give up.

For women in the martial arts, there's a power that develops that your muscles alone can't bring you. Development can go a lot further if you stay with the internal arts. Obviously you develop self-confidence, and that brings a lot more emotional mobility into your world. Vince Black said to me that women are initially at an advantage. We have the element of surprise, the softness and the quickness. For instance, Kim Black has hit me so hard, I was shocked that it wasn't coming from one of the big guys. Her power came out as fast as a whip with a cannon's force, and it blew my mind. So this higher expression of martial power definitely can be achieved by women.

I had an interesting experience a while back when I was doing push hands with a woman half my size. I told myself to take it easy on her because I didn't want to have too much of an advantage by using a lot of force. As a developmental exercise we began with pushing softly and soon we were asked to increase our strength of force. The idea was to get our muscles exhausted so that our sensitivity would be different when we were not relying on our power. I noticed that she was pretty strong. As we continued my arm was getting a little fatigued. The more we kept pushing hands the stronger she became, and I started getting really tired. I began to override with my muscles to compensate. Even though she didn't fit my picture of what strength should be, she ended up totally overpowering me. I asked her later what she'd been doing. She said she stands forty-five minutes a day in a posture called "Holding the Ball." That conduit of energy clearly wasn't muscular. The more she engaged the energy, the stronger she became. I'm pretty strong, but as I watched her partner up with others, men and women, she was able to repeat the same scenario. Her body structure and size didn't warrant that kind of power. That is the benefit and the beauty of the internal arts.

I'm not saying that people who work out and have muscle strength aren't at an advantage. You have got to be in shape—it's not all qi. The "Holding the Ball" exercise is a great way to build up your arm power. What you do is relax and extend your arms out as if to hold a large ball in front of you. At first you may feel shaking in your legs, like an old radiator clanging with rust moving through the pipes. The more you practice consistently, the greater the flow of energy gets. The more you relax into it, the more energy you are able to move in your body. It's important to breathe, to relax the places where you're tight. The rough spots we feel are where the qi wants to move through but the tension is stopping it. Stay with it. The tension is impeding you, not lack of qi. That's where practice gives you some insights. Don't get too analytical, though, just do it.

Martial Arts As Physical Therapy

INTERNAL MARTIAL ARTS CONDITIONING starts out very physical, and it looks like any other hard-style form. But from the start there is the idea that you relax with the breath. You don't force it. If there's unnecessary tension in the abdominal area it can cause people to get hernias, so when you're exerting you exhale. When I don't hold my breath I'm more relaxed. When we work with the breath, we don't strain and injure ourselves from trying too hard. It is a constant refinement and checking to make sure the body mechanics are correct. Check yourself: how are you breathing? Are your shoulders and elbows relaxed? Are you coordinating hips with shoulders, knees with elbows, and hands with feet—in other words, are you practicing the six harmonies? Qi development is a part of all this, but you need a starting place. Movements can look just like any other style from the outside. That's why Xing Yi looks linear but it's not in actual usage. Its expression looks hard, but it's not straining.

When one of my patients has a problem with their hips I may ask them to do the duck walk exercise from our system. I say, "Here is an exercise that's going to increase the flow of blood and qi in your hips. And that's going to help the pain go away because you're going to have a greater range of motion. You need to try and do this." They're often very enthusiastic when I approach it from the medical point of view. They would never try to do these exercises on their own! Once they know what it's doing internally, once they know the benefit of it, they are motivated. Of course, nothing speaks better than the results they feel.

Vince Black has had many patients whom he strongly encouraged to do Xing Yi and Ba Gua, even if he knew they didn't innately have the ability of a natural martial artist. Surprisingly, overcoming their pain and illness keeps them motivated. The perseverance, heart, and the character all comes from within them. Then, like me, they didn't have sense enough to quit and they just kept plugging along. Pretty soon it's years down the road and they're a whole different person because of it. There's an entirely different way they move in their body. They have an internal sense of themselves. They have a strong sense of self so that they aren't pulled around as easily by other people. This is because there's an internal reality that's just as real and solid as the external reality.

It's wonderful to see that metamorphosis. I think that's why Vince will take a patient whose shoulder is really screwed up and teach him some Ba Gua or sword work. What's that sword going to do? Extend and open up the joint that needs to be opened from the weight of the sword and the extension of it. Some patients might ask why they're doing that if they aren't a martial artist. Well, guess what, they're doing medicine. It's a powerful healing art! If they keep it up, what eventually starts to come out of them is a certain sense of personal power. Many of these exercises can be prescribed for rehabilitation, and I do! There are entire wards in some Chinese hospitals that specialize in practicing *qi gong*. That's the physical therapy they give people with chronic illnesses. Ultimately it's all about working with the life force and restoring imbalance so you can have more vitality. The internal arts are that doorway, whether you use it for benefiting your health or as an effective fighting art or both.

Bruce Kumar Frantzis

Bruce Kumar Frantzis is well known in the martial arts community due to his popular writings and international seminars. Originally out of New York City, he now makes his base in northern California. After years of traveling and training in the martial and healing arts of Asia, he has focused on creating a core of trained instructors who can bring the numerous benefits of internal style martial arts and qi gong *to the public in a very concrete, non-mysterious fashion.*

Mr. Frantzis is a direct, sometimes blunt teacher, and although his methods are deeply rooted in the traditional way, his teaching is always concerned with the here and now. To feel and live within your authentic self is emphasized above and beyond aggressive fighting techniques.

Although much of what he does is beyond the ability of students to replicate, he is ever insistent that what he can do, all can do. It's just a matter of methodical and dedicated practice. Quality above quantity is the focus, as throughout his teaching the feeling and sensation within your body is fundamental. Without this inner ease and poise, all martial or healing arts will only function partially. When the mind and body are united, the internal arts can then flourish.

During my meeting with Mr. Frantzis, I was impressed with his ability to clearly demonstrate the essence of each of his arts, while maintaining the thread of continuity between them. He notes that the spontaneity required in free fighting demands absolute liberation of the mind, yet to develop that freedom requires disciplined training. His execution of fighting applications is fearsome and totally alive, yet consistently takes the shape of the classical postures. After experiencing this firsthand I came to realize that the Chinese martial arts can indeed fulfill their promise of making body and mind function with a seamless fluidity.

Bruce Kumar Frantzis
APRIL 30, 2002

Stages of Martial Arts Practice

I DON'T THINK there's just one purpose in practicing Chinese martial arts. Like anyone else, I went through many different stages. Training usually begins as one thing for people and ends up being something else over time. There are a couple of different things that can be had out of it, but your personal goals are up to you. The first and most important thing is that any practice you do ought to be something that makes you healthy. I say that because a lot of martial arts will basically destroy your body. They may make you good at fighting, but you can get hurt in the process.

In external martial arts the goals are well-defined. You become fit, you get some discipline, you learn how to fight reasonably well, and you gain some confidence in your life. It's not just that you can stop somebody from beating you up; it's that you can accomplish goals, period. You are given very clear, measurable tasks. When you can kick somebody in the head or kick a bag and send it flying, you have now done something that you can measure.

Photo by Caroline Frantzis

Bruce Kumar Frantzis with his teacher Liu Hung Chieh.

Many people who become good at internal styles start with some base in external martial arts and have already gained the experience of self-generated inner discipline, training hard, and the sense that "I can do it." You need that sense because in internal practice some of the goals might seem a bit nebulous. You need to know what it is when someone says, "Train until you get it," for this not to be an abstract idea but something you can actually go and accomplish.

Practicing internal martial arts should first make you healthy and full of energy. If it gives you *qi,* it will make you healthy and it will fill you with energy. *If you have inner discipline,* you are being taught properly, and you practice enough, you will get qi.

The second thing is that the internal arts are going to develop your mind. Because the way in which you get qi in the martial arts is through applying your mind to do very specific procedures. Whether it's a fighting technique or a way of doing a form or a posture, it's your mind that ultimately is going to mobilize the qi and enable you to do these techniques. As the Chinese phrase goes, "The *Yi* moves the *Qi.*" The mind moves the qi, the qi moves the blood, and the blood brings strength.

This is at the most gross level of practice. Once you make your body healthy and strong, you are in a realistic position to learn the fighting techniques of internal martial arts. Some people only learn to get healthy; they never learn the fighting stuff. If you learn the whole program, which makes you go to the furthest extent of your abilities, you learn the fighting. But doing so means overcoming your fears, it means learning how to train, it means learning how to focus, it means getting over the fact that you think you're the best or worst in the world, and just going and doing it, win, lose or draw, until you start winning.

Fighting the Enemy Within

A T THIS POINT we have another issue. You can have very strong qi running through your energy channels, you can have a punch that can knock out a horse, but your mind could still be fairly messed up. You could be an emotional wreck and lack all the qualities that are normally associated with spirituality.

The next stage of practice in the internal arts, which also helps you to get more qi and refine your mind, involves the meditation side of the martial arts. Here is where you're going to learn to get off of most of your negative attitudes and self-images and the real insecurities that you have, which may not be very obvious to you. Here is where you're going to go into very pristine mental and psychic states, which are at the very beginning of learning how to truly integrate yourself on all levels.

Maybe you just have an interest in fighting, because a lot of people, men especially, have had that interest since the dawn of time. But how do you come to peace with the fact that you have this incredibly aggressive biology? You need to deal with it and work with it and have it become your friend, instead of an enemy that rips you apart and gives you a heart attack at an early age.

So you have a strong punch, but do you have it with uncontrolled anger, or do you have it with peace of mind? Are you able to integrate to the point where fighting or combing your hair or studying or typing at your computer all have the same smoothness, or is it that each of these has this stressed-out, manic spike to it? This becomes a very big issue when you enter into the world of meditation within the martial arts. As you start getting into more advanced

Photo by Jaimee Itagaki/CFW Enterprises

Ba Gua Zhang application against side kick. The force generated by the step allows the Ba Gua practitioner to throw his opponent without the use of a backward leg sweep, leaving him free to contend with additional attackers.

qi work, you start going into the mode of meditation. But the fact is, you could just do internal martial arts and get a lot of qi, and not actually work on transforming your mind, spirit, or soul. What it ultimately comes down to is having the qi of your body and mind be very, very full, and that doesn't require fighting.

I started off with an interest in fighting well. I liked it. I didn't even particularly think about it making me healthy, because I started in external martial arts and in those days health wasn't an issue. But even in the earliest stages of martial arts I had an interest in meditation. I did my first Zen *sesshin* when I was about fourteen, where you sit twelve hours a day for about two weeks. My motivation wasn't spiritual. I wanted the one-pointed concentration that Zen gives you. That's really why I did it and I got it. Applying that concentration to martial arts stood me in good stead throughout my whole training in the West and in the Orient. It gave me a kind of relentless focus, an ability to persevere that very few people get.

In my late teens, I went to university in Japan and did very heavy traditional Judo and Karate training. I also trained with Aikido's founder Ueshiba O-Sensei for two years. Along the way I learned some interesting and pretty wild techniques that I was told were Tai Ji, but were really from White Crane. They made me incredibly powerful, but I came up against the fact that they also made me slightly crazy. I personally experienced what was called *Zuo Ho Lu Muo*, or "Fire Goes to the Devil." This means that if you do qi gong incorrectly it makes you physically sick or mentally crazy. I didn't get sick from it, but I did get a little bit crazy. And I started finding out, "Wow, I have this anger, all these destructive emotions inside me." I said to myself, "Wait a second, this is ridiculous, are you just going to become a powerful crazy person, or are you going to deal with this and be a positive force in the world?"

Daoist Meditation

A T THIS POINT I started getting involved in Daoism. I also went to India for a couple of years. I did practices to find out how to make my mind smooth and clear, which is the goal of meditation, on the road to enlightenment. Although I had an interest in the abstract concept of being enlightened, I also had a very pragmatic interest in making sure that my mind and emotions were very clear and very smooth. So I meditated.

At this juncture I was somewhere in my twenties. At the time, I was involved in the real fighting game. I wasn't just joking around or playing it as a contest, but doing it for real. And I was very good at that, and as a result I had confidence in my abilities. So I wasn't too worried about protecting myself physically.

But then I started really becoming interested in what would happen if I focused on a different enemy. Instead of an external enemy that you can beat up, what about taking on everything that is a lower part of your nature, and making that the enemy and trying to raise that up to the higher possibility of a human being?

So that became very much my focus, and the interesting part of it was, the better I got at the meditation aspects, the better my physical fighting skills became. Not because I was doing anything extra physically, but because when I lost the internal resistance that is inside all of us, my natural abilities started coming out. Even if you train like a maniac, if you have enough internal resistance, your best can't come out. And that's ultimately where you find the barrier to really advancing.

I also became a healer. I learned how to use qi for healing and I became a doctor in hospitals and clinics. Again, even from the perspective of healing, what are you really dealing with? You're dealing with how to make your body really work, how to make your mind really work, how to make your energy really work. But instead of your opponent being somebody you need to punch, kick, or throw, the opponent now becomes fighting somebody else's disease, either physical or mental. How do you balance their qi so that they no longer have this disease?

So my process went from having an enemy that was a physical opponent, to the opponent being the basic nonsense and destructive emotions in my mind, to the enemy becoming other people's diseases. And to accomplish all these things meant learning how to deal with my higher nature. Eventually, with my last teacher Liu Hung Chieh, the whole thing became about accomplishing and embodying emptiness, balance, and compassion.

Subtle Energies

WHY DO MOST PEOPLE take up martial arts? Some take it up with the fantasy of being able to be a super person, or for physical protection. What most people are really after is to increase their confidence and get rid of their insecurities. All the bogeymen that are in their psychic garbage can, all the things that they have left over from their childhood or from bad experiences in later life. They want to get over the feeling of being powerless.

Who in this world likes to feel powerless? But in reality, everybody is to some degree powerless. So much of real life is beyond anyone's control, as much as we would like to pretend otherwise. This said, when you get to a place where you have enough sense of your own power and how it can be used as a positive and constructive force in the world, you ultimately understand how knowing that allows you to live comfortably with the powerlessness.

Internal martial arts, especially Ba Gua and Tai Chi, have the possibility, but not the obligation, to naturally develop in the direction of enlightenment and spirituality because they are philosophically connected to Daoism. Xing Yi is different and in my experience it is not, nor ever historically has been, primarily built around spiritual growth. However, it can wonderfully engender very strong and stable confidence, make your body incredibly strong, and focus your will just like a laser. The basic philosophy of Xing Yi is to conquer the other person's territory, to fulfill your worldly goals. *Xing* means "form," *Yi* means "mind." I train my mind to make my body and actions assume a form that will accomplish my goals. The way in which I do my physical actions or mold my thoughts produces the mind that will accomplish my goal. Xing Yi is totally about achieving goals, period—goals usually worldly rather than necessarily spiritual.

However, because Xing Yi balances your qi and builds an incredibly strong body, it can create a good foundation if you want to do something higher. Many forget that if an airplane is going to lift off into the sky, it first must go down the runway. You need to use your own effort to turn the key that starts the engine and your basic training gets you down the runway. To become highly skilled in the basics of martial arts you have to start somehow, with either an external or internal method. You must go through some process until you can realistically recognize what your body is doing when fighting or practicing by yourself. From the Daoist perspective especially it is extremely important to have a basic understanding of how your body works.

Photo by Jaimee Itagaki/CFW Enterprises

Xing Yi Heng Quan defense against multiple punches. The circular Heng Quan motion crosses the attacks, deflecting while simultaneously striking the attacker. This requires the skill of sticking. Heng Quan is the most difficult of the five Xing Yi Quan fists, integrating all of the first four elements.

Overcoming Fear

YOU ALSO NEED to get past the instinctive fear of being hit, punched or kicked, so you don't freeze up in the clutch. Whether you get that from doing sparring practices, or you go and get that from fighting in the roughest ghettos of the country, or by being in military combat, you have got to get to the point where you can say, "So what?" So what if somebody is attacking me? Maybe I'll win, maybe I'll lose, but I won't freeze.

One reason Tai Ji has a hard time getting going as a martial art in the West is because most of the people who take it up don't have sufficient experience of fighting to get over that fear. People who go through Karate, Shaolin, or boxing become used to physical contact as part of their training. For example, there's a phrase in Western boxing called "getting your face wet." That's where two people put on gloves and for the first few minutes of sparring just hit each other in the face without really defending themselves. This practice helps you get over the emotional fear of getting hit because you learn to deal with the reality of what's happening.

Self-Hypnosis

WITH EXTERNAL TRAINING, the way you use your muscles can become a form of hidden self-hypnosis. You get habituated to all the emotional rushes caused by the screaming, yelling, tensing up, the making of animal-like contortions that help you focus your power. Effectively, these very strong hormonal rushes act like a form of hypnosis.

My teacher Liu Hung Chieh always used to say, "What you practice, you become." If you practice becoming tense, you become tense. Practice relaxing and you become relaxed. Being addicted to an external way of movement or fighting comes largely from how you do your solo forms. If every time you decide to do a punch, kick, or throw during a form or sparring, you tense up, lock up, or make a certain kind of a scream, all of this creates a certain mindset that constantly trains your body to tense. Over time, this develops into a habit, an adrenaline addiction to unconsciously and continuously recreate this tension within your body. In the West we would call this adrenaline addiction. If you have become accustomed to that rush, you won't necessarily look to anything that isn't going to give it to you, even if a different approach makes you a more effective fighter. It's a very rare person that gets interested in looking at what the art of fighting really is rather than how to further extend the adrenaline rush.

"From posture to posture the internal power is unbroken"

THERE IS A PHRASE from the *Tai Ji Classics* that addresses the fundamental difference between internal and external martial arts. In Chinese it goes, "*Shr Shr Shang Cheng Jing Bu Duan.*" The translation is, "From posture to posture the internal power is unbroken."

Look at the way most external martial artists do a typical punch, such as a snap punch. They usually put some kind of attention on how they tense while doing a technique and then how to relax the muscles at the end of the strike. It's like a staccato drum beat—an ever-repeating pattern between relax, recharge, tense, relax, etc. Very often, without most people realizing

Tai Ji Quan defense against high roundhouse kick. *Tuo*, lifting, is used to catch and break the attacker's balance, followed by a kick or stomp to the supporting leg.

Photo by Jaimee Itagaki/CFW Enterprises

it, there's an unconscious time lapse between when they stop and when they recharge. And in this gap or pause, the mind often unconsciously goes temporarily blank, leaving the body without power, if only for a very small amount of time.

In the internal martial arts, first and foremost, you never have a second where you don't have power. Your power never turns off. So rather than being like a drum beat, it's like water coming down a waterfall. The water's never disconnected; it never stops and starts. Regardless of whether you are yielding or attacking, there is no time when you lack power in your arms or anywhere else in the body. There is variation, like a dimmer switch that you can turn down to where it's almost dark, or up to as bright as it can go. But you never turn it off.

That's how the internal martial arts are done, and it has many practical benefits. For one, it prevents exhaustion. Because when you're constantly doing/releasing, doing/releasing, you can easily get tired and drained. Second, a really smooth flow can occur, which allows you to put out full power at relatively no distance—called in many martial arts circles a half, quarter, eighth, or zero-inch punch or open-hand strike or kick. This is a very important thing because the goal is to make sure that your mind never loses awareness or gaps out.

If you reach a stage where your mind ceases to disconnect, you start noticing how other people disconnect in almost invisible, micro-interval moments of time. When you catch someone in the gap between a disconnect and a re-connect, a stop and a re-ignition, you will find that they are frozen and defenseless, if only for microseconds at a time. If you look at the subject of timing and fighting, victory or defeat is measured in thousandths or ten thousandths or hundred thousandths of a second. That's the difference between you getting in with enough momentum to succeed, or not getting in and being hit.

This issue of unbroken power is a pretty basic difference between internal and external martial arts. A lot of this awareness training appears to be like meditation, but only in the sense that, within meditation, the first stage is having continuous concentration. The second stage of meditation, in any form, is about how you are going to transform and change all the stuck emotional stuff that's inside of you.

Every place inside that you have anger and fear, some bad memory, or some limitation inside your mind is where you're going to have a gap. Your mind and body will be incapable of functioning with a smooth flow. Overcoming these gaps is a major goal of the spiritual side of internal martial arts. Most martial artists don't do their practices with this goal; hence practicing these arts usually doesn't actually do the things necessary to get rid of those glitches or blockages inside one's spirit.

This is a big subject in internal martial arts, and all its techniques are geared toward allowing the mind to make your power continuous. You end up at: "From posture to posture the internal energy is unbroken"—not just the qi, but also the mind, also the body, so no part of you goes to sleep. Your physical power never shuts down; it's just that you go down to the least amount of power that's required to maintain either the structural integrity or effectiveness of any posture or technique.

Traditional Ba Gua Zhang

I WAS VERY FORTUNATE to learn the methods of two different branches of the Ba Gua Zhang tradition. First was the Ba Gua martial tradition. All my main teachers, Liu Hung Chieh, Hong Yi Xiang, and Wang Shu Jin, and a number of other people that I dealt with knew the martial tradition and knew it very well. As much as I was able to learn from them I did.

However, another Ba Gua tradition is derived from the Daoist monasteries, the original energetic source that created the martial art

Photos by Jaimee Itagaki/CFW Enterprises.

Ba Gua Zhang defense against a left side kick, punch combination. The defender captures the attacking limbs, stretching his opponent's leg out and thereby destroying his balance. This makes the attacker vulnerable to either a downward chop to the head or an upward palm strike to the ribs.

Alternately, the captured leg is used as a lever to throw the attacker while stepping through his space.

of Ba Gua. I was able to learn that method only from my last teacher, Liu Hung Chieh.

This Daoist Ba Gua tradition also contains parts that aren't only about making your mind, qi, or spirit stronger, but include Daoism's transformational methods that impart how to make your spirit completely free, clear, and open.

These Daoist spiritual practices weren't done as a martial art. The whole practice of walking the circle was designed to manifest the energies of the *Yi Jing*. It wasn't about fighting. Its energetic techniques became adapted to fighting three or four thousand years after the basic method was developed.

As previously said, martial arts encompasses many purposes. You can desire to beat someone up; you might want to defeat a disease; or you may want to conquer and overcome the weaker parts of your nature that prevent you from becoming fully aware, at peace with yourself, and enlightened. The Daoist practices within Ba Gua Zhang can be used for all these purposes. In the monasteries, monks used it to try and overcome their lower natures and become totally aware.

As with all internal martial arts, it's not just what you do with your qi, it's also what you do with your mind, and your mind has many different levels to it. There is energy running through the qi channels of your body, but what about your mind that is running through the same channels? Or your emotions? So the next step is to look at the nature of the mind and spirit that is running through the channels. Buddhists use the term "Mind," Daoists more often use the term "Spirit." They look at the same phenomena slightly differently but are essentially talking about the same thing.

As you get better at working with your channels in meditation, an interesting thing happens. As your body loses its general resistance and gets rids of emotional glitches, it gains mental clarity. Now you can begin to effectively use this clarity in real situations because you have the foundation to develop your skills to the greatest extent.

From my experience, the best way to get into this is to find a good Daoist teacher and learn how to do it. The first thing they most likely will take you through are various detailed methods to open up the energy within your body. You're not going to find what's inside those channels if those channels aren't open and full to begin with. They're going to get you to become aware of, open up, and develop what's inside of you. Rather than the inside of your body being something that you're not experientially aware of, your insides start becoming something you are consciously aware of.

For example, start with the body until you can feel the inside of your joints, the inside of your internal organs, the inside of your spinal cord within your vertebrae, the inside of your brain. Then you learn how to coordinate the different anatomical and energetic things inside you that are real but normally hidden from your awareness. Because you're one person—you're not only an arm, you're not a leg, you're not your Tan Tien, you're not your eyes, you're not your foot. You're one whole person. However, in order to actually fully integrate this one person, the Daoist perspective is that there is a need to be consciously aware of each and every single part. If the inside of your liver, the inside of your brain, the inside of your blood vessels are conscious living things to you, only then can you start discussing, "How do I make it all integrate?"

In Chinese they call that *Nei Wai Xiang He*, "The outside and the inside combine." In the beginning everyone focuses more either on the outside or their insides. Eventually, however, they bounce back and forth until they arrive at this place in the middle where there is no difference between the inside and the outside. They are fundamentally the same, they are just like a coin, you've got one side and you've got the other, and in the middle they join. That joining point is essential to eventually finding out what it truly means that "from posture to posture the internal energy is unbroken." Within the Daoist tradition I belong to, meditation, fighting, healing, it's really all the same thing. The basic method is applied to different situations.

Liu learned the monastic tradition after his thirties. Before then, he was a qualified master in the martial art of Ba Gua and one of the last members of the original Beijing Ba Gua school headed by Cheng You Lung.

Photos by Jaimee Itagaki/CFW Enterprises.

Ba Gua Zhang defense against high side kick. Ba Gua stepping allows the defender to capture and sweep or kick the attacker while in continuous motion.

In Sichuan Province he took his practice to the next purely Daoist level. He didn't do it just by "investigating, exploring, and inventing" the material on his own. Rather, he learned from a refined tradition that had been developing and specializing for thousands of years.

There are two general ways to approach Ba Gua practice—from the outside in, or the inside out. The method of doing a lot of qi work (walking your circles, practicing slow movements, etc.) eventually starts to awaken you to some of the spirit and mind that's inside your body. That's from the outside in. But what I've been talking about so far is a few notches higher where everything starts coming from the inside out. It just depends on where your main focus is, what "enemy" you ultimately wish to overcome.

Cheng You Lung. From *True Transmission of Ba Gua Zhang* by Sun Xi Kun.

Integration: "First Separate, Then Combine"

ULTIMATELY, INTEGRATION is the most central aspect of the internal martial arts. The phrase "first separate, then combine" from the *Tai Ji Classics* sums it up really well. First become aware of something that's separate inside of you. Then combine it with the rest of you, the totality of everything else you are aware of. If you're disconnected from your body, first you have to become connected to your body. If you are disconnected from your energy, you've got to get connected to your energy. If you're disconnected from your mind, you've got to get connected to your mind.

Then you've got to find out how to start connecting all three of them, so that each brings out the other, until everything that's in you comes awake and you now have everything consciously combined. But along that path, there are millions of little mini-combinations and little mini-separations before you start getting into the larger and more spiritual ones.

At each stage every external movement has inner forms and outer forms. Your outer, external form is where your torso, head, arms, and legs are moving through space. Your inner form is what you are doing inside your body with your mind and with your energy. Your awareness of how little body parts move is also part of the inner form. Most people in the West are not terribly aware of inner forms. And if you're going to go from the stage of form to no form, everything in this form has to become awake before you can drop it. You have to know how to ride a bike before you can forget about it and just ride. There's no free lunch, although lots of people who read martial arts books fantasize that there is.

The nature of a specific situation determines how the various training methods are done with all the minor details. The minor details are all the important details. The most talented have the natural ability to see something and make all the parts just come together. Others get it better by clearly being taught in very specific, articulated detail. My teacher in Beijing, Liu Hung Chieh, took me through the entire process until I understood everything as specifics, so that I could pass it to the next generation and be able to adjust to a wide variety of people's natural inclinations. This is because most people aren't able to just naturally bring it all together without being shown how. I wasn't one of these chosen few naturals, nor did I know anybody who was one.

Early Experiences Learning Martial Arts

I BEGAN MARTIAL ARTS IN 1961 at the age of twelve. I got into it because I lived in New York City and either knew of or saw a number of extremely violent incidents. I personally knew people in junior high school and high school who got mugged and killed. When I was twelve I saw someone murdered on a street I happened to be randomly walking down. In a second incident, a student in my school-yard on the Upper East Side of Manhattan got his stomach sliced open for verbally ridiculing a fellow student. I watched his intestines fall out. I didn't want this to happen to me. I didn't get into martial arts for fun, I wanted to make sure I didn't get killed.

Shortly after the second incident, I saw a sign that said, "Jerome Mackey's Judo: Fear No Man," and I thought, "That's me, I'm afraid, I'm going there." After I started, I just fell in love with it. Call it a karmic calling, I took to it like a duck to water. It was like the first time a person realizes they are going to become an artist by seeing a certain painting, or a musician that is inspired by someone he hears play. Once you start, you've just got to do it. I was very fortunate, especially when I first started, to learn from teachers that were really good.

Mr. Ito was the person who gave me my first Judo lessons. Mr. Ito began Judo at seventeen and by twenty-two had won second place in the All-Japan Judo championships. In my first two lessons, Mr. Ito taught me how to fall. The first day he asked, "Can you fall?" I arrogantly said, "Yeah, kind of, I guess." He must have thought I was the typical disrespectful kid, because he then proceeded to pound me. I guess he thought I would admit that I was arrogant and that no, I don't know how to fall, but I wouldn't give him the satisfaction! At the end of this pulverizing first day, when he finally let me go, I couldn't even walk upstairs. I was so stubborn. The good part of perseverance is tenacity, but I was just stubborn. The reality was that Mr. Ito was an amazing, if unorthodox teacher. During the second day of training he taught me how to take hard falls, and this skill has stood me in good stead for my entire life.

My first Jujitsu sensei was an eighth degree, an old-time samurai. My first Aikido sensei was a close student of Ueshiba, the founder of the art. He was the first Aikido teacher to come to New York. My first Karate teacher was a legend in Okinawa before he came to the States. Everybody was really first-rate.

Ba Gua fighting
application. From *Ba
Gua Zhang Applications*
by Yan De Hua.

Learn the Basics

MY EARLY EXPERIENCES taught me to respect martial arts
as an art. You don't get people that train three, four,
five, six hours a day for decades on end, all without getting
massively paid for it, that aren't artists. The great martial
artists had the same drive and motivation that makes
painters paint, that makes musicians play. They may change
what they do through different phases of their lives, just as
some artists have blue, red, and orange periods as means to
fulfill their artistic expression. Personally I relate to this. I
also went through different stages; it's an evolutionary thing.

Picasso and Gauguin were both great painters, and at
times they shared the same house and inspired each other
to do their best. Both had really different approaches to art.
But both were trained at an early age in the fundamentals
of art. They used similar tools and oil paints and had the
same structural understanding of painting. And it's out of
that that the genius of their art grew.

That's why in all martial arts, there is a constant, never-
ending emphasis on getting your basics right because without those basics, you'll never become all that you could be;
you'll never reach the high performance that you may have
a natural gift for.

Many martial artists never reach their fighting potential
because they are busy collecting new fighting techniques
with lightning speed. They're not doing the needed amount
of repetition to truly assimilate them so they can effectively
use them under real pressure. They have not taken the time
to find out what the real grit of a fighting technique is. They
haven't learned the central point that it's not in the movement itself, but what the movement is capable of creating

inside of you. Some have accumulated so many poor martial techniques that they would be better off doing a lot less movements and extracting more quality out of them than to continue doing a lot of movements and having minimum or no quality within them.

They have a phrase in Japanese called *"Tokui Waza,"* which means "your special technique." Those are the one or two that you win all of your competitions with. But you learn hundreds of other techniques, because by learning them you get to recognize little tiny pieces that are inside your few special techniques, and it is this knowledge that gives you the winning edge. Being able to do something and having it work well for you are two different things.

You need to have good basics. Don't be concerned about learning so many moves; learn a few well. If you want to expose yourself to the different ways people do it, fair enough. But remember, you've got to have something that you practice regularly. It's like practicing chords for a musician—it's something that keeps on bringing you back, and takes you deeper. It's only from your depths that you're going to draw up and develop your creativity and power. It's not going to come from your surface.

Especially during the initial ten years of training, an immense emphasis on basics is what allows you to hit real pay dirt in terms of your body, energy, and spirit. Because eventually, good teachers can only teach you to the level that the strength of your basics will allow them to. They can't do anything more, it's impossible.

Do Less Better

THE BEST THING you can do to succeed in internal martial arts is to take the primary technique of the art you do (in Tai Ji it's Grasp Sparrow's Tail; in Ba Gua the Single Palm Change; and in Xing Yi, Pi Quan) and really practice that technique to death, ad infinitum. Not like an unfeeling mindless machine, but more like a musician playing chords until you really get what it is. It's going to be from that foundation that your natural creativity, talent, ability, and insight are going to truly emerge. Many excessively bounce around learning the next "new" form or movement set without ever extracting the real internal value from any of them. As my first Ba Gua teacher Wang Shu Jin used to say, "It is better to do one technique well than ten thousand poorly."

Over time you go progressively deeper into each one. You extract real value from each one, gaining more real internal power and the ability to apply it across a wide variety of contexts, such as fighting, healing, or meditation. This organically happens by going though what seems like a thousand different profound micro-stages—until while still doing the same simple movements you are playing the internal martial arts equivalent of Beethoven.

Speed and Power

IN TERMS OF FIGHTING, internal and external martial arts have many points in common, such as the absolute necessity for functional speed and power. Speed is of two kinds. The first is how fast you can accelerate from point A to point B in space. For example, if you start with your hand at your side, how fast can you punch somebody in the head and retract your hand to its original position?

The second kind of speed is speed at touch—how fast do you move when you're touching the opponent's body? Speed at touch is different from speed when not touching. Speed through empty air is very different from how fast you change direction or accelerate when your hand, leg, or torso is in bodily contact with human flesh that can instantaneously react, give resistance to, and thwart your attempts.

Internal martial arts focus much more on speed at touch for two major reasons. First, initial physical contact with your opponent's hand or body gives you real-time intelligence, allowing you to accurately feel and know where your opponent's weapons (hands, feet, or swords) are located. Second, you become able to accurately extrapolate from tell-tale but subtle signals (that can be felt but not seen) what their next move will be and to counter it. This ties into an important phrase from the *Tai Ji Classics:* " I start after my opponent begins but arrive before him"

Speed at touch enables you to control the enemy better, especially when fighting multiple opponents where there is an even greater need to know where your opponents are by feeling and touch rather than sight. However, the biggest thing in the internal martial arts is power not speed. The curious point is that as you get internal power by developing qi, you get speed automatically. Internal martial arts don't depend on pre-programmed combinations. Your movements work at the same speed your mind does. You can be very fast if your mind doesn't gap. The more your mind gaps, the slower your actions are.

Internal and external power are different. Internal power is invisible, so subtle you can't see it. External power can be seen; you can tell it's happening when it's being exerted. As you develop internal power, you start to intuitively feel the qi of a person. You can also feel where their qi is absent, weak, or fluctuating. When you attack, these are what you go for. After all, why would you bother to hit something that's not a vulnerable area? You become very conscious and sensitive to how your qi is interacting with your opponent's qi. You don't just throw your fist because you see an opening of unobstructed empty space. That's a little like launching a bullet from a gun, or a stone from a slingshot: the projectile's movement is fairly mindless and predetermined so it has a trajectory that will not vary. A punch that goes out from your internal power is more like a heat-seeking missile: it tracks and adjusts its trajectory accordingly until it hits, or finds a better target.

In internal martial arts, the power is like a bullet that doesn't really leave the gun; the power never fully releases, it sticks with you. You first learn this sticking ability by touching and adhering to someone's skin. Over time this progresses to where you do not need to stick to their skin but can do so without touching, by sensitively tracking the qi emitted by different parts of their body, feeling it, not just looking. That's how internal power works. Or at least that's the way I and many internal masters I met in China experienced it.

The Waiting Game

THE SINGLE MOST IMPORTANT fighting skill in internal martial arts is waiting. You wait until your opponent gives you an opening as a gift. Look at joint locks, which are hard to do in full-speed fighting, particularly if you go for them aggressively. Some martial arts like Jujitsu and Aikido make joints locks look deceptively easy and make them out to be a perfectly reasonable fighting strategy applicable to a majority of situations. In their training practices one partner willingly lets the other grab his arm, usually with a decent grip, deliberately making himself vulnerable. This is a foolish and potentially suicidal strategy in a real confrontation with a well-trained opponent.

Internal martial artists don't go there. They develop training methods such as silk arms where they can twist and bend their joints like a piece of silk, making their movements highly fast, reactive, unpredictable and mobile, which makes it hard to grab or lock their joints. This is why in China it is known that it is almost impossible to put internal martial artists into any kind of joint lock.

However, joint locks can be very easy to do if you just wait for a natural opportunity to spontaneously appear. Their hand has to be in just the right place and your hand has to be in just the right place before you can take the opportunity. But you don't go looking for it because joints can fold, and if your opponent understands this science (and Tai Ji and Ba Gua people do), not only will your joint lock most likely not succeed, but you will be wide open for a nasty counter.

Ba Gua Zhang defense against a side kick. The defender begins by stepping into the opponent's kick to capture his leg.

Photos by Jaimee Itagaki/CFW Enterprises

The power of a slight forward step is used to strike with a palm to the face. This could knock the opponent out, or with a waist turn, he could be thrown backward. Alternately, the defender steps forward, turns the attacker's body, and applies a leg lock, driving his head into the floor.

Therefore vis-à-vis joint locks, it's better to wait for good opportunities than to assume or expect them to be there.

To put it another way, when a practitioner of the external styles attacks with a lot of combinations, what they're doing is setting up patterns of rapidly turning a light on and off, three or four times in a row, so their actions appear to be continuous. But they're not continuous; there's a certain level of stop and start, an unconscious gap between each individual action when it is done three or four times, and if the opponent is awake during those gaps they can catch the attacker in a vulnerable position. That's when waiting can be a very powerful advantage.

I'm not saying that the internal arts are ultimately better than other martial arts. Because in a car race, there's the person and the car. The best car in the world with a lousy driver won't work, and an exceptional driver can do wonders with a junk heap.

The Mind behind the Form

BEHIND EVERY LIVING martial art form is a way of thinking, a mindset, a kind of strategy. These strategies teach you to think in terms of moving this or that way, or to this or that angle. But when you start moving into free flow, these strategies only become possibilities. They should not become expectations of what will happen during the free flow of fighting within each microsecond of time. It's not like if he does this, I *should* counter with that. This will destroy your spontaneity and stop you from adjusting appropriately to what is really happening. In free-flow combat each microsecond is new, alive, and unique. Internal martial artists need to give up preconceived expectations, as real life has a nasty habit of not fulfilling them.

The reason why there are many forms and so many strategies is that they catalog most of the ways any two fighters can shape, fold, and interact with each other. The movements are options to use in specific circumstances. Hopefully your teachers or your personal creativity serve you well enough that you have sufficient technical variation to start to understand what's far, what's near, what's close, what pressure causes this or that reaction for what reasons, and you can extrapolate appropriately in unpredictable circumstances.

Now you have the next issue: once your body has enough technique and has learned many possibilities and options, it's time to understand that it's the mind that's telling your body what to do or not to do. When you are doing specific single techniques such as the Single Palm Change, Pi Quan, or Beng Quan, or different forms within Tai Ji, Xing Yi, or Ba Gua, you are developing a kind of mind, which is something distinctly different from the physical movements themselves.

Is your mind able to perceive what is going on in the here and now, or is it just projecting ahead of itself? Let's say you start to reflexively do a three-step combination. Projecting ahead about how to deal with this is OK, but what if your opponent at the second step doesn't do what you expect? If your mind is awake you see it, adjust and change to something else. If your mind is not awake, you just go through the third step and between the second and third one you are now vulnerable. Consequently if the opponent is good enough, you'll lose.

The central point of internal martial arts is mind, not qi, as most seem to think. You need mind to get to your qi, just as you need to really develop your qi to empower the

Xing Yi's Lian Huan form. From *Xing Yi Five Element Connecting Links Boxing* by Li Cun Yi.

mind. It's like a circle. You also need your body because your qi has got to function through something. Your physical body, qi, and mind are all connected. The first step is doing the necessary Nei Gong work to be able to get qi to really energize your body, so your body can properly work so that if you mentally ask it to do something, it does it.

As you develop this qi energy further, it both starts making your unconscious mind more conscious and also causes your mind to gradually wake up. Your mind waking up intuitively tells you what to do with your increasing energy. Mind and energy dance with and reinforce each other. One does not exist independently of the other, although at times either can dominate or appear more important. Sometimes getting your body to be energized so that it can move more speedily is important, but then there's your mind's ability to just be capable of accurately seeing what's going on. Then if you have good timing, if you have a strong enough punch, you don't have to do fifty movements—you condense all the possibilities into one action. Make one cut, hit him, Boom... it's over, down he goes. Enough already with all the screaming and excessive movements. Just do the job, get it over with, and go on to the next thing.

Xing Yi Quan finishing technique against a punch. The lower hand pulls to open up the opponent's chest for a downward blow, which can drive him to the ground.

Photos by Jaimee Itagaki/CFW Enterprises.

Intention

THIS STUDY OF THE MIND is a major focus of the internal martial arts. Using the mind in internal martial arts is central to how you find "from posture to posture the internal energy is unbroken."

For example, look at Xing Yi. You have a thought or an intention, your mind tells your body something, and your body morphs into that shape. It's not "I practice a technique, so my body goes into that shape." If you actualize the philosophy of Xing Yi far enough, wherever your mind leads, your body instantaneously assumes the shape that your intent dictates. You reach that point by going through many practices, the main point being that I want my mind to make my form become a certain thing.

Can you do this in the beginning? Hell no! At first you move your muscles, but your mind doesn't go along. Eventually, however, your mind moves with your muscles. Your body does the form because your mind wills it to. After this goes far enough, you next begin recognizing the link between your mind, your body, and your energy. Then if you change the direction of your mind, your body just responds. Not because you learned specific physical movements; maybe it was only by watching someone do it once and finding that you can also do it. Rather, it becomes a question of whether your mind can encompass what the end function of your intent is, and can your body do what is physically needed to fulfill that intent successfully? This implies that you first had your mind directly interface with your neurology, which tells your muscles what to do. You first had your mind interface with the energy that moves your body. When they're both fully awake, there is no difference between thinking and doing.

Most people can't see the mind; they see its signatures or shadows. In actuality, it is possible to see the mind, but you have to be really developed to do that, and the central issue is how awake you are. This is the bridge between internal martial arts and meditation. Practice first makes you aware of simple things like punching, kicking, throwing, and moving energy to be able to do them. Practice can be understood as a process of moving from the most external part of internal, to the most internal part of internal. The least internal part of internal is that you learn how to physically move not only primarily from your muscles, but from your joints, spinal vertebrae, and internal organs, until you can physically move things below your skin.

Gradually you learn more and become able to move energy through your channels to hyper-charge any given movement and make it much better. You learn to control the energetic field around you, your aura. This is more internal.

Moving even more internally, you start considering the mind that runs through your channels. What mind, motivations, emotions, thoughts, attitudes, and primary instincts run through your channels? Now you begin to take conscious control of what is going to run through your channels, rather than being controlled by what was previously put in and remains there. Now you choose and train what you want to run through those channels—be it ferocity, creativity, clarity, love, or compassion. To many, it's transcending what was conditioned into you during the past. If you want to break your dysfunctional and destructive inner programs and move on, you have a method to do so.

This is yet again a more internal part of "internal," which is moving into the area of what in the West is commonly called enlightenment. The Daoists don't usually use the term "enlightenment." They talk about going more internal. But "internal" doesn't have just one meaning, it's all a matter of levels.

Classic Nei Gong, Integration, and Degrees of Internal Clarity

BY THE SAME TOKEN, what does it mean to be clear? Yes, there are levels of that as well, but something more serious than levels in a computer game. We're talking about what level of human development your life is at, for real. Not at an intellectual level that you would chat about in a coffee shop, but what is your day-to-day living experience? I teach the classic Daoist sixteen-part Nei Gong system, of which the sixteenth component is integration: integrating everything

Ba Gua diagram.

you've done, going through the first fifteen parts and having them integrate into one fully connected coherent whole. This goes back to the Tai Ji idea of "Separate and Combine." If you go from one to two, you've got to integrate one and two. When you go to three you've got to integrate one, two, and three.

A central phrase from the *Tai Ji Classics* describes integration in another way: "One part moves, all parts move. One part stops, all parts stop." For my money the two most important phrases in the internal martial arts in general, and in Tai Ji specifically, are: "From posture to posture the internal energy is unbroken," and "When one part moves, all parts move; one part stops, all parts stop." These are more or less a description of enlightenment. If something is enlightened it is true in all places, at all times, and in all circumstances. That means it is connected, unbroken. Anyone can use the words to fantasize and distort the true meanings behind them. This said, there's an immense amount of training and an immense amount of wisdom and knowledge that have accumulated over thousands of years to teach someone who wants to learn how to precisely accomplish this.

The qi work, the Nei Gong, is special in that it contributes to all these considerations, while also giving you additional resources to heal your body. The alphabet of Ba Gua is Nei Gong. The alphabet of Tai Ji is Nei Gong. The alphabet of Xing Yi is Nei Gong. The alphabet of Qi Gong is Nei Gong. The alphabet of Daoist meditation is Nei Gong. You can look at Tai Ji and Ba Gua as types of writing based on these fundamental letters of the Nei Gong alphabet.

But all Daoist systems have to integrate with everything else that's in the system, all the defenses, all the set-ups, all the training of how you get the power. All martial arts are integrated to some degree— some much more, some considerably less.

Nobody owns Nei Gong, qi, or spirit. They are gifts that antiquity has given to the human race. Some people have the good fortune to wake up to them sooner; some people's luck is not so good and they wake up to them later on. That's about all there is to it. The West will sooner or later find out about parts or the entirety of Nei Gong. However long it takes, it is inevitable.

Paul Gale

Paul Gale teaches in the redwood region of northern California, outside the small town of Arcata. His efforts are dedicated to teaching the essentials of gung fu *practice. Unusual among many who've reached a master level, Mr. Gale continues to train daily to perfect his own art outside of his regular teaching duties. The emphasis at his school is on basic training, the fundamental building blocks laid from the ground up that create not just a fighter, but an authentic human being. The understanding of balance, coordination, and connected strength is continuously built into the body and naturally overflows into all aspects of his students' lives.*

Paul Gale is a man of humor, penetrating insight, and seemingly endless patience. This patience manifests in helping his students strive for the best they can be, but he has no patience for phonies of any kind, including fantasy martial artists and tough guys who see fighting as their way to dominate others. Paul Gale has lived through the reality of what violence is and the core of his teaching comes directly out of that experience—the understanding that to hurt another human being is to utterly deface one's own humanity.

Paul Gale
August 15, 2001

The Cultural Context of Chinese Martial Arts

ONE OF THE GOALS of Chinese martial arts is, first, good health. Live a long life. The best way to defeat your enemies is to outlive them. You're here, they're not, you win, that's it! The first aspect is good health and fitness. This brings long life, longevity.

Along the way, you try to fulfill your potential as a human being. It has nothing to do with being Chinese or anything else. Ultimately, training is a way to express what you think a human being is, to move like a human being. To feel yourself as a human being, and what that means. Whatever you think the human species is supposed to be, you're it. Training is a way to figure out what it is to be a human being, and to move as a human being. To express that humanity. We're the only ones that can do it! It's not that we're humans trying to be animals; we're animals trying to be human. Training is a way to figure out what that means.

Paul Gale.

All martial artists are born into a certain cultural context. That's something about martial arts in America that people seem to forget. They imitate things, but they don't duplicate them. There are certain cultural contexts that you can't duplicate if you're not born into them. People get lost in theater, thinking, "We're back in nineteenth century China." No, you're not. You never were! You weren't even ever in twenty-first century China! So where are you?

Photo by Mike Stengl

These ideas go beyond a particular culture. Balance, posture, and coordination are not a nationality. Being on your legs and being coordinated does not depend on an ethnic origin. You either are or you're not. There's no such thing as a Chinese humerus. If you're balanced and on your legs, you're on your legs; it doesn't matter where you're from. That's really what the arts are trying to get us to, not all of the ceremony.

In some ways, Asian culture has too much tradition, and we're a culture that has no tradition—people are starved for it. A lot of people get involved in martial arts because they want the ceremony, they want the tradition, they want the trappings. That's usually what they're best at. When it comes to doing a martial art, they can't move, but they can go through the ceremony, they can recite the mythology and all the stories correctly, and pronounce everything right. That's when it just becomes an imitation. Because you will never be able to duplicate the cultural context. I grew up in Canton, Ohio, not China; there's no way I could ever duplicate that and I'm not interested in imitating it. Then I'd be an alien in two cultures—mine and theirs.

The martial arts have become so fantasized, so full of mythology and nonsense and mumbo jumbo that people forget about the physical reality part of it. You have to put all that nonsense aside and do the labor, do the work. People have been fighting all over the world for a long time; it's not exclusive to Asia. Somebody in Scotland, six foot five, two hundred and forty pounds, will pick you up and throw you on your head, and he's wearing a skirt. Fighting arts are found all over the world.

I don't know that it's only fantasized here in the West, to tell you the truth. I haven't been anywhere else, but I don't think it's much different. My teacher Sifu Woo said to me once, "If there's a million people doing Tai Ji in Tianamen Square, nine hundred ninety-nine thousand, nine hundred ninety-nine aren't doing a damn thing." It's no different there than here.

The advantage that we as American martial artists have is that we can take the best of all traditions and put them together. You're not chained to one way because that's how you've done it for generations and you're not allowed to change. You don't have to follow that tradition. You can change, you can take the good ideas from everywhere and put them together. If you're involved with a throwing art and you keep getting hit in the face with a jab, you'd better find an answer to that! You should say to yourself, "I'd better fix this" instead of saying, "It's just our tradition to get punched in the face."

The idea in training is that you become something. Not that you do Tai Ji or do *gung fu,* it's that you become *gung fu.* You become Tai Ji, you become something. That isn't a skin color, that's not a nationality, that's not an ethnic origin. When you run into people that have become something real, you don't fight. You either sit down and have a cup of tea or you go your separate ways.

There's an irony to training in a fighting art that a lot of people seem to have forgotten. You're not training to be an assassin. Most Chinese martial arts come out of a family system as opposed to a military system. The system was, your grandfather said, "Hey, come here, do this. OK, now go get me some food." It wasn't boot camp, it's what you grew up in. That's the cultural context—some kids are born with a soccer ball in the crib.

The First Step

THE FIRST STEP is to begin on a very physical level: put your body in alignment and move it in harmony with itself. That's posture and coordination. Without that, you can't do anything anyway. That's the first realm, that's the physical realm. Then all the other stuff comes out of that. The emotional, the philosophical, the esoteric, all of those other things come out of that physical experience. Without that, all you ever feel is that you are off balance. All you're ever feeling is your

Paul Gale teaches the warm up set.

conflict, all you're ever feeling is your discomfort.

Are you a body that learned to think, or are you a spiritual consciousness that's taken physical form? Well, you're both, and one evolves the other. We participate in our own evolution. Most other creatures adapt, but we have an ideal of what we want to become, and we keep trying to evolve into that. Politically, socially, economically, spiritually, physically. We have the longest childhood of any mammal, and that in itself is a big lesson. Creation is trying to tell you something—that you need a lot of help. Training is a way to do that. You're constantly being born again into your own potential. Because as you fulfill potential, you create more potential. So the first goal is to live a long life, and to express what it means to be a human being. First, on a physical level, that means you are moving as a human being.

Martial Arts and Sports

YOU CAN TRAIN YOURSELF in any sport, martial arts or not. The difference is that the fighting aspect of it is a way to resolve violence. See, you can do it in ping pong, you can do it in football, people do it in art, you can do it in plumbing, if you seek that within it. Within the mundane is the extraordinary, if you seek the extraordinary within the mundane.

I have trained with people who never sought any of those things. To them martial arts is just about making a fist and hitting somebody. That's all that it ever was. There's no metaphor to it, there's no symbol, there's no parable, there's no philosophy, no application outside itself, nothing. If you don't seek those things, they don't exist. You have to seek them in what you're doing. Otherwise, what's the point? Then it really is just about punching somebody, and you don't have to train to do that. Just do it. You get hit back, that's part of what you get.

You can find the physical aspect of it in any athletic endeavor. The difference is that it's a fighting art. Not to fight, but to be able to if you must. So the lesson is to know when you must. You see, most people fight *about* things, they don't fight *for* anything. Most people fight about nothing! There are things to fight for, and everybody has to make up their mind about that. That's specifically a martial art. That's not ping pong. In martial arts you're hitting a human being, not a ball. You have to understand the consequences of that. It doesn't take very much to hurt somebody. You start to understand how fragile we really are. How precious we really are. You don't feel that the ping pong ball is really precious.

You can find a lot of life lessons in other sports that are the same as what you find in martial arts, because each one is a discipline. The work ethic, the physicality, the dedication, the perseverance of it. Having to use your body in a coordinated, aligned way. All those things are the same but then they go in different directions.

Paul Gale's students practice kicking.

Art

CHINESE MARTIAL ARTS are a human art. You're the canvas, and the painter, and the paint, and the person viewing the painting all at the same time. You're a blank sheet of paper, you put your poetry on it. It's a self-contained art form, and what you're expressing is what it is to be a human being. What it is to be alive in context of where you are. All in one, that's the ideal.

Along the way, the fighting part is really the easiest aspect of it. Once you can do it, it's the simplest part of all. First of all, the majority of people in the world have never been in a fight in their lives. Which is a good thing, don't misunderstand me, that's how it should be. But, most people are completely defenseless. So what does it take to hurt a defenseless person? Not much. If you go through the rest of your life and you never have a fight, you'll be a better martial artist than me. Because I've had too much violence.

The great general wins the war before he even fights the battle. But the first requirement is that you have to have an army. That's what training is, to become an army. You first have to be willing and able to fight. That comes first, then you choose not to, and it becomes the last thing you want to do. In order for it to be the last thing you want to do, it has to be the first thing you train for. Then you put it aside, then you do everything else not to use it. Use your humanity, your humor, your intelligence, bribes, whatever is necessary not to go to war. Because you always know that if worse comes to worst you can do this.

Some people think that this parable about the general means that you just don't fight. That's not what it means. The real issue is, you only have a choice if you are able to do it. Otherwise it's just something you can't do and it has nothing to do with a choice. So the lesson is that you learn how to do it so that you don't have to do it.

Action and Reaction

WHEN YOU MOVE, all of you is in it. Nothing is left behind, nothing is stagnant. Everything's connected and moves as a unit. Just like creation itself, all the different parts involved are constantly interacting to create a whole.

People who move in pieces are always off balance. They're always disconnected from themselves. Physical training teaches you to connect things and move them as a unit. You becomes something greater than your individual parts. Your different components have a relationship, an oversoul to it which is true in all relationships. A third thing is created when two people come together: the relationship. It should be greater than the individual parts. It should be an obligation, a dedication, a commitment to "the relationship." Not just to what I want. Hopefully, if it's a productive relationship, it makes you better together than you could be by yourself. If it's a bad relationship, it makes you less. In training you're trying to make yourself more than you could be separated in different parts. Because that's off balance. You put it all together and it becomes holistic. Then when one thing moves, everything moves. There's a total commitment to everything you're doing, or you don't do it. That teaches you about fighting. If you have any doubt, that's the answer, you don't do it, because when it's justified there will be no doubt—it will be reflexive.

People already know how to fight. There's a fight or flight mechanism in everybody. Training is to allow you to respond to that instinct. The training should give you the physical wherewithal to do what your instinct is telling you to do. That may be to turn around and run away, but most people can't even run away. They fall down, or they don't move at all. Because they move with the top, they don't move with the bottom. That's what training teaches you—move your feet, move your legs.

Do what your body tells you to do. The great art of martial arts is in reaction, not action. It's reflexive—that's the art of it. Confrontation is not a reason to fight. You're not training to fight because someone said something about your mother, or flips you off on the freeway. It's when it's twelve o'clock at night and you're trying to put air in your tire and somebody jumps on your back and hits you on the head—that's when you find out what's real, what's reflexive. You find out how you react and then you'll know what you've been training.

Pre-meditated techniques don't work because they're actions, not reactions. They were originally reactions, but people take them out of context and standardize them. Someone comes in and attacks me and I do one, two, three and four and he's down on the ground—it's reflexive. If you take it out of context and try to repeat it, then there's no reaction to it any longer. You're just practicing the end result.

You might be imitating the moves, but you're not duplicating what it took to do them. The art is to respond reflexively, second nature, on the breath. It's a non-thinking intelligence. It's not pre-meditated in terms of "I'm going to put my hand here and then I'm going to put my hand here, and I'm going to do this."

That's what most people find out about their training. A real situation happens, and they don't do anything. It's not so much that they do something and it doesn't work. It's that they do nothing, they have no reflexes. It's because they trained that way. Do you realize how many times you have to do something to make it reflexive? How many thousands of times you have to repeat something for it to really be there? More than people think!

Structure

WITHOUT STRUCTURE, you can't do anything. And people with skill, they don't care what technique you're doing—they're busy exploiting your physical structure. They're not going to attack your strength, they're going to exploit your weaknesses. The weaknesses are just in how you move yourself. If you can't move up and down the floor without losing your balance, what can you do with somebody kicking and biting and punching and poking you in the eye? What chance do you have? People kick and fall down all by themselves. People punch a bag and break their own wrist!

Without a good foundation, what can you do? We accept that in any other art or physical discipline there's a certain foundation. You have to be able to get your fingers to work to play the piano. Without playing scales, without playing chords, you'll never make music. We accept that in any other discipline.

Without the basics, without the fundamental structural realities, nothing will work. It just takes longer to build good basics than it does to learn a few techniques. You can learn tricks fast, but to develop real

Photos by Owen Tipps

Students practice the Three Star drill.

structure takes longer. That's why magicians practice, while martial artists train. You're not just doing tricks, you are training to become something. You should be moving differently from somebody who's never trained. You should be put together differently. And if you're not, what's the difference between you and somebody that's never trained? The tricks, that's all. If somebody comes along who truly has that foundation, and truly is on their legs and has that structure, the tricks won't work.

What you eventually come to discover is that motion is just motion. Once you have a structure where you can move your arms and your legs and your body simultaneously and not lose yourself, then motion is motion. A punch can be a push, a push is a throw, a throw is a kick, it's all just motion. When is it a block and when is it a strike? It depends on the moment that you apply it.

When you watch somebody with real skill move, there's a certain structural integrity to how they move that's different from some-body who's just a thug. There's no denying a thug can hit you hard and hurt you—that's not it. Where's the elegance, where's the grace, where's the art, where's the expression of what it means to be a human being in movement? It's a beautiful thing. To move the body that way is an important part of training. That's what feels good when you're training all by yourself. That's why you can move and move and move because it feels so good to be able to move that way. It's like how good it feels for Michael Jordan to leap into the air and dunk the ball. Or somebody who can really and truly hit the sweet spot on a tennis racket.

Someone who's really on their legs doesn't need to overpower you—it's purely structural. It's not that he's bigger or meaner or stronger, or anything else. It's that he's underneath you. He'll uproot you all the time. To uproot a person you don't even have to knock them down. It just means you have to get under. At that moment in time they're not doing anything because they're falling, they're grabbing, everything chokes up. They can't hit you, they can't kick you, they can't move out of the way, they're defenseless. Once you disconnect a person like that, once they're disoriented, they're defenseless. They can't see you. If you're good, you're always exploiting a person's weakness, never fighting their strength.

The secrets are in all the basics. The secrets are what you should be learning in the beginning class. The secret is, I'm on my legs while you aren't. The secret is, my arm is coming off my whole body, yours is not. That's the secret. It's hard for people to accept it but that's the only secret. In an art like Tai Ji Quan, the way most people do Tai Ji, it's not a martial art. They could never use it the way they're doing it. Because there's no legs, everything's in their hands, they just fill in the rest with the fantasy talk.

In order to really develop true fighting skill, there are certain things you have to teach yourself. That's the lesson, that's what's important. You can dance through things, you can live in a fantasy, and you wouldn't have to teach yourself anything. So that's really what you're missing out on. What's really important has nothing to do with fighting. Because the training has a relevance in your life every day and the fantasy doesn't.

Hard versus Soft

IF YOU TRAIN LONG ENOUGH, hard and soft arts become a third thing. When people get into arguments about which is better, hard or soft, internal or external, the question should be "when is it better?" If you train long enough, they become a third thing. The bulb isn't light, the electricity isn't light, its when they come together that they create light. They are constantly interacting, you don't know which is which.

If you train only one way, you usually go too far that one way. Hard training can get to the point that you become rigid, and the rigidity becomes brittle. You look at people who've trained only that way and as they get older they can't move; they're all broken down. Everything hurts, they have tendonitis everywhere, they've been hard in the wrong way. People also go the other way and get so soft that they have absolutely no structure to what they're doing. When you hit them, they fly like a kite; they have no foundation.

Tai Ji is iron wrapped in cotton, or iron wrapped in silk. Most people do circle in a circle Tai Ji—there's no square in the circle, there's

Photos by Jason Henry

Students practice the Yi Chi Kuen Chak form.

no iron in the circle. They're doing silk wrapped in silk, with no internal structure to what they're doing. Whereas most people in a hard art are too hard, and that's why they hurt themselves all the time.

When hard and soft start to interact they become a third thing. If I were to do a punch or a block, I don't know if it's a Tai Ji punch or a Gung Fu punch. I don't know if it's a Tai Ji block or a Gung Fu block. I don't think of it that way.

The essential aspects of true internal martial arts take a long time to manifest. You know, you can pound on somebody with brute strength if you have it. Truly, the internal arts take longer to develop. It's not just visualization techniques, either. People think that internal means you just imagine something happening. There are things internally going on within the body, real physical things that you're doing. That's what the training's supposed to be, not just that you can imagine it. You can imagine it forever, but if your body's not doing it, it's not happening. Internal expansion, the intercostal muscles lifting and expanding, those are physical realities, not just "I imagine it." There's also energy, life-force energy that you're moving. It's not just brute strength, it's Shen force, spirit force.

Ideally, you put hard and soft together into a third thing. For me the ideal martial art is Yang long form Tai Ji legs with Southern Gung Fu arms. Put them together, what can that do? Is it striking? Is it kicking? Is it throwing? Is it grappling? It's all of those things. Is it internal or external? Yes! Is it hard, is it soft? Yes!

Mohammad Ali was right about "Float like a butterfly, sting like a bee." You also want to be a bee that floats like a butterfly, and a butterfly that stings like a bee. That's hard/soft, internal/external coming together. That's being a two-hundred-pound butterfly.

Physical Reality

ONE IDEA WITHIN Chinese martial arts is the sense of feeling what's going on inside your own body. It should be present in all martial arts, but most of all it should be part of being alive! That's what I mean, being a human being. You really can't feel the outside unless you feel the inside. It's a physical reality that you're feeling. Do you feel the bottom of your foot? For real! If not, why not? Can you feel your spine? Can you feel those things for real? They're a physical reality, and the more that you can feel them, the more insight you can gain, and it becomes the foundation of a fighting art. You're able to feel the opponent more than they can feel themselves, so that when the opponent does not move, I do not move. When the opponent thinks about moving, I move first. What does that mean? Not that I'm reading his mind, but I'm stealing his own feeling. As soon as he strikes, I've hit him.

You have to begin by feeling yourself, then you can go out from there. Otherwise what can you feel? If you are numb to yourself, then what can you possibly give to someone else? And what can you receive? In a way, you are the center of the universe, but you must acknowledge the universe. What you're trying to achieve is the inside looking out. Not the inside looking in, that's having your head up your ass. Not the outside looking in, that's a non-feeling objectivity, that's just you watching you like a TV show. You want to see from the inside looking out. You need to literally feel yourself as what it means to be a human being. Then you train that to a specific discipline.

The exercises will help you find that feeling. These arts are designed to do that using very specific exercises, not aerobics. It's designed to build a structure in a very particular way. That's what's lacking in most people's training: they're not putting themselves together so that they can find these things. They're just doing the outside. If you seek the truth outside yourself it just keeps getting further away.

First and last, it's a physical discipline. Your body has to be able to do these things. Then visualizing can enhance it. If you visualize that you're going to run a 9:5 hundred-meter dash, you'd better be able to run a 9:6 first. Otherwise visualizing doesn't mean a damn thing. I can visualize playing for the NBA from now until the end of my life. It isn't going to happen! First you have to have the physical reality of things to a certain degree. Otherwise you're just in a TV show. There's really nothing going on from your head down.

That's the labor that most people don't want to do. That's where you reveal a lot about yourself to yourself. You can BS the world about a lot of things and get away with it. Don't BS yourself about martial arts. Because you put yourself in a situation where you might get hurt. It's better to know "I'm going to run real fast right now, as fast as I can and get the hell out of here, because this guy's going to kill me." You should know that instead of saying, "Just yesterday I learned a technique that'll work—watch this!"

Mindfulness

THE MORE YOU CAN feel yourself, the more you can use yourself, the more useful it becomes to enhance what you feel, and you are able to enhance what the body does naturally. You have to be able to feel that first. Most people move out of habit and don't feel themselves at all. Until they look in the mirror and say, "I look like I don't feel too good." But they don't really feel what they feel. Training is a way to get you to feel yourself. Doing what you're doing when you're doing it. Then it has an experience, and experience gives it meaning.

If you go through the whole day and you never feel what you're doing and don't experience what you're doing, at the end of the day that's self-inflicted Alzheimer's. You have no memory of where you were or what you did. It's totally a blank space that day. Wasted, gone, and it'll never come back. There will be many days at ten in the morning, but never this day at ten in the morning. Each moment becomes precious, and that becomes a fighting art—you're right there every moment. Somebody loses their mind for a second, that's when they're hit. They lose their focus, they lose their concentration, they lose where they are for that one moment. And the other person doesn't. That's why all war is based upon deceit. You distract the person, take their mind, then hit him. The training is, don't lose your mind. Mindfulness of yourself, mindfulness of your own existence, mindfulness of the experience of what you're doing.

Feeling what you're experiencing for real is part of the mentality you train in the martial arts. It's called mindfulness. You don't empty the mind just to lobotomize yourself; it's not mindless-ness. People just space out and they think that that's it. You empty it so that it can be refilled by what you're experiencing. It's empty of the chatter, it's empty of neurotic anxiety, it's empty of preconceived notions, it's empty of opinions, it's empty of politics, it's empty of social conventions, and if you empty your mind of all that, it's a cleansing process. Then you can allow it to be refilled by the true experience of what you're doing. Then you can do something with it; it becomes skillful. The more mindful you become, the better your body can move and respond in a certain way naturally.

Sometimes if I was training, working on a form, Sifu Woo would say to me, "What are you doing?" I would tell him the name of the form and he'd say, "I know the name of the form! I'm asking, what are you doing? Where's your mind? You're just dancing around! If you're not going to be mindful in what you're doing, then forget about it, let's go eat." I would end up saying, "OK, let's go eat!" That's the difference.

When you practice, your mind should be in exactly what you're doing. It's not that if you're punching your mind should be in that punch; it should be in the whole structure, in the structure that you're building, in the structure that you're connecting. In the sequence of everything that's moving, in the sense that things are moving from the bottom of the foot through the legs, through the body and out the arms. Most people are moving the other way; they're moving their hands first.

You're constantly connecting things and you're monitoring things. You almost have a CAT scan going; you have the insights into all the things that you've been working on, and you want to try and keep them connected. The exercise is to keep things connected. Then you work on individual parts. A specific exercise may work on just one thing. You put all the things together through the use of forms. That's when you take on the structure that the exercises taught you. Then you throw away the exercise and keep the structure. The next step is when you move it, that's transportation. You find things when you're still, but then you lose them when you start to move. Gradually you are able to keep the structure and move. First is balance, posture, and coordination, then comes transportation. Be able to move on a person, and be able to make them move when you want them to.

Balance, Posture, Coordination

BALANCE IS YOU in relationship to the earth, to your circumstances, to your situation. Posture is you in relationship to gravity. You live in a world where the first external force is down, so the first force you want to feel is up. Eventually internally, up creates down creates up again. Coordination is you in relationship to yourself. Physically, mentally, emotionally, spiritually, however you choose to apply it. You develop those things, and there's an inherent structure to those things. Then you move the structure—that's transportation, and that's what has to come from the legs and the feet. If it's not coming from the feet and the legs, then you're off balance.

Some people talk about the Tan Tien, but what moves that? That's the center of gravity, but you have legs. You're not sitting and doing this. A lot of kinesiology students say that walking comes from the hip, but what moves the hip? Your legs and your feet! They're what's moving the center. The foot is the root, the leg is the power, and the waist is the control, meaning it releases all that power. The arm and hand are just expressions. That's what the Tan Tien means—it's a command center. It's where you're steering things and guiding that energy, but it has to come from the leg and the foot. Then that internal expansion is released through mindfulness, and you can decide where you want it to go.

The root, the power, the release, and the expression are all what is being exercised. The coordination is that sequence of actions. When you are out of sequence, you are uncoordinated. If you're going to start things with your hands and your shoulder and your head and your chest, you're uncoordinated, because there's no foundation supporting it. You're awkward, you can't move, and that's why people get thrown on the ground all the time. They're falling all by themselves but they don't know it.

Students demonstrate Moving the Horse stance.

That's why a lot of people in striking arts can't shoot more than three or four punches in a row. They aren't balanced. So they have to grab, they have to stop themselves and regroup, they can't keep moving. The ideal is to shoot a thousand punches and never be off balance. If you practice a striking art, you should be able to strike somebody and keep him off of you. In order to grab hold of you, they have to come to you. You completely throw away the supposed advantage in a striking art if you can't shoot more than one punch.

If you understand balance, posture, and coordination, you will see that it has nothing to do with fighting. It has to do with executing a correct kick so that somebody can't grab it, and that requires a certain balance, a certain coordination, a certain structure, a certain way of doing things. That's what you want to learn, not kicking somebody. That's really what the teaching system is trying to get people to understand about training. If you train for those things, those qualities are in everything in your life. There's no place where you want to throw yourself away. There's no activity you want to get involved in and throw yourself off balance when you're doing it. One thing reflects the other.

I emphasize basic training because without those basics, without that foundation, nothing will work. I teach very, very little, and what I teach is not everything. Some people tell you they teach everything: ten thousand weapons forms, ten thousand katas, ten thousand techniques, ten thousand punches, ten thousand kicks, clairvoyance, everything. I don't. I teach a very little thing, but that little thing is the basis of everything. What could a martial artist possibly do without balance, posture, and coordination? What could you possibly do without truly being on your legs? Without truly being rooted and having a foot? Without having your body connected and moving correctly? It's a physical discipline first and last. If your body can't do it, it doesn't exist, it's not even an idea. It has to be a physical reality.

The Bottom Moves the Top

As you start to understand that balance in all things, you see how the bottom has to carry the top. What does it mean w the leadership loses the people's trust? They lose the bottom, t the foundation, they lose the base. Because that's why the As the bottom becomes discontent, the center starts top. Now they've lost everything. That's what it how you start to see things. The people who a the boss is the whole thing, that without hi apart. No, without the workers the company would fall apart. Leadership can be visionary, but the work has to come from this foundation. The bottom moves the top, the back moves the front. The inside moves the outside, the weighted side moves the un-weighted side. For real! Not just in a philosophical ideal, for real.

Then you start to see this principle in all things. Just as the center, the Tan Tien, the waist, is the control and the release, there's a line of communication between the top and the bottom in all things. It's the center in politics that allows the extremes to communicate with one another. It's the center, the middle class that allows the rich and the poor to communicate. Otherwise they'd never have anything to do with each other—they'd always be at war. These ideas are in all things. Once you experience it in yourself, then it's really clear that it's in all things.

Common Sense

YOU HAVE TO ... e about what you're training
at everybody can do this if
this if they learn the tech-
do it. That's very undemo-
hat's the truth. Everybody
hat tells us we can, and in
e have to be individually
n sense.

around, but you should
r. You should have some
ou're coming through the
y. Otherwise you're just
ı'll be sold whatever the
ne common sense, some
k that. And you'll find

somebody that's genuine. Not "The Best," but genuine, authentic. Then you don't have to imitate anything. You just keep pursuing that excellence, see how far you can take it. You don't know where it will take you, and that's the fun of it.

Put all the mystical hype aside. You see, there's real mumbo jumbo in the world, and if you're ever lucky enough to get to it, the first thing you realize is that you couldn't make it up. There is a spiritual consciousness that gives you an insight, enlightenment, understanding beyond the physical limitations of our world. There really are those things. When you first get to them you realize, "I couldn't make this up, and what I was making up actually diminishes the real thing."

If spirituality is so easy that you could really learn it in six months, or in a seminar weekend, then why isn't everybody doing it? If you could really just touch a person and paralyze them, why don't boxers do it? Why club each other to death for twelve rounds? Why not just touch a point and paralyze them? If you could just wave your hand and cure cancer, then why isn't everybody doing it? The amount of time and dedication it takes to get to those things is a lifetime's work. It really isn't "I took a semester and I got it." That's not how it is, but for the most part that's how we're being sold on pretty much everything.

Gung Fu

IT'S THE DEDICATION, the perseverance, the commitment to something that really teaches you. No matter what it is that you're committed to in your life, work, or an endeavor, or a relationship, or a cause, it's that lifetime commitment that teaches you all the lessons. It isn't even so much accomplishing it. It's that path of dedication, that path of having virtuous commitment to something. People who live their lives that way, that's what they have in common. Not so much that they are dedicated to the same thing, but they share an

Photos by Jason Henry

Students practice the Yi Chi Kuen Chak form.

understanding of dedication. Their mutual respect is not so much that they're aspiring to the same thing, but that they respect each other's perseverance, they respect each other's commitment, they respect each other's authenticity to what they're doing.

All *gung fu* means is hard work. A skillful hard-working person as opposed to a hard-working idiot. A lot of people are *gung fu.* Luciano Pavarotti is *gung fu* in opera. The guy who drives a truck eighty hours a week to support his wife and kids is *gung fu.* In a broader sense, *gung fu* also means two skillful hard-working people—the person you are today and the person you aspire to be tomorrow. That's how you train every day. You are constantly evolving into what you want to be tomorrow and the next day. To be a better human being. Today is practice for tomorrow.

That's why there's the old saying, if you wake up and you feel good, train hard. If you wake up and you feel bad, train hard. How you feel is irrelevant: get up and do what you're supposed to do that day. Some days you do it slower than others, you have to stay within what you have, but the point is that you do it. That's the commitment, that's the dedication. That's why mountain climbers don't look up! Put one foot in front of the other, because that you can do. If you look up you'll quit.

Teaching

I'M VERY BLESSED because I do what I am. I never take that for granted, it's a great gift I was given in my training. Every day in my prayers and meditation I give thanks for that. If I could give people one gift, it would be that you do what you are. Because that's what training revealed to me, warts and all, exactly who I am. Inside out, no secrets, no illusions. Nobody can say anything about me that I don't already know.

That's what it takes if you're going to teach. You had better turn yourself inside out. No one wants to study with somebody that's walking the path for the first time. They're supposed to have walked the path and come back so they can tell you where the quicksand is. If you're both taking the journey for the first time, you're in big trouble!

I was very lucky when I first started to train because I was totally ignorant, my ignorance was an asset. I'd never been in a martial arts gym or dojo or kwoon in my life. I'd never seen a martial arts movie, I'd never heard of Bruce Lee, I never saw a martial arts book or magazine, I didn't know anybody who'd trained in martial arts. I was completely ignorant. My ignorance was an asset in that whatever Sifu Woo asked me to do, I just did it because I didn't know any other way to do it. I had no argument in my body, in my mind, no argument period. If he said, "Do this," I just tried to do that, and I assumed that everybody trained that way. The first time I went into a gym and everybody had bare feet in gi's practicing on a mat, I didn't know what I was looking at. I thought everybody trained in cotton-soled shoes on a slippery waxed concrete floor. I'd never seen mirrors in a gym. I had never seen sparring equipment. I didn't know what belts were, I had no idea. People were in boxing shoes on carpet, people in bare feet on mats—I'd never seen any of that.

My preconceived notions didn't get in the way. Almost everybody I trained with had trained in other things. They had all kinds of martial arts stories and I just listened. I didn't know what they were talk-ing about. I didn't have any frame of reference at all about martial arts. But I had been born into a lot of violence, so I knew what fight-ing was. My best friend got killed in a street fight when I was eighteen, so nobody had to tell me about fighting. I saw a lot of terrible violence in the streets, so I knew what that was.

I kept asking Sifu about other styles. Somebody would tell me a story about some martial art and I'd ask Sifu Woo about it. After about a year he said, "Get the phone book out and go around and look at all the other gyms." So I went around to all the other different kinds of martial arts and I just watched. I did it for about three weeks, and I came back and he said "Well?" I said, "I don't know what they're doing." He said, "Neither do I." I said, "I tried to be open-minded because I don't know anything about any martial art, but I know about fighting and I can tell you one thing: what most people are doing, they're going to get killed!" He said, "Right."

As hard as I am on the martial arts world, there are good people out there who are real and authentic. What you find is that they are all training for the same things. First of all is structural integrity in the body. That's what they have in common. I've known boxers, people in Aikido, in Kenpo, in small-circle Jujitsu, in Karate systems whom I respect. I respect them and they're real, what they're doing is real, they have real skill, and they're all training for the same things. Balance, posture, coordination, to be connected, to be truly on their legs, to have internal expansion, all those same things.

Fighting

PEOPLE THINK THE DIFFERENCE in martial arts is a difference in fight-ing styles. It's not, it's a difference in teaching styles. A style isn't really a system, a style is just how you happen to move. Your idio-syncrasies, your particular personality, your physical ability, it's just you. A fighting style is Mohammed Ali versus George Foreman. Making a fist correctly is what they both had to learn, and that's the teaching system. The tradition I am true to is the teaching system.

You have the opportunity to take the best ideas from all worlds, all systems, and incorporate them into what your life is now. The thing I'm most committed to in what I teach isn't that I continue Sifu Woo's fighting style. How could I do that? What I continue is his teaching system. Because really, that's his contribution to the martial arts. Not a fighting style, a teaching system—that's the tradition. A fighting style is just you, it's how you move.

From a fighting standpoint, if you're already disconnected, I don't have to do anything but make you move. The wheels will come right off the cart. If a guy is connected, you have to disconnect him in some way, you have to take his mind. You have to uproot the tree before you can move it. And if you can't do that, buy him a cup of tea, because a man that's truly focused and connected and moving as a unit is hard to beat. It's called "fighting clouds." You can't get in, and if he moves on you, he's moving like a tornado. Most people, if you truly can move, can be overwhelmed with sheer motion. They get to the point where there's too much going on and they just stop. In order to do that, though, you have to be able to move.

The longer you train, by embracing your own violence and teaching it something else, the more you start resolving the conflicts within yourself. The more skill you develop, the more you realize how easy it is to hurt somebody, and therefore, how very precious we are. The last thing you want to do is ever hurt anybody again. It's the people who are numb to that who are willing to fight about nothing.

People who have already been to war are the last ones who want to go again. The people who've never been there say, "Go get 'em!" No, YOU go get 'em! I already went! I know what it is. That's why you always treat a victory the same way you treat a defeat, like a funeral. Because it's ugly! What you start to understand is that there's

nothing romantic and glamorous about fighting and hurting somebody—it's ugly. Whether you win or lose, it hurts. So those ideas are
very specific to martial arts training. Different from baseball, different from ping pong, different from bowling.

Giving yourself to the system evolves the man—it's designed that
way. You notice as time goes by how people's balance and posture
and coordination improve. You can't lift your knee and touch your
ankle every day for an hour without sooner or later finding that alignment. Most people are off balance as soon as they lift one leg up. That's
why they fall down when they kick.

Wing Woo Gar

SIFU WOO DOESN'T TEACH the way he was taught. He was taught
the old way in China, where you just followed along. If you could
follow, fine, and if you couldn't you were ignored. That's it! You follow and follow and follow, and if you could do it, fine, you could do
it and that's it.

Sifu Woo's way was to train until he could beat the teacher, then
he'd go somewhere else. That's why in the teaching system that he
created there are so many influences in the forms, because they come
from all around southern China. The teaching system that he put
together was not how he was taught. It was to teach the people here.

The study of anatomy, kinesiology, the warm-up set, all of those
things compose a teaching system that he developed to teach people
here. The one responsibility of the teacher is that you have to teach
the people in front of you. I'm not teaching in China. You have to teach
Westerners differently, you have to explain things to them, they won't
just follow. For better or for worse, you have to approach them differently. Teaching is really about linguistics. You have to find the word,
the language that clicks for somebody. Sometimes the language is the
study of anatomy or kinesiology, sometimes it's a story, sometimes

it's a metaphor—it's different for each person. Sometimes it's hands-on, a physical thing. What clicks for each person is different, but you're trying to get the same thing across to each them all.

Some teachers follow a lot of philosophical things like "Absorb what's useful, discard what's not." Well, how do you know that? That's what you're supposed to be taught. "Express yourself." What does that mean? People end up throwing out what they can't do and then they call it their style. They're not really continuing a teaching system. They're trying to continue a fighting style. That's why in the end, it's all about techniques. "This is our fighting style, this is what we use." But there is no teaching system. So you're really not developing a human being. You're just teaching them some tricks, and they'll work on people who are defenseless.

All I can say is that time will tell. I would say to Sifu Woo, "Yeah, that's what I want to be able to do" and he would say, "We'll see." We'll see if you'll be able to do it, I don't know. I do know that if you don't train this way, you'll never do it. And if you do train this way you have a chance. That's what I know.

Most people in the martial arts fall into two categories. Either they understand more than they can do, or they can do more than they can understand. I was in the second category. I had no idea what I was doing, but I could do it. Then I had to break things down and figure out, "What am I doing? Why does this work and this doesn't?" Sifu Woo had to do the same thing when he started to teach so that he could get somebody else to do it—that's the idea of teaching. It's to get YOU to do it. I can do it, that's not the point. It's a school! How do I get you guys to do it? Because you have the same body. Not the same personality, not the same nature, not the same idiosyncrasies, but the blueprint is the same. So everything must start from the question of how do you use this blueprint? Then you add yourself to it, your own characteristics. But first and foremost, get this blueprint built the way it's supposed to be built. Move it the way it's supposed to be moved.

That's first, because if you aren't doing that and you face somebody who is, you won't have a chance.

The Teaching System

ONCE YOU'VE BEEN through the system you can do whatever you want with it. In any training, everybody has to get to the point where they sit down and figure out for themselves what they're doing, and why they're doing it that way. Sooner or later, no matter what they're training in, the student has to sit down and break things down for him or herself. You reach a point where you have to take it as far as you can on your own. There are things that cannot be taught, they can only be experienced.

The teacher's responsibility is to put somebody on a path where they have a chance to experience it. You know that path will take them somewhere that's real, somewhere that's useful, that's productive, that's relative to their life, that they can use every day. Most people are on a path with a dead end. They train ten years and they end up with nothing. To me, that's immoral. There's a certain code, an ethical code, that says you want people to end up with something. It doesn't mean that they're the baddest ass on the face of the Earth. It has nothing to do with being invincible, it has nothing to do with being unbeatable, it has nothing to do with any of that. It has to do with attaining something that's real. You are truly on your legs. To what degree, I don't know, but it's there.

In the long run I don't teach Chinese martial arts. I teach American martial arts—what else could it be? That's where I am and that's who I am and that's who I teach. The seed of it, the root of it is Wu Shu, the Chinese martial arts I've learned. But there'll always be ten thousand things about Chinese martial arts that I'll never know, that I've never seen, that I've never heard of. There are people who can do things that I can't do, know things that I don't know, and this will always be true.

That's why every day Sifu Woo says, "I just figured something out!" You see, I'm not a master of martial arts, I'm a student of martial arts. Otherwise, how else could I learn anything more? The only people who are masters of martial arts are dead. Somebody says, "I've trained with a master." I say, "How could you learn from a tombstone?"

These are the concepts of belt systems. All "black belt" originally meant was that you finally became a student. It didn't mean you retired and became a very important person, that you now make appearances at tournaments, which is what it seems to be these days. It just meant that you trained a long time and were rolling around on the ground and your belt was black because it was dirty. That's all. So I'm only a student of martial arts. My training and my study are equally important as my teaching. When most people start teaching, they stop studying, and they stop training. They just become important. For me the teaching wouldn't be enough. I know that there'll always be more to learn. I never have to worry about "I got it!" I ain't got it! I just train, keep trying to acquire it, just keep adding to it.

Tradition

EXAMINE THE TEACHINGS that have been passed down and try to understand the physical reality of those things. These traditional sayings carry a lot more weight with people than if I came up with them myself. If I say "the teaching," people have a tendency to pay more attention than if I say "I thought of this last night." I would say to Sifu Woo, "People weren't listening to me so I said to them, 'Sifu Woo used to say…'" So everybody listens because it came from a wise old Chinese man. He would say, "Well, whatever it takes to get their attention." How you get their attention is really irrelevant. What's relevant is the teaching, whether it comes from my mouth or Sifu Woo's mouth or from one of his teacher's mouths.

One teaching says, "The bottom of the foot is the back." There's a physical reality of it that the bottom of the foot *is* the back, meaning that the bottom of your foot is pulling your back forward. You're not pushing the front forward, you're connected. The front is hugging into the back, the back is wrapping to the front, and the bottom of the foot pulls the whole thing forward. The bottom of the foot is pulling your back forward. It's not pushing the front forward. You have to learn to move that way, otherwise there's no foundation. You'll always get swept and knocked down because you'll be top-heavy.

The pictures we use are symbols showing that the foot being the root, and the head holding up heaven, are what get your alignment to stretch up. It's to achieve a posture, using the metaphor of a certain picture. For some people the picture works, and for somebody else another explanation works better. It's always to achieve a certain end: use the bottom of your foot and your leg to transport yourself, keep the front and back connected, make the back go forward, your head holds up heaven, meaning hold your head up! Your head should feel suspended, your neck should feel empty. Holding something up, as if you were carrying a book on top of your head.

Holding heaven up has something else to it as well. It connects you to something. Your foot is rooted to what you've come from; your head holds up divine aspiration. Because whatever people's view of heaven is, it's usually pretty nice. I've never heard anybody tell me, "Oh, heaven's a terrible place." It doesn't matter how they define it or what their beliefs are; for the most part that word is a pretty enjoyable idea for most people. You need to connect to that enjoyable idea. You want the Earth to reflect that.

It's not that heaven is like the Earth. That comes up as a misunderstanding in a lot of translated Daoist writing. It's not that you're trying to make heaven like Earth; you're trying to make Earth like heaven. You have this divine aspiration and whatever your definition of heaven is, try to reflect it. Here and now, take a little heaven home!

In order to do that you have to hook up to it.

In this it's not a game and it's not a ball or a basket or a racket—it's you. You're trying to move with a certain grace and elegance that feels good, and you want to keep feeling it because it's you. The fact that it's martial movement is what makes it a fighting art. All of these "teachings" are to get the physical reality of things, so that you can find all of these other expressions that come out of it.

It's not a tournament. It's martial arts, in life, for real. You win because you didn't get hurt, and you didn't have to hurt anyone else. That's the idea. When people talk about what's authentic in traditional martial arts, what's most traditional, what's most authentic is to do what works. Which means you have to keep updating things. You're not involved in eighteenth-century warfare. So if you're learning techniques that were taught in a military system to go fight an eighteenth-century war, you'd better update them or throw them out. People aren't attacking you with eight-foot spears. So in some ways the techniques are obsolete. You upgrade them and update them, or else you throw them away. Military systems are for getting people ready to go fight a war, and they were fighting a very specific kind of war. They're not fighting it now! Where's the relevance? You'd better answer that question for yourself, or else you're just in a movie. Two hours a day you go into a time machine.

One time Sifu Woo said to me, "You know what you're doing?" I said, "No." He said, "Right. Just keep doing it. Eventually you'll have to figure out what you're doing so that you can teach it to somebody else."

Fong Ha

Photo by Eric Nomburg

Fong Ha

Berkeley, California-based Fong Ha is a frequent sight at Thousand Oaks Park, under a large cedar tree, carefully instructing students in the arts of Tai Ji Quan, Yi Quan, and Qi Gong. For decades he has been a stable presence in the Bay Area internal martial arts scene, bringing up generations of students, many of whom have enjoyed practicing with him for years. Mr. Ha's humor and joy in practice are infectious, and his students learn by example. He always practices alongside his class, doing numerous hours of standing and Tai Ji every week. His accessibility and good nature have led many people with chronic health problems to discover relief from pain with his practice methods.

We began evening class with an hour of sitting and standing meditation. Fong Ha's teaching emphasizes accomplishing more result with less effort. This is achieved by preserving one's energy for its most essential uses, reducing the amount wasted on frivolous thoughts and unconscious tension in the body. Mr. Ha insists that the most effective way to gain more energy is to stop wasting it. Once the qi is free and plentiful, the body can begin to naturally heal itself. After performing the gentle movement and awareness exercises of Yi Quan I found myself relaxed, stable, and energized. Fong Ha's vitality, compassion, and continued enthusiasm for the internal arts are a testament to the efficacy of his practice.

Fong Ha
FEBRUARY 27, 2003

Feeling in the Internal Martial Arts

I COME FROM A TIME and place where practicing Chinese martial arts
was quite popular among young people. When I was very young
my father referred me to my uncle, so by five years old I was already
familiar with martial arts. However, I've found that to do Tai Ji Quan
is quite another thing.

Martial arts, even in these modern times, are still important. For
one thing you have military service and other jobs where you have
to use some kind of skill or technique to cope with physical situations.
If you are a policeman or a security guard you must learn self-defense
and how to control an opponent, so I don't think the martial arts are
any less important today than before. Actually today Chinese martial
arts have become more popular and widely accepted than ever before.

But Chinese martial arts have a wider scope than just being an
offensive and defensive art or a sport. They are also considered to be
useful for human development, similar to the Yoga practice in India.
Some martial arts, especially internal martial arts like Tai Ji Quan,
Xing Yi, and Ba Gua, besides the sport and self-defense aspects, include
the practice of meditation. This involves cultivating awareness of the
mental as well as physical parts of yourself. Since the internal arts are
a Daoist practice, I guess you could call it Daoist yoga.

In reality there's nothing that's really internal or external; all actions
contain aspects of both. For example, if you're walking around holding a good posture, that's external. But the senses of equilibrium and
balance in the way you walk and being comfortable in dealing with
your breathing—all that is the internal part. There is an external and
internal element even in just standing up. You can make a solid posture, hold up your chest, and put your hands in the right place—that's

external. But how you feel inside, if you feel balanced, if you feel comfortable, if you feel less tension, this is the internal aspect.

Therefore everything has both internal and external; it seems to be that one affects the other. When practicing what's called internal martial arts, people seem to become more aware of what is happening inside themselves while they are doing the outside movements.

Wang Xian Zhai's Yi Quan

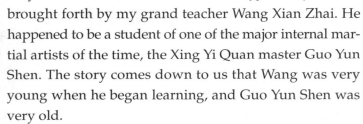

YI QUAN, also conventionally called Da Cheng Quan, is relatively new. It only surfaced with this name in the 1930s or '40s when brought forth by my grand teacher Wang Xian Zhai. He happened to be a student of one of the major internal martial artists of the time, the Xing Yi Quan master Guo Yun Shen. The story comes down to us that Wang was very young when he began learning, and Guo Yun Shen was very old.

Guo Yun Shen was one of the three major titans or giants during that golden age of martial arts. He was in the same category as Yang Lu Chan of Yang style Tai Ji Quan and Dong Hai Quan of Ba Gua Zhang. When people talk about internal martial arts they talk about these three major systems. Guo Yun Shen had retired, and Wang Xian Zhai was supposed to be a young kid with not very good health. He was sent to Guo Yun Shen to learn something about improving his strength. He gained Guo's confidence and affection by taking care of him, and eventually Guo transmitted all of the essential knowledge of Xing Yi Quan to him.

One of the major things that Wang Xian Zhai later shared with the world is a very important practice called Zhan Zhuang, or "standing stake still practice." This is

Wang Xian Zhai.

holding a posture like an *asana* in Yoga, except that you are standing straight up. It is geared toward developing tremendous energy, awareness of the central equilibrium, and other fundamental practices of Xing Yi Quan. Yet Wang Xian Zhai had further perfected it and made it into a practice that is very unusual when compared to most traditional martial arts. It is designed to uncover how all the finest abilities of internal martial arts were derived. He discovered that these skills all originate from a kind of meditative state. Later on when Wang Xian Zhai began to outgrow traditional Xing Yi Quan he didn't make up a new name for his art; he just took away the word "Xing," which means "form." He called it Yi Quan, because it's focused on the "Yi" or intent. Later on he supposedly gave it the name "Da Cheng Quan" since it's so complete, meaning "the great accomplishment boxing. "

It may seem unusual to include standing still in martial arts practice, but it is actually quite well known. Everybody at one time has heard the old stories about people that go to the Shaolin Temple and before you learn anything they make you stand for three years! This shows that standing, Zhan Zhuang, was a major fundamental practice. Of course when the art was passed on to the layman, most people were more drawn to the skill and the power they could develop in the system. They immediately went to the more fascinating things like movement and techniques while forgetting the very important awareness training. Zhan Zhuang is like meditation, and most laymen at the time considered that the practice of the monk. Monks meditate, whether sitting or standing, which was not for the layman to do. Therefore, for whatever reason, the students were not prone to the meditative aspects, so the teachers started just teaching the movement.

The Art of Central Equilibrium

AFTER MANY YEARS of Yi Quan practice, the concept of central equilibrium came to me almost as a little awakening. Central equilibrium is your own sense of balance, when you are standing up and you feel comfortable; you don't feel like falling down. In short, you are in perfect balance. And everybody in general has that after they get to be about one year old. They take it for granted until they lose it, until they are sick or they get old or they lose the ability of spatial balancing.

When you try to acquire the ability of standing on a balance beam, that is central equilibrium. The ability to maintain your balance in any situation is central equilibrium. So any kind of skill is nothing more than discovering central equilibrium while putting yourself in a difficult position. You could be standing on a tightrope, or standing on a parallel bar, and you would feel as comfortable as if you were sitting on the ground.

We practice being aware of central equilibrium to get more and more comfortable with it. For example, a finger banging on the piano gives you sound. But to be a pianist, you don't just use the finger to bang on the piano—playing music is an art. To be able to stand up and not fall down is the central equilibrium. To be able to stand and move in every way and still be at ease in your daily activity, that's an art. Standing in central equilibrium is at the core of all the physical arts. Discover how to maintain the central equilibrium in every situation. By yourself or in tandem with another person, if you make that the central idea, all the skills and techniques will come out of it.

Wang Xian Zhai, although he was not a

Photo by Eric Nomburg

Fong Ha practices Zhan Zhuang.

Photo by Eric Nomburg

Fong Ha teaches Yi Quan.

large man, was able to win many contests because he had mastered his central equilibrium. It's the same thing with the founder of Aikido—he was not a big man, either. Anyone in Aikido knows that by manipulation of the central equilibrium of yourself and your opponent, you can achieve great success.

Yi Quan's Four Practices

O F YI QUAN'S FOUR MAJOR PRACTICES, the primary one is Zhan Zhuang. *Zhan* means "standing," *Zhuang* means "a posture that is polar in nature," like a stake or pillar. Within Yi Quan there are a number of different postures. As you hold each position, you relax into it and allow your body to balance within it. You allow the qi to circulate freely—that's the major body of practice.

The other one is Si Li, testing strength. While keeping the posture,

Photo by Eric Nomburg

Fong Ha teaches Yi Quan.

how do you move the body slowly and gently while at the same time remaining grounded in your central equilibrium? While practicing Si Li, you will be able to observe yourself in motion. The third stage is Fa Li or Fa Jing. Fa Li means you are delivering or issuing your energy. The fourth stage is called Yi Jai or "realization." From your practice you slowly start to realize the true nature of your body, the true nature of your mind. We say that "this small art will lead you into the Great Way, the Dao."

Qi Gong

WHEN YOU SAY "QI," different people have different concepts, different ideas. It's easiest to look upon qi as energy. The general word *qi* means "energy." But energy exists within everything. This energy is the energy that creates matter. A scientist will tell you that everything on Earth is composed of one hundred-some elements. Each element is composed of a different atomic structure. Each atom is nothing more than electrons moving around a nucleus. The thing that's moving that electron is energy, what we call qi. That's why energy is so hard to clearly define. Energy exists in everything, in all organic matter, in gas, solid, and liquid form. Our body is also made up of matter, therefore qi is within our body as much as in any living thing.

We have only limited control over the energy of the things outside of us. But within our body, we can get in touch with it. Where we manifest ourselves there is feeling and sensation. If your energy is good, you feel good. You feel full of vitality, full of hope. When your energy is down, you feel hurt, pain, you feel discomfort, and if the energy is totally gone, you're dead. That is qi. How you cultivate it and nurture it and gain more of it is the practice of Qi Gong.

When we practice Zhan Zhuang, we are immediately in touch with our current state. Immediately because you are not thinking about outside things. If you are seeing, you see outside yourself. If you are hearing, you hear outside; if you feel, most times you feel outside yourself. If you stop this, immediately what you feel is yourself. You recognize whether you feel good or bad; you are in that state already. It is a state you can do something about. Doing something about it is the practice of Qi Gong.

Once we have a definition of what qi is, we can talk about it, we can do something about it. For one thing, to replenish the qi we can eat food! This gives energy to the body. There are ways to get rid of bad, toxic energy that disrupts the body. You can exercise, and when you move it gets the qi circulating. Of course, you can get more and more detailed about where qi is moving, the path of the various meridians and so on—people found them out long ago. But really, the theory you wish to follow is up to you. You still feel good or bad no matter what theory you have. If you want to feel good, that doesn't need any theory. Not just if you do martial arts: if you do anything, such as using your computer or playing music, you need good qi, good energy. Especially if you do a martial art, you need a lot of energy, therefore you need good qi.

The human body is a very complicated organism. People can become very particular in their understanding of their own internal sensation. You can feel inwardly and watch your body from the inside, experiencing the sensations and feelings of how this energy moves.

Be Still

ANY TIME YOU USE one of your senses—if you see, hear, smell, taste, or feel with the skin, any effort that you emphasize—you are using qi. In Yi Quan practice the first thing, whether you're weak or strong, good or bad, is to stop doing that. I call it "Be Still." Be still with the body and be still with the mind. To be still with the body means you don't move, externally as well as internally. To be still with the mind means you don't continue to produce thoughts. The ones you are aware of that come into the mind, you don't continue to support them with your energy; you don't follow them. You are like reading or watching as the thought comes by, and after a while it becomes like you're merely witnessing it. That will become very interesting, more like a philosophical thing. You'll witness your thoughts and your mind. Someday you may discover your real self! All of the techniques will be discovered from there.

Anytime we do not use conscious effort, our real nature will come out. Nature is always working for you already. Being still is the very simple entry level of *qi gong*, but it's also the final level. It can be the beginning of martial arts, depending on what you want to achieve. The movement at the beginning and end of internal martial arts is always standing still.

The Yi Quan of Han Hsing Yuan

WHEN I WAS YOUNG I was interested in martial arts like anybody else. If you want to learn something, the only way is through lots of repetition. Any movement, any posture, any thing in the world you want to learn must be trained through repetition. It doesn't matter if you do music, dance, or whatever, if you are instructed correctly and you keep on doing it, you will be good at it. But to an extent you must know what you want to achieve. In the beginning most people's objective in the martial arts is to be better than someone else—you want to win, you want to control others. Some people just stop there.

When I was growing up I heard about Tai Ji Quan and all of the wonderful results that you could get from practicing it. I also heard about all these Daoists who studied not necessarily to be a great martial artist or great swordsman, but through doing Tai Ji Quan they achieved great understanding and ability physically, mentally, and spiritually. I have seen a few good teachers in my life, and they were relatively prominent people who practiced the Yang style of Tai Ji Quan. And I made a lot of friends who studied that style. But within myself, I wanted a little bit more than just correct movements. So that led me into the internal work.

In the process I began to get exposed to other cultures, like the Yoga practice in India. I also identified the fact that Tai Ji Quan and most internal martial arts seem to have their fountainhead in the Daoist tradition. The Daoist practices are sort of the Chinese version of Yoga. But the contemporary Tai Ji Quan I practiced didn't seem to give me any of this. And I remember seeing the great accomplishments of my teachers, in push hands and other things, so I thought I would look until I found a way to replicate that.

That's when I came upon a book a friend gave me by Wang Xian Zhai, and I read this dissertation on the art of Yi Quan. It was so extraordinary, so out of this world, so different from the conventional

Photo by courtesy of Fong Ha

Han Hsing Yuan and
Fong Ha.

Photo by Eric Nomburg

Fong Ha practicing the Tai Ji Saber form.

talk about martial arts that I got very fascinated by it. In 1971 or so I had the opportunity to go to Hong Kong. Then I heard about one of Wang Xian Zhai's disciples, Master Han Hsing Yuan, who was teaching in Kowloon.

At the time I was studying with Yang Shou Chung, who was the eldest son of Yang Cheng Fu—he was a great contemporary Tai Ji master. I had been corrected in the postures, doing the push hands and everything else in his system. I thought at the time that I wanted to go for more awareness and feeling of the qi energy that we all talk about. Finally I met Master Han, and then I started standing. The practice was very simple; you just stood there holding postures for forty minutes. During that time you would move through eight different postures, one every five minutes. It was so unusual compared to all the things I'd done before. I'd do the Tai Ji set, I'd do the saber, I'd do the sword, I'd do the San Shou, I'd do the push hands, but I had never achieved the awareness I did when I simply stood there in meditation. Then my awareness during my other practices began to change. I started to get an inner understanding of why the moves are done in their particular way.

That led me to the pursuit of Yi Quan. Eventually I came to the understanding that Yi Quan as martial art depends on who is practicing it. As in any system, you develop the technique of how to use it for fighting, how you use Zhan Zhuang, Si Li, and Fa Li. But there is always the danger that the more focused people are on the martial and competitive aspect of it, the more the ego takes over. You start wanting to show off or prove your technique is better and so forth. As I got older I began to appreciate the other aspects of the arts. Tai Ji Quan contains a certain beauty in its flowing movement, and Yi Quan has a kind of stability in its austere, still practice. Both of them work quite well. Yi Quan gave me a new dimension. It's a form of expression in just standing, and eventually I came the point that I do Tai Ji like I do Yi Quan, and I do Yi Quan like I do Tai Ji. In short, I've come to understand that there's no such thing as different systems.

The Yi Quan Tradition

A TRADITION MEANS THAT SOMEBODY did it this way and people consider that way to be good. So we try to conserve that way. However, I feel that it can sometimes limit creativity. The way you hold your head, the way you move, the way you do everything is given to you by your teacher. Hopefully the one you imitate is something of an enlightened person, somebody who already has great knowledge. For instance, if you don't know better you might end up imitating somebody who's handicapped. If you never knew how to walk, and you imitate someone with only one leg, you end up spending a lot of energy distorting the natural way you walk. And you will think that that's the correct way. However, a good system can liberate you. If it leads you back to your own true nature, it'll be a good system. If the system enslaves you and makes you have no feeling for anything, with no freedom for thinking, the system is a closed, dead-end tradition.

Fong Ha and student demonstrate the Tai Ji San Shou form.

Yi Quan does not emphasize the tradition that much. The focus is on the principle and the theory, how to get the results. How you feel is the most important thing, not perfect imitation of the postures, holding the hand this way or that way. To me it's a very wonderful tradition, and Wang Xiang Zhai, given that I know of him only indirectly, influenced his immediate students greatly—they all were very liberated, very open. Even though most of his disciples were already well accomplished in other systems, once they got to him they all seem to have been liberated. I have met quite a few of his students and studied with them. But none of them do it in the same way! It doesn't puzzle me though; instead it opened my eyes to the fact that they didn't have to do it in exactly the same way. For this reason I think it's a good art for freeing yourself. That's why I say that to sit, stand, walk, and work with another person is enough. All the techniques are the outcome of that training, and everyone should become their own master. You are already your own master! Yi Quan is really teaching the principle of returning to your own nature.

Therefore it leads me to feel that the essence of Tai Ji Quan is found in the principle. The Tai Ji principle is a very refined principle, and the Tai Ji Quan movements are its manifestation. Now, some masters are much better than others in manifesting this principle of Tai Ji. You can imitate the external form and it may or may not make you realize the principle. If you realize the principle first, then you can manifest it in every move. But even if you do every move correctly like your teacher, you may not have any understanding of the principle behind it.

Photo courtesy of Fong Ha

Yi Quan teacher Cai Sai Fang with Fong Ha.

The Nitty Gritty

I N Yɪ Qᴜᴀɴ you get right to the nitty gritty of what makes martial arts work. Stand up in any posture very naturally. You're comfortable, like you stand every day. At this time, your innate nature is getting energy from the atmosphere, from the air that you're breathing. You are standing in the posture very comfortably without using any effort. This is the most economical way of standing in that particular posture. You are doing it at its best, so any unnecessary effort added to your posture is counter-effective.

Now, nobody in their right mind will just stand there holding their hands out because they'll get tired. But if you put your hands out and cultivate it, it's possible to increase the time, even if at the beginning you are comfortable for only five seconds. Your body is integrating, learning how to deal with the situation, provided that you are not forcing yourself. So gradually continuing the next time you do it for two minutes. You are increasing your internal energy—that is the cultivation.

People can misuse it. This happens when you just force yourself to hold the posture. Perhaps to a certain extent you will develop some ability to endure by numbing yourself but this is not the optimal way to learn. That is why I am always against "no pain, no gain." Because pain is always the body rejecting whatever you are doing. It's your body telling you, "I don't want to do it, it's not right for me." But people can force themselves to do it, sometimes because they come from a hard life, and have had to work so hard just to survive. That becomes the mentality, therefore anything you do must become hard, uncomfortable. That is not a good thing.

Yang Style Tai Ji Quan

Dong Ying Chieh on the right.

Fong Ha teaching Tai Ji.

Photo by Eric Nomburg

WHEN I WAS VERY YOUNG I was fortunate to learn from the Tai Ji Quan master Dong Ying Chieh, who was relatively old at that time. It was 1953 when I was first exposed to his Tai Ji. I was initially drawn to his mannerisms and his way of quiet serenity. He was living on Hennessey Road, Wanchai District, Hong Kong. I was living on Lockhart Road, so he was only a couple of blocks away from my house. I had had a long-time admiration of internal martial arts, as I read many books and novels on the subject. From my reading I knew the name Yang Lu Chan of the Yang Family Tai Ji Quan. One day I looked at a sign, and it said, "Ying Chieh, Disciple of Yang Cheng Fu." I recognized that Yang Cheng Fu was the grandson of Yang Lu Chan; it had some relationship to the stories I'd read.

Of course, Tai Ji Quan hadn't had any attraction for me when I was young, since most of the time what I saw in the park was the kind of Tai Ji Quan that old people practice. Most of them weren't really expert in Tai Ji, and I didn't understand why it was done in slow motion. But I was drawn to what I read, and finally I got up the courage to go knock on the door. When I saw Dong Ying Chieh his mannerisms were very nice and I could feel a personal affection. I told him that I wanted to study Tai Ji Quan. And so from that time forward he taught me one on one. Eventually his grandson came from China, so I had another young guy to practice with. I learned the techniques and the form; I studied quan, sword, and saber; and I also studied his personal art, which is like a fast Tai Ji Quan. He created it supposedly—it's called Ying Chieh Fai Quan, and it's part of the Dong family system.

During the time I learned from him, I never saw him practice. Traditionally you never see your teacher practice, he only teaches you. It was the same with Yang Shou Jung. I don't know anybody who ever saw him practice the whole set. I never saw him myself. I asked my peers, but nobody ever saw him do it. He only showed you a few moves at a time. Then he would move your hand from here to there into the correct positions.

I came to the United States in 1968 and then I went back to Hong Kong in 1970. Dong Ying Chieh had passed away. I discovered that Yang Shou Jung, son of Yang Cheng Fu, was staying in Wanchai. He was a bit closer to me on Lockhart Road. So I began to study with him every summer. We were studying the set, but I was fortunate enough that he allowed me to join his push hands circle. He hardly ever allowed people to join it, but I told him that I had studied with Dong Ying Chieh, so he allowed me. Not only did he allow me to do it, he allowed me to take a movie of a push hands session.

I have had the opportunity to see a number of great masters do Fa Jing, and among them there are differences that you can definitely feel. Fa means "release" and jing means "energy," so Fa Jing means to release energy. It's all dependent

Photos by Eric Nomburg

Fong Ha teaching Tai Ji.

Photos by Eric Nomburg

Fong Ha teaching Tai Ji.

on timing and precision. I only move when I've got you, when you're already falling down. That's when I insert energy and move your equilibrium.

True Tai Ji skill means that your opponent cannot even lay a hand on you. I remember reading about this in Dong Ying Chieh's book. The first thing in his book seems to be almost like a fable about the old master Chung Fa. They went up to the mountains to see the master at Wu Dang. There the old man kind of made fun of them, and challenged him. So Dong tried to get him, but he couldn't touch him—every time the old man was standing at his back. That is the kind of quality that is fascinating—how is that possible? I feel that it is possible, it is a skill that can be developed. The Tai Ji principle is verifiable, and it can be cultivated.

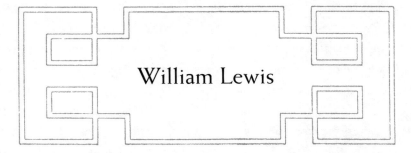

William Lewis

I first met William Lewis on a sunny day in a local Oakland park. When I asked for a demonstration, he performed Xing Yi's Pi Quan, and I was unable to defend as his sudden, severe palm strike drove me back. After recovering my breath we practiced his outwardly simple training routine. Focus is on basic body movements and the Wu Xing, or Five Elemental fists, of the Xing Yi Quan style. Through this practice Lewis' students develop power, agility,

Photo by Eric Nomburg

and most of all, dual freedom of movement and mind. This is the foundation of his martial arts teaching.

Based in the San Francisco Bay Area, William Lewis is one of the "underground" internal martial arts teachers that are rarely heard from. Preferring to stay out of the limelight, he teaches a few private students who are more of a family than an official class. Part of the young generation of martial arts teachers in the Bay Area, he has had experience in many different competitive venues. His speed, precision, elegance in motion, and unshakeable frame of mind belie the efficacy of the movements he practices. As anyone who has experienced it on the receiving end knows, the simple beauty of Xing Yi hides a tremendous power.

William Lewis.

William Lewis
MARCH 2, 2002

Efficiency

THE PRACTICE OF MARTIAL ARTS begins when people revert to the primal instinct to protect themselves. Initially, being able to use your own body if you have nothing else available seems to be desirable and practical. When you are able to use weapons, that's an added advantage, but we're not born with weapons, we are only born with what we have. Using that efficiently makes sense to me.

Personally I find any use of the body beautiful. I love watching dancers, I love watching any athlete move. Movement just interests me a lot. Internal martial arts particularly interested me because every movement has a purpose. In my art, Xing Yi Quan, there's no wasted movement of any kind. It combines something that's beautiful with something that's useful, creating many health, psychological, and spiritual benefits. Just as importantly, it suits my personality.

The science of body mechanics is a beautiful thing. It can be very exciting: no matter how much progress you make, you never quite reach the mountaintop. If you do reach the mountaintop, there's always another mountain. In looking at life as a child does, you are able to get more out of the arts. If you think you know it all, you can't get much farther than where you're at now. I choose to stay like a child, to have an open mind experiencing what my art and other arts have to offer.

Evolution

MANY TIMES PEOPLE GET INVOLVED with martial arts out of insecurities, to protect themselves. Hopefully we can evolve past that, but most people don't. They are interested in dominating another person, and through their insecurities they feel that having an added advantage will assist them in doing that. Being able to change the way that you move, being able to change the way you think, those are things that deserve more attention than feeding your insecurities.

The problem is, most martial artists are not especially evolved people. They don't let their practice have an effect on them, because they're busy battling these insecurities within themselves. That's why sometimes when you go to martial arts tournaments, there's less sportsmanship than you'd find at any other sports activity. Envy, anger, ego—all those negative emotions and behaviors that we exhibit often get amplified at tournaments.

You can look back at the way you were as a child: you grew, you evolved, you changed. Those changes brought you into adulthood, and with that you should become more knowledgeable and wiser. It's the same thing with practicing an art like Xing Yi. You become more knowledgeable and wiser because you are looking at things in a more truthful way. You are looking at reality and trying to get a glimpse of it on its terms and not necessarily on your terms, through practicing something that's very structured. Once you gain that structure and you don't have to think about it, your mind is free to pursue other things. With the structure that's developed over a period of time you gain a tremendous amount of freedom because your mind doesn't have to focus on those things that hold that structure together—they become totally natural.

There are many changes that go on within your body through all this practice. Your energy passages open up, your circulation is increased, your breathing is different. By lowering the breath you are using more lung capacity. You begin unifying the upper and lower portions of the body with the breath, to develop whole body power.

The Essence of the Art

MOST MARTIAL ARTS consist of more externally oriented styles. People tend to gravitate toward those styles because they offer more of a quick fix; there's more immediate gratification. You learn how to fight faster and the movements are more flowery and pretty for tournament usage. But when you look at the essence of most external martial arts styles, in their original forms they were simpler. Forms were added on purely for economic and ego reasons. One instructor changes something and adds things to it so he can keep more students. If a style just taught you one little form, and then you had all these different applications of just doing the same thing over and over again, people would get bored, especially in this society. They don't have the patience to endure and get the true essence of an art. They are too busy looking at the flower, instead of getting to where the root is.

Martial arts are a very individual sport, and everyone has something in particular that motivates them. It's different from other sports mainly because the activities that we do in this country are generally of European origin, and martial arts are generally from Asian countries. Sometimes it's the cultural influence that interests people. Other times it's the perceived discipline that draws them.

When you practice internal martial arts you discover a way of using the body's intrinsic force or intrinsic energy. You are using body alignment and whole body power as opposed to having the body segmented, using the upper body and lower body individually. This is a way to get the maximum

Photo by Eric Nomburg

William Lewis demonstrates Xing Yi's Pi Quan.

amount of force using the least amount of energy. It takes more time to learn how to use your whole body, like learning how to crawl and walk all over again.

The person who takes the time to learn an internal martial art is generally someone who is coming from a more (for a lack of a better term) intellectual path. They are not looking for so much immediate gratification; they're looking for health benefits, they're looking to settle themselves in some way. In external martial arts they may use the same terms and may have similar goals, but the arts are taught with the intention of dominating another person. Many times internal martial arts aren't even taught from a combative perspective. Internal martial artists don't usually learn to fight until they have a solid foundation. And most of the people that go to those schools are interested in gaining more knowledge about themselves, about their bodies, trying to get in touch with their spirit in some way.

There are different objectives when looking at the internal and the external, and looking at the types of people who do those arts. Not to say that there aren't people in external martial arts that are trying to do the same thing as internal martial artists—there are, they are just addressing it a bit differently. Ultimately there's not that much difference between the internal and the external, they come from the same root. It's just that different instructors emphasize different things. On the other hand, you'll find some "internal" martial arts that don't really focus very much on internal training at all. They don't practice so much lowering the breath and trying to cultivate internal energy, *qi*. They may concentrate on the mechanics instead. Any way a person chooses to grasp whatever they're trying to reach for is fine.

Xing Yi Quan

XING YI TENDS TO BE more aggressive than the other two main Chinese internal martial arts; it's done at a regular speed, and it tends to look more linear because in most cases it's done in straight lines, or criss-crossing. When you break it down and look at the movements and the angles, though, you find many small circles. The turning around in Xing Yi to reverse direction is like a Single Palm Change in Ba Gua. In practicing these very small circles, I look at using the angles within those tight circles in as many different ways as possible. I find that it gives me a lot more freedom, and by breaking down each movement, each turn, each angle, there are infinite possibilities.

I notice that a lot of Xing Yi styles don't feel comfortable backing up. In some forms there's no back-up step at all. Backing up, stepping to the side, moving forward—to me they're all the same. I feel comfortable moving in all different directions. It gives me a lot more freedom while remaining true to the art. Being able to move within the traditional stances and make transitions from one to the other while feeling comfortable takes some creativity. It takes breaking everything down and putting it all back together like a puzzle.

The focus during practice is different at each stage of development. A beginning student is just going to be trying to get the basic form and movement together. Generally they're going to be very stiff. They're not sure of what they're doing, so you get them to try and relax, more and more. "Relax, relax, relax," you'll say a million times. Once they

Photo by Eric Nomburg

William Lewis demonstrates Xing Yi's Beng Quan.

feel comfortable with what they're doing, they learn to relax. Then maybe they start relaxing too much to where they get limp. That's sort of a middle phase where you have them focus on extending a little bit to where they start creating more of a firm energy.

Once you establish that firm energy you enter a third stage of Xing Yi practice, where you are able to feel what's going on in your body, you are able to feel when you're getting too tense, you end up feeling things from the inside out. There's a lot of fine-tuning that goes on as your body changes. Your back ends up getting a little bit rounder, because you are extending your shoulders a little more. Your shoulders also end up dropping, because generally in this culture we hold our upper bodies in such a way that we have a lot of tension in our shoulders. By letting your shoulders just relax and drop, and then rounding the back, you get another couple of inches reach.

Looking at the alignment when rounding your back, your shoulder muscles are being supported by your back muscles, so with that you have an upper foundation that you then connect to the middle foundation, which is the center, the Tan Tien. That center unifies the upper and lower portions of the body, so the body acts as one solid unit. The hips and shoulders are functioning together as one; they're not working independently. That's where the whole body power comes in.

An art like Xing Yi requires you to do things a certain way to reap the benefits. Even if you think you are doing something right, unless you can apply it properly and efficiently, chances are it isn't right. You have to keep working on it until all these things come together and you can apply it. What that teaches you is that sometimes you may think things are right simply because that's your perspective. In most cases that's because you are ignorant and you haven't taken into consideration that you are just looking at things from your own specific point of view.

You train to position your body in a way that you can penetrate the opponent's body, and with Xing Yi that involves occupying someone else's space. I'm looking at where you are, and I want to occupy that space. I have to penetrate your body and remove you from that space so I can occupy it. It's different than throwing a punch or a kick, because I am putting myself where you are; my intent is to move forward whether you are there or not. I want that space.

If the movements are broken down, all the different elements of fighting are found in Xing Yi. There are locking techniques, there are throwing techniques, and there are striking techniques. If you break down the art that you are doing and you look beyond the surface, you'll see those things present themselves. I don't teach my students techniques, I teach them to feel what's going on in each moment. If you're moving with someone in something that's not choreographed, you don't know where they're going to be. A slight adjustment on their part means that your whole game plan could go out the window if you are counting on them doing certain things. If you are used to working out with one type of person and you have to work out with someone of a different size, you need to be adept at changing and feeling what's going on or you're going to be in trouble.

Intrinsic Power

YOUR CONNECTION TO THE EARTH is very important. That's where all the intrinsic power comes from. The root is down in your feet. From there you channel the energy from the ground, through your legs, hips, shoulders, and out through your arms and fingers. You use whole body power, but in a way that's not so noticeable to a person watching from the outside.

William Lewis demonstrates Xing Yi's Pao Quan.

Photo by Eric Nomburg

To move with the whole body engaged, you use your weight in a compressive action, where as soon as you compress it releases, so it's almost a slight bounce. This compression is not easily noticeable, but someone who is knowledgeable about body mechanics can see a compression, a sort of rippling through your body. Some people think you should be trying to project yourself forward, whereas for me that's not really what it is; instead, you are going downward. The byproduct is that it can propel me forward. But my intent is not necessarily to push myself forward. The compression gives me a direct and powerful connection to the earth, and by transmitting that energy from the earth through my body I can do something very tangible that people can feel if I'm touching them. It tends to have more of a penetrating feeling that jars you to your core.

With the Earth element form of Xing Yi you are getting a centrifugal, almost circular movement. It has a curve to it, whereas the Wood element is very linear and very straight. The Fire element has a slightly upward and explosive aspect. Look at these different energies and the directions that you are going. You are projecting through your whole body in that direction or at that angle to maximize effect with minimum effort.

Sun Lu Tang practicing San Ti. From *Xing Yi Quan Xue* by Sun Lu Tang.

Standing

X ING YI STANDING MEDITATION is really good to begin with because you end up having to listen to your body. It's uncomfortable at first, but what happens is that you get into a meditative state for a while and you separate your body from that discomfort. Standing in San Ti is especially beneficial, because you are in the main stance for the art of Xing Yi, the one that you are going to be using more than any other position. It helps you build a root and get your body connected. Whether you are moving or still, you want to have a consistent posture, something you have done over and over thousands and thousands of times so that it gets to feel very natural for you. You don't have to think about it; it's something that becomes a part of you. If you ever have to use your art and you don't feel comfortable with it, you are going to revert to primal survival skills. However, if you train your mind, body, and spirit to focus on something that you've been working at for a long period of time, that something becomes very comfortable and that's how you can use it effectively.

Standing postures are very difficult. They not only create really good body unification, but a lot of strength as well. Over time you are able to hold these postures for longer and longer periods, and you develop a lot of strength in them because holding the postures becomes very familiar to you. Standing postures end up being striking postures; your body in that instant of contact can almost turn to stone. When you are using these postures in a more fluid nature—through rooting, and transferring that energy from the Earth into your body—you can recall that same type of static imagery and power, even when you are moving. It takes a lot of time, but that's what you strive for. That's how the movements in Xing Yi become like moving meditation: you end up doing the same thing moving and still.

Learning and Teaching

I LEARNED FROM MY TEACHER by really watching and listening. When you see someone who is very skilled with their body mechanics, you try to emulate that. Of course, you have to make adjustments because everyone's body type is different. Taking something and making it your own makes a big difference. It's not just copying something, it's breaking it down, feeling what's going on and experiencing it for yourself.

Over a period of time, you will look at other people and see that their body type may be different than yours. Their legs may be shorter, they may not be as flexible in the hips or the shoulders—adjustments have to be made so a person can end up benefiting from the practice. Gaining knowledge from other people, just being able to absorb that and make it your own, is one thing. It is another thing to be able to transmit that knowledge to someone else and give them the opportunity to do the same thing.

Being able to give something beneficial to someone else is a joy. I don't see enough of this as far as the transmission of knowledge between teachers and students. At the core, most people don't want someone else to have what they have, and so they tend, sometimes unconsciously, to put up barriers so the knowledge isn't transmitted. A lot of times that's from their own insecurities, not wanting someone to be as good as they are.

What is a teacher, what is a sifu? You are supposed to transmit knowledge to people who are ready to accept it and cultivate that with them so that they can be as good or better than you. So that the art can flourish and live beyond you. You don't try to keep everything for yourself. I notice that with a lot of instructors, when a student starts to get very good there tends to be a falling out between the two. Oftentimes it's because of a lack of maturity within the instructor—ego and that basic need for self-preservation.

When people ask me about my teacher Peter Ralston, the first thing that comes to mind is his spirit. He has great ability, but his spirit really stands out. He can play around with it. He could be joking around and then immediately shift gears and be ferocious, all within a split second. That's a very useful attribute in self-defense, because it's very unsettling not to know where someone's coming from. It's not something that everyone can do; it definitely requires an accomplishment.

I teach in a low-key way intentionally. I want students to be comfortable. In order to learn you have to be relaxed and comfortable. It's more difficult to learn when someone makes you uneasy, and I want my students to get it; I want them to be as good as I am; I want them to be better than I am. So I create an atmosphere that I feel they can benefit from.

A person's martial arts ability has nothing to do with them being a good teacher. There are a lot of really good martial artists who aren't very good teachers. People tend to lose sight of that. Teaching is about transmitting knowledge effectively. If a person has won a lot of tournaments or fights, it doesn't mean that they are going to be a good teacher. Just because they've had famous teachers, it doesn't mean they are going to be a good teacher. Teaching simply isn't meant for everyone.

Look for someone with a refined spirit, who is willing to give of themselves and share what was given to them so that other people can benefit from it. Those are really important things in a teacher. A teacher has to know what they're doing, they have to be proficient, but being able to transmit the knowledge is paramount.

Internal Martial Arts

THE THREE MAIN Chinese internal martial arts—Ba Gua, Tai Ji, and Xing Yi—are not really that different. There's a particular flavor to each, but basically all of them are using whole body power. Maybe different types of energy are emphasized more in the different arts, but they have a lot in common. More and more these different movements all become one. They become smaller and smaller within yourself to where when you are moving in general—just walking down the street, opening a door, being in a crowd of people, and moving and flowing and being in that mix—those things are all done consistently with internal principles. Instead of taking time to practice my internal martial arts, at this stage I'm practicing all the time. When I'm moving and when I'm sitting I'm always breathing from my lower abdomen.

Most fighting styles are very simple in nature. You do patterns of things over and over until they've become reflex. I can understand and relate to that because initially, when I started internal martial arts, I didn't see the benefit in it. I thought, "OK, maybe this is cool for health, but how can you apply this in a real survival situation?" It is applied by becoming comfortable, not having to think about it, and having everything you've got come together at once. The nature of using your whole body is something very exceptional because we are

Photos by Eric Nomburg

William Lewis
demonstrates an
application from Xing
Yi's Pi Quan.

not used to using our body in that way. When you can use whole body power you end up using less effort, but getting maximum effect. Because there's a lot of static exercises in internal styles, you tend to be able to concentrate and focus your attention on one spot or in one area, and that concentration is also a great benefit as far as issuing power. You are extending, penetrating an object, as opposed to trying to hit it on the surface and shatter it.

Internal martial arts are about cultivating a smooth, calm mindset, so that you are able to respond in the moment without having any preconceived ideas. When you are dancing with someone, doing something that isn't choreographed, you have to maintain a distance that you are comfortable with. Similarly, in conflict you aren't taking things personally because you can't think straight when you're angry; you can only think straight when your mind is clear. Being able to quiet your mind and quiet your body so that you can feel what's going on gives you an advantage. Being angry and frustrated, you tend to make mistakes. When you're relaxed and able to mentally step away from a situation and deal with it, things can move almost in slow motion.

The human body can only move in so many ways. If you look at it and break it down for what it is, there aren't too many surprises. We don't have three legs and five arms; we have two legs and two arms. When you are looking at those things coming toward you, they can only come from so many directions and they can only be thrown in so many different types of combinations. Being aware mechanically of how the body moves can give you a slight advantage in that you are not so surprised. When you're not being surprised you are able to relax, and when you relax you are able to think more clearly. That can be an important advantage in self-defense.

The training isn't training at all after a while—it's part of your lifestyle. You are doing most of these practices, if you choose to, for the rest of your life. Whereas you can't practice a lot of other sports or martial arts for the rest of your life—they tear your body apart.

Internal martial arts use your body in a way that is healthy and structurally sound so you can practice until you are old.

Awareness

HAVING A HEIGHTENED SENSE of yourself is an important survival skill. It helps you in your interactions with people on so many different levels. It helps you in many different relationships—in friendships, work relationships, combative relationships—and they are all important. Your survival can depend on them. Being aware and being in touch with yourself means sorting through a lot of the static and the junk that you have inside, looking at your own personality, and breaking things down. There are certain behavior patterns that we have, certain things that we do that are very positive, and other things that are very negative. Break the negative things down and look at why you do them, where that comes from, how to address that. Overcome those things so you have more control over yourself.

It's a lot about your intention. That's why with Xing Yi you don't really spar in the competitive sense. When I'm doing a technique my mindset is the same whether someone is there in front of me or not. That intent and focus give you something extra that I don't see in a lot of other martial arts styles. They're doing things on the surface, where in Xing Yi you are doing it with your whole being projecting outward.

Over a period of time you can practice and become very skilled, but eventually you will have to make contact with something. Making contact is different from practicing in thin air, because if that's something you aren't used to, you can knock yourself off balance. In fighting you're actually making contact, and a person is not where you want them to be. There are no rules. Making contact with someone when they're moving into you or moving to the side alters your body, and you have to be able to adapt. Hopefully with your attention to feeling you can adapt and feel comfortable moving with someone else in an adversarial relationship.

Martial art is like a dance in this way. The difference is that your survival may depend on the way that you move. The dance can be beautiful and advantageous, or it can be ugly and destructive. Being able to use an internal martial art is practical self-defense, but many people are led into a false sense of security because they are so used to doing it in theory. To apply it requires a different type of training, a

Photos by Eric Nomburg

William Lewis
demonstrates an
application from Xing
Yi's Heng Quan.

different type of mindset, and you have to have your foundation based in a certain degree of reality, because reality will slap you in the face without it.

For me, I have no desire to dominate anyone else, to fight with anyone else, or to show off to anyone, but there have been times in the past where I had to rely on my skill to protect myself or someone else, and you learn a lot through that. Those aren't situations that come up very often, but it's an experience that I can share with someone else so maybe they won't have to go through the same thing.

Effortless Power

EFFORTLESS POWER has to be felt to be understood. When you make a breakthrough, something that you get really excited about, it's what I call a mini-revelation. They come in stages. First you'll start to get something and the general feel of it, and by relaxing and feeling more comfortable and more open to what's going on within your body and your practice, you can become so comfortable that what used to require a lot of effort doesn't require as much any more. You really start to notice effortless power when you are relaxed in your body alignment, your intrinsic qualities are coming together, everything is moving as one solid unit, the timing and rhythm along with that, then everything sort of comes together like an explosion. It takes time, your body has to coordinate itself, and your mind has to coordinate itself with the body. Most people at first are a little disjointed, things aren't quite working together, they're out of sync. When everything gets in sync it becomes a more explosive movement and at the same time more effortless.

The tricky part is to have all those things come together at once, and to unify all that with the breath. It's a pretty remarkable thing—there's a lot going on, and when you don't have to think consciously about it all, that's when you've made progress.

Getting to that stage is going to require starting with the physical aspects, feeling comfortable with what you're doing first, and then with the alignments and the mechanics. After that you're talking about feeling the tension from the inside, and the breath, and cultivating internal energy. Those are the things that usually take time, and everyone isn't interested in doing all of those things. Some people are interested in the physical movements, some people are interested in more of the internal exercises, the *qi gong* exercises, breathing exercises, or stance training. There's nothing wrong with just being interested in one or more of those aspects, because you can definitely benefit, but the opportunity is there to be involved with all of them.

Qi and Health

I FEEL THAT THE IDEA of qi is very important. Everyone doesn't necessarily feel that way, but the ability to cultivate and circulate qi helps you feel what's going on inside you. This is an old technology, that has been worked on by priests and sages over thousands of years, in cultures spanning from Africa to Asia. The essence of the practice is to unify mind, body, and spirit. The fruits of the practice are health, longevity, balanced emotions, and spiritual growth.

The basic steps of the practice are simple. Qi exists in all living things, so first we develop an awareness of our own body through proper body alignment and lowering the breath. By lowering the breath to the center body area (the area, two inches below the navel, called the Tan Tien) and keeping good alignments, we can begin to cultivate our energetic awareness. This is really the gateway to *qi gong* practice, but on a less esoteric level it also makes good sense. Deep, clear breathing maximizes lung capacity, and enhances the circulatory system's intake of oxygen. Oxygenation of the blood improves just about all body processes. Food is broken down more easily, and wastes are eliminated better.

Qi is directed by the mind (or the *Yi* in Chinese.) Conscious attention directs a bioelectric current to the joints, muscles, and tendons. When these tissues are healthy, relaxed, and loose, circulation is improved, and it becomes easier to direct the current. It will only go as far as your body lets it go. If you have a blockage in a certain area, qi won't flow through as effortlessly. Once you open the blockages you'll be able to circulate it through your whole body.

Part of the reason that people are unhealthy is because of blockages of energy circulation. Freely circulating your energy creates a healthy little universe, because everything is dependent on something

William Lewis demonstrates a Xing Yi application.

Photos by Eric Nomburg

else within your body—it all works together. When your energy is flowing freely and properly, your glands are nourished, in turn supporting healthy function of your organs. Your immune system is boosted, and you don't get sick as much.

For me personally, I've gained a lot health-wise over the years, and it's something that you really wish that everyone could benefit from. There are so many people with illnesses that maybe could have been prevented if they had a different lifestyle and were aware of internal health practices.

Qi and Sex

WE ALL HAVE ENERGY, but those that cultivate it build a reservoir. Instead of dispersing it and wasting it you are able to concentrate it more. What people don't realize, especially for men, is that being in control of your sexual energy, your seminal essence, is related to the cultivation of your internal energy. You might notice that after you have sexual relations you generally feel a little weaker. The next day when you wake up in the morning you feel less flexible, your back may ache a little bit, you're a little lazier, a bit sluggish. That's because you've let your battery run low by dispersing a lot of energy.

Part of the discipline of internal martial arts is cultivating and retaining your seminal essence. That's something that most people don't want to hear. Now I'm not saying you need to be a monk about this, but it really does make a difference. Old men in martial arts will tell you to stay away from women when you are training, and with experience you notice it more. The flipside of this is that if your energy is healthy and free-flowing, your sexual function improves greatly. You become more sensitive to your own internal sensations, as well as those of your partner. Let's just say that there are ways for you to have your cake and eat it too, but they take a lot of discipline to attain.

Qi and the Martial Arts

THE BODY MECHANICS of internal practices rely on fairly specific alignments. One part of the body supports the other with minimal effort. In practical terms, by lowering the breath and awareness to the Tan Tien, the upper and lower portions of the body are unified in to one solid unit.

When you are using martial arts you don't need to think about qi. When you are actually doing a movement you have to be focused and let the energy passageways and your circulatory system operate naturally. When you are doing a technique, qi is not something that you have time to think about. You should be concentrating on your objective. If you've been doing your practices and have your system functioning properly the energy will take care of itself. Energy will go where it is needed.

But this doesn't come overnight. You can work toward guiding it to different places and clearing blockages when doing static postures and meditation. You can stay conscious of your breath, stay relaxed and calm, keep bringing your mind back to your Tan Tien. Over time the preparation trains your body and mind to experience internal sensations and structural relationships, as well as moving with unified body and mind. Once you start to experience this, it becomes more tangible. Then when the roadways are opened up and you're ready to go, step on the gas.

Freedom

WHEN IT COMES TO THE FUTURE of martial arts in the West, there's not much that people in this culture are going to do that's really going to enhance what's already there. The foundation is there, and it's up to each individual to take it where they want to go. Everyone's going to have some strengths and some weaknesses, that's the way it has always been. By staying true to the art they practice, people will find that they develop a lot of freedom and creativity within that structure. They will find that all these different arts have much in common, and that it's really beneficial to look at that instead of their differences. In that way you will gain more understanding of your own art.

The important thing is loving what you're doing and becoming a part of what you're doing, then it's not so hard anymore. I like taking the easy way, making something easy for myself. When you don't waste a lot of energy and movement, you end up doing things in an efficient way. Xing Yi is very efficient, that's why it really suits my personality; I don't like wasting time, and I don't like wasting energy. At the same time I like to be comfortable and I like to be clear. I can take all of those things out of this art.

Photo by Eric Nomburg

William Lewis demonstrates Xing Yi's Dragon stance.

Luo De Xiu

Mr. Luo is best known for his expertise in the Chinese martial arts of Xing Yi Quan and Ba Gua Zhang, both of which he teaches in his home town of Taipei, Taiwan. I was first exposed to his teachings in Berkeley, California, on one of his yearly seminar tours that take him all over the world. I was immediately impressed with his uncanny ability to move in a most fluid, connected, and open fashion. I was soon to learn that this fascinating type of movement translates into immensely powerful and amazingly fast attacks and defenses.

Photo by Eric Nomburg

Luo De Xiu demonstrates Ba Gua.

Once I made contact with his body, I found that there was no escape. Try as I might, his percussive strikes, baffling locks and whiplash-inducing throws were utterly effective.

One of the first major concepts that Mr. Luo likes to emphasize is the idea of "whole body power"—the ability to put everything you've got behind every move you make. This is what enables the less powerful internal martial artist to overcome a stronger opponent. Even if someone has a strong arm, by making all of your body's muscles unified against it, you can be even stronger.

Mr. Luo spent a lot of time and hard work putting together the pieces of the Yi Zhong system. He now passes it on by presenting the entire program without holding back, in the hope that others can progress even more rapidly than he did. His endless enthusiasm, helpfulness, and genuine good humor make it a pleasure to practice this wonderful art with him.

Luo De Xiu
JULY 18, 2001

T'ang Shou Tao

WHEN I WAS A CHILD my great-uncle from the country introduced me to martial arts. They called it the Temple style because it was always demonstrated inside a temple. I learned for one day and it was fun, but it was too hard so I had to give it up. Growing up I saw books about Judo and Karate, and I always liked their nice uniforms. Then in junior high school I had a classmate who learned from Hong Yi Xiang. So my classmate and I talked about it, along with the other classmates who trained there. I started practicing, and in the beginning I didn't really want to learn the fighting. I just liked being there with everyone. It was nice, there were a lot of students there, we all had the *gung fu* clothes, and everybody respected each other. I thought to myself, "Wow, maybe someday I can become a senior student!" I wasn't really thinking about fighting much. We would learn at the martial arts school at night, then we'd go back the next day to our regular school and that's all we talked about. So I was beginning to get interested.

I learned for a couple of months but I stopped because my mother wanted me to. A lot of times in the Chinese culture when you are young learning martial arts, people think that it's just for fighting. She asked me, "Do you want to learn so you can fight?" I told her, "No, I just want to learn!" But I had to give it up. About eight or nine months later, I asked her, "If I do my homework and be a good boy, can I go back?" Fortunately she said yes. That was in 1971, and it was then that I really began to practice.

At that time Hong Laoshi ("Laoshi" is Chinese for teacher) had already established a number of schools and was training a lot of people. One of the senior students was my school classmate, so every day we talked about martial arts. A lot of the time when I would learn new stuff I'd test it out at the school. Sometimes I'd get hurt, but it was always interesting.

At the T'ang Shou Tao school Hong Laoshi created some forms as a program for the beginners. We all wore Japanese-style uniforms with the belt and the gi because he wanted it to become a bigger, more popular school. We started at the beginning with what looked like Shaolin forms, but they weren't really Shaolin. They were modified Xing Yi and Ba Gua forms, changed into a more Shaolin style. At the higher levels, we learned the traditional Xing Yi forms. We didn't practice Ba Gua, but we did learn a lot of the Ba Gua fighting skills. At that time I didn't know which martial arts were supposed to be better than the others, it was just fun.

The Chiang Kai Shek Memorial Cup

A FTER A YEAR OR SO, in 1972, the school wanted to fight in a tournament. We had someone for every weight division except one. I was chosen, even though I was new. Actually, at first they wanted someone else to go, but he didn't want to, so I had the chance to train for the tournament. The first stage was a regional contest among the schools in Taipei city, which was separated into four areas with us representing one particular district. Sometimes people say I must have been taught something extra because I won, but it's not true. I was just scared—for a couple of days I couldn't sleep! But in the regional tournament I won first place. The next day, every inch of my whole body was in pain!

Luo De Xiu demonstrates Ba Gua in the early 1980s, observed by his teacher Hong Yi Xiang.

We had three or four month's training before we went to the nationals. At that time the national tournament was called the Chiang Kai Shek Memorial Cup. It included people from Singapore, Hong Kong, and Taiwan. The tournament champion had a fourth dan in Judo, so I was scared because this guy was good. I ended up with second place and I was really happy!

Afterward everybody said, "You're really good!" But I tell you, if you really want to fight in a tournament, have at least six months of hard training beforehand. The body and the energy need to be well developed. Spar with different people, again and again. The first round is OK, but in the second round your energy gets used up, and by the third you are so tired that your will power starts to get weak, and things really start to hurt. If you can beat somebody quickly, it's easy; you have your full power available. But sometimes you get struck back, so you are scared, too. Every second passes so slowly, thirty seconds becomes a long time!

This was a very good experience for me. After that tournament my position in the school got higher, so I started helping Hong Laoshi teach the new students. After a while I started getting a lot of teaching experience.

At Hong Laoshi's school we all got the same training, but it was up to you to develop it yourself. Because if you do one thing really well, and the teacher sees you, he'll teach you more. That way you gain more knowledge, and find more things. In my life I always try to do this, a little bit at a time.

Learning Experiences

SOMETIMES JAPANESE STUDENTS and other foreigners would visit our school. The teacher gets to choose who has to fight challengers, and often he would select me. Also, when we had exams for belt ranking we had three people take part in the test. I was always testing the fighting part, not the forms. If you wanted to become a black belt, you had to fight me. I gained a lot of experience from those encounters.

I always tried not to make the same mistake twice. If I got hit I would think about it and learn from it.

During these years I was happy because I had a couple of really good classmates. But it's funny, sometimes among classmates of the same generation, when you learn something special, you don't want to trade that knowledge with each other. In the Chinese society, everyone has to save face. Some people want to try and say, "I am the senior student; you are younger so I can tell you what to do!" So, sometimes I had to be the dummy for their techniques, but I still learned.

The situation is much the same now—we have not yet opened up the territory as far as martial arts in the Taiwanese society. There is the idea that if you learn from one person, you cannot learn from anybody else. Here in the West it's easier; people can learn whatever they want. In Taiwan, you cannot do that. When I learned, we didn't ask many questions of our teacher. We would just practice and the teacher would watch. If the teacher was happy, he might give us something more. If we asked too many questions, he became very angry. That's the old style of training.

The senior students were also hard to approach. It was OK if you were accepted and became a good friend. If not, they would become angry if you asked questions. Now I know why they were angry—they didn't quite understand it themselves at the time. They felt that you were challenging their position.

Hong Yi Mian's Ba Gua Zhang

WHEN YOU BEAT SOMEBODY in a tournament, everybody suddenly respects you. But in the depths of your heart, maybe you are still scared, because there is always someone more powerful or faster than you. So, I sought some way to learn to find more power, and I turned to Xing Yi Quan. We practiced it in Hong Laoshi's school. It's an internal martial art, so we learned about the *qi* and the *jing.* It was actually very difficult to find the power within it at first. When you are young, you don't always like the quiet, peaceful practices that are required. We wanted the power! Even though we learned a lot, we determined that it still wasn't enough, so we wondered how to get it.

We decided to go see our *gung fu* uncle, Hong Laoshi's brother, Hong Yi Mian. He was a teacher of Ba Gua Zhang. One morning we found his practice area and we watched. However, the brothers' relationship was not always very good. Even among brothers, students training with more than one teacher was frowned upon.

We'd go to different places where Hong Laoshi's brother practiced, to talk and have a cup of tea. But every time we'd sit down to watch, Hong Yi Mian would quickly end the practice. He knew that we were there. To show him respect, we would go there with a small snack and say, "We have a snack, could we join you?" Even though we students didn't have much money, sometimes we'd buy a cigarette, put one on the table for him, and every time he smoked one we would put out a new one.

It's kind of funny—we knew Hong Yi Mian would always end class if he knew we were watching, so we tried to watch with binoc-ulars from far away. We would do anything! My friend worked at a film company, and even though movie cameras were expensive and hard to get at that time, he managed to borrow one. We put a box over it and when we went to tea we put it out on the table to record him practicing. However, the angle was no good, all we got was his head bobbing up and down! But it was fun.

Sometimes at lunch time we'd go back to the park and try to run into him.

Photo by Eric Nomburg

Luo De Xiu demonstrates a Ba Gua defense against a kick.

We would walk around a tree and say, "Oh, goodness, uncle! You've come!" or something like that. This was so we could begin to make a relationship, and get to know him. We were curious, just like anyone else. We would go to the parks to watch everybody practice. Sometimes we would get confused and wonder about the difference between our style and theirs. But a lot of times they didn't want to share what they had. Some people just become a master and don't want to talk anymore. But with enough experience, maybe the grass grows up, people become more open. Even myself and my classmates.

At one point we saw Hong Yi Mian give a demonstration with his students, and his attacks were very fast. We thought, "Wow! Why does he do it like that?" Hong Laoshi would strike on the center line very well—he was a bigger man. Seeing his brother gave us another viewpoint. We were impressed because this was a different way of thinking. He used multiple fast strikes to all sides.

Luo De Xiu demonstrates Hou Tien Ba Gua.

The Line of Tradition

EVENTUALLY WE FOUND OUT that our grandmaster was Zhang Zhun Feng, and that Ba Gua was among his martial arts. We wondered, "What is Ba Gua? Why does it use a circle?" By thinking about it we found another piece of the puzzle and, very slowly, a little bit at a time, we tried to copy it. I came to realize that each of Zhang's students was different. Hong Yi Wen (Hong Laoshi's eldest brother) liked one thing, Hong Yi Mian liked another. So we tried to take a little bit of his art from different places, and tested it in the school.

After high school we had to split up and get jobs. Military service came first because in Taiwan at that time everybody had to serve in the military. But we students still had a close relationship, and we started to have a little bit of income. So we put our money together, five or six people, and we went to learn from Hong Yi Mian. We asked him if we could follow his practice on Sunday mornings as serious students, paying with a red envelope. He agreed, but only one or two of us at a time. After a few months, someone tipped off Hong Laoshi and he came over and caught us. He was so angry, and that was the end of it. We let things cool down for a little while and then returned to our habit of bringing snacks for teatime after Hong Yi Mian's class to chat with him. We also kept up our habit of arguing aloud amongst ourselves over things we weren't sure about so that he would jump in and correct us. You know, if you really want to learn something you have to use a lot of ways to get it. This meant that we really wanted it. We weren't bad guys trying to steal something—we just wanted to learn! Hong Yi Mian appreciated that and thought we were good, but he also had to think about his relationship with his brother and his own students. These are good memories—we had a lot of fun.

During that time we also visited some other teachers, as well as Zhang Zhun Feng's wife. Hong Laoshi was one picture. His brother was another picture. Each person has his own specialty. One perspective is not enough; you have to find everybody so the whole picture comes out. Finally you can say, "Oh, so this is how it is arranged."

If you really research you will find that everybody has their own style. If your teacher says, "No, you must follow me—I'm the best one," you will find that maybe his style is right, maybe it's wrong, maybe it's his own style only, maybe it's not complete. At a younger age I sometimes did things a little differently. But I kept this line of tradition. Everything, the material, the tradition, I keep this and follow Hong Laoshi's teachings. We didn't change it because we always researched Zhang Zhun Feng's Gao style system. Before Zhang Zhun

Feng died, he made a recording saying that if you're looking for his martial arts, go to the three Hong brothers. Hong Yi Xiang was the top at sticking hands and close-range fighting. Hong Yi Mian was best at long-distance fighting and getting good angles. Hong Yi Wen had very powerful structure and Fa Jing and helped Zhang Zhun Feng to explain martial arts philosophy. He was well trained in the classics of Chinese literature and culture, so he understood the martial theory and poetry very well.

Sun Xi Kun's Ba Gua Zhang

M Y SECOND BIG EXPERIENCE was during my military service in Kaohsiung. In the Navy I was teaching school, so I didn't end up on a war ship. I worked nine to five so I had a lot of time off and weekends as well. I met one guy who did Ba Gua, but it looked really funny. A lot of times people are quick to say, "Oh, this guy's really not so good." It's a natural human reaction. But if you cool down and look at the form, you can try to understand what the meaning inside it is. Just because someone isn't very good at it doesn't mean the form is bad. At first I thought this style was terrible. Then I watched for another couple of weeks and I thought, "Maybe it's not so bad." It seemed like some of the pictures in the book by Sun Xi Kun. So I went back and found the book, brought it to the teacher, and started learning.

Sun Xi Kun. From *True Transmission of Ba Gua Zhang* by Sun Xi Kun.

I told him, "I don't have much time, you must teach me quickly." He said, "OK, you want to learn? Let's go faster!" The first day we did four forms, the second day we did four forms. After those two days we were finished. But I went home and found I had

Sun Xi Kun demonstrates Single Palm Change. From *True Transmission of Ba Gua Zhang* by Sun Xi Kun.

nothing, it was just a couple of forms. What was the original meaning? So I went back. He said, "OK, I think you are genuinely interested. I just do it for sport; our teacher is really a martial artist." That's when they introduced me to Liu Qian. From him I started to get a sense of the principles behind the Cheng Ting Hua Ba Gua system.

Before that, I had learned a lot about Ba Gua from Hong Yi Mian and other classmates of Hong Laoshi, but I still hadn't linked it all together. In Kaohsiung, I learned the whole concept of the Cheng Ting Hua school. So I went back over everything I had learned and put it all together. Hong Yi Wen had once said to me, "You are never linking things together. What is the purpose of this or that, why or why not?" Suddenly it became very clear why each part is practiced and how to put it all together. If you can make your thinking the same as Zhang Zhun Feng or Gao Yi Sheng, you can get a clear view of the proper training method.

The Cheng Ting Hua system is very well ordered. Sun Xi Kun and Zhang Zhun Feng were in the same generation of that lineage. Sun Xi Kun learned from the son of Cheng Ting Hua, and Gao Yi Sheng learned directly from Cheng Ting Hua himself. The whole Cheng Ting Hua way of thinking emphasizes a lot of body movement and a lot of internal training. The basic training is always very important, and even if it's not fun, you have to do a lot of it. Because if simple actions are perfected, you can combine them to make more complicated ones. If it is complicated from the start, how do you combine it all?

When I went back to Taipei, I talked about this concept with everybody. At the beginning though, nobody could accept it. Some people thought that by making connections between the different styles of Cheng Ting Hua Ba Gua, I was implying that our school was somehow lacking. So, we argued at first, but everybody eventually adapted and recognized that all the schools have something to offer. About that time I decided to put everything into Ba Gua. It was a really big change for me because I had done a lot of Xing Yi, but not nearly as much

Gao Yi Sheng.

Ba Gua. Even though we had a lot of information, for me it had been nothing but a form, because I hadn't developed it yet. About 1979 I started to really practice like crazy, several hours every day.

To me Ba Gua isn't just for fighting, I think of it as an art. So sometimes I don't talk so much about applications, I just say "play this game." Try to discover how to control the situation by understanding the body's behavior. I focus on controlling the opponent; I don't have to beat him up. This art is still only a couple of hundred years old, it's a very recent creation. In a short time it has become very respected. It's also really good for the body, so I want to keep it intact.

The Ba Gua Zhang of Zhang Zhun Feng

H OW DO YOU FIND OUT if you learned something correctly? Hong Laoshi had learned the techniques of Zhang Zhun Feng's martial arts, so every time we did a demonstration people would say, "You do it just like Master Zhang used to do." This meant that we conformed to the style. Even if you think you've got it right, you must demonstrate for some other masters. If they say, "Yeah, I've seen that before; Zhang Zhun Feng did that one," it shows you are doing it right!

Sometimes you have to use a different route to get information from your teachers. Often if

Luo De Xiu demonstrates a Ba Gua technique.

Photos by Eric Nomburg

you ask a teacher, "Please show me the fourth form," they just shake their head and say no. However, if you say to them, "How did Grandmaster do this? I heard Grandmaster did it this way." Suddenly he replies, "Yeah! He did it like this!" and he shows you everything! If you ask directly, nobody wants to answer you. If you ask about their teacher, then it's "My teacher was the best! Do it this way!"

When I asked about Zhang Zhun Feng, everyone who knew him said he was very special. Zhang Zhun Feng used a number of different techniques. You can see that many of his students have the same moves. If five students all use the same technique again and again, this must be one of the best ones, because every student copies their teacher's best moves. But research like this is not really done in one day—it takes many years. A lot of time is needed to become proficient.

Ba Gua is complicated and can be difficult to practice correctly. There is a process, but only the indoor people usually understand it. People think, "Ba Gua is just a circle. It's very strange, why do you always do the circle?" But there are basics, very important basics that must be built first. Then you can go to the circle.

The Ba Gua way of thinking is like this: You have raw materials, and you have a machine. Ba Gua training is the machine. When you put material in, it comes out as high-level skill. But to begin with, what kind of material do you have? If you don't have anything you must make the raw material first. If you take any kind of martial art, and you pass it through this program, this machine, you can jump to a higher level of ability.

Dong Hai Quan.

Dong Hai Quan was a very smart guy. He developed this special training. Every time he took on a student he would say, "Show me your form, show

me your martial art. Oh, you have a problem with this and this. See?"
He gave each of them one or two concepts that helped change the student's thinking. Then the student could give the material to his own group. This training helps to restructure the body and then everybody can improve. This is why one guy who does Shaolin Quan can become good at Ba Gua. Another guy has Shuai Jiao ability, yet he can become good at Ba Gua. If I have something else, I can become good at Ba Gua.

As far as creating the raw material, some people use Xing Yi, some people use Shaolin, it doesn't matter. I don't care whose material it is, if you learn any martial art you can go and learn Ba Gua. If you follow this way of training you will upgrade your skill. If you don't have previous experience, you must do a lot of additional basic training.

In traditional Chinese culture, when you went to see another class, you were supposed to stand a little bit further away to show respect unless someone introduced you there. If the teacher looked at you, you should just bow and leave. If you looked aggressive or practiced your own form in front of them, that was very rude and might be considered a challenge. Touching anyone's weapon without them inviting you was definitely a challenge. But if you were polite and stayed aside, the teacher might invite you to come over and talk to him. Nowadays, everything is more open, which is good, but there can also be a problem. With the traditional ways of showing respect fading away, sometimes the respect itself goes too. We should still try to be respectful sincerely, even though the rules aren't so strict anymore.

Luo De Xiu teaches Xian Tian Ba Gua.

Photo by Eric Nomburg

Foundation Training

Tai Ji looks too slow, and you might wonder how it is used for fighting. But if you have good material to begin with, then pass it through Tai Ji training, you come out a lot better. This requires training your mind and qi to combine together. In Tai Ji you want to develop soft, sticky hands. There's not actually that many techniques—only five movements and eight forms. But by using this training a lot of stuff can come out. If you only want to use very pure Tai Ji, you must have a lot of foundation training to begin with.

Among the indoor students, whether in a Tai Ji, Ba Gua, or Xing Yi school, the specialty is not in the forms. It's not a matter of how many forms you have. In Xing Yi the forms are the same among most schools. In different Ba Gua styles the form are performed with the same principles. Tai Ji forms are all the same. There's really only one difference, and that's found in the basic training methods of each school. Henan style Xing Yi has a lot of Fa Jing. Shanxi style has a lot of sticking. Hebei has a lot of fighting skill. Knowing this you can focus better in your training.

Indoor training always emphasizes the basics. They don't usually tell you that, but before you can learn martial arts you must do the basics. Even after you learn the martial art you still do the basics. The form is a form, it's a training program. But there is more detail in the background that people don't often know about. On the surface they see the forms practice and think it's very nice, but the real question is, what supports it? People say, "I want to learn this form and that form." If you want one hundred forms, OK, I'll give them to you. But even if you have all those forms, you still have only one body. What supports your form, what supports your movement, what supports your fighting skill? What part supports the rest? You can learn every kind of martial art, but basics are always the most important. Forms allow you to combine everything—mind, structure, movement, qi, and power.

Body Alignment and Relaxation

I N TRAINING there is a traditional phrase, *"Han xiong ba bei chen jian zhui zhou."* It refers to body alignments—cave in your chest, round your back and all the other instructions. However, above all you must relax. But what does that mean? Equality. This means that the power in every part is the same. You can read these instructions in a book, and after you do them you may end up aligned but tense. When I say "relax," this means that within every part the power is the same, but not locked up. Even when relaxed you must keep the structure intact. Sometimes when people relax, they get floppy. Instead, keep the limbs extended, with the whole body and tendon structure unified. Don't let your structure collapse when you relax.

Relaxing the structure is one thing, but how do you relax the mind? It's easy—smile. People tend to only relax the outside. At some point you must balance it, relaxing the inside as well. Some incoming students are too tight, others are too relaxed. It's always the teacher's job to help the student find a balanced way. Smile inside to relax deeper. Your teacher will always check your level of relaxation.

Another factor to consider is the mind. In martial arts we say that the mind is to be feeling. But feeling what? What parts am I supposed to be feeling? This point, this point, or this point? No. First you must feel the whole body. So keep the structure correct, that's all. If you are already able to pay attention to the whole body, you can go back to one point and feel it more easily. But if you pay attention to one point only, it's not easy to check the whole body.

Photo by Eric Nomburg

Luo De Xiu demonstrates a Ba Gua opening technique.

If you can combine all the alignments correctly, the whole body becomes smooth and moves naturally. If you already have the ability to feel the whole body, one point is very easy. But if every day you only focus in one area, then unifying your whole body becomes a problem. Both application and form can seem very well done, but if you do one thing with this hand, and something else with the other, you have forgotten to unify the whole body. You never put it all together and become one.

It's clear that you must pay attention and unify the whole body. But how is this accomplished? One way is for someone to test your posture. Put yourself in any equal, whole posture and I push on you a little from different angles. If the structure is correct, anywhere I push becomes your center. Once you have a sense of the center, you must have a feeling of the whole, then relax and hold this structure.

Some Western people like lots of detail, which can be useful. But it's too confusing sometimes—you have to try to hold the posture while remembering all of these details. Rather than thinking so much, just keep the whole body structure. Become the one. In Chinese internal martial arts it's always said that heaven and the human being must become one, so that everything comes together. Then you can talk about the details.

Qualities of the Internal Martial Arts

IN INTERNAL MARTIAL ARTS, you must have unification. Some external martial arts have it as well, but I think internal martial arts teach it very clearly. How do you compare internal and external martial arts? Actually, they are the same. Everything, including the body movements, are almost the same, except for one thing. Internal martial arts require the Yi, the mind, and Jing, the power, to work in harmony. This means following the progression of Jing, Qi, Shen as a requirement. It's easy to get the Jing, Qi, Shen to work properly if you follow the correct structure and alignments. In Shaolin, they have a very powerful outer form. But it's not the same power that's developed through Jing, Qi, Shen.

In internal styles we train to relax in a fast way. A stronger outer posture is too difficult to maintain for long. Stiff body posture affects your emotional stability. External styles have *qi gong* training, just like internal methods, but it is kept separated from the martial practice. They cut everything apart and at the end put it all back together. Internal martial arts from the start combine *qi gong* and martial training.

From the beginning we try to keep mind, power, structure, and movement all together. To make everything become one, focus first on the structure, then the movement. Then the movement and power are combined together to create the Fa Jing. Xing Yi Quan has this, as does Tai Ji Quan. Internal martial arts don't teach you many movements because the structure is more important at first.

One benefit of forms training is that the movements can be trained like you are really fighting, fast and powerful. Throughout the movements you must use the minimum effort to keep the structure you have. From beginning to end you keep this structure in place with as little effort as possible. Good, relaxed structure helps you to move fast in a dangerous situation. That's the internal martial arts.

Now, as far as fighting, suppose I am more powerful, faster, and stronger than you. If I have a lot more skill than you, I will win. This is normal, anybody can do this. But what if it's the other way around? If I am in that situation, I have to ask myself

Photo by Eric Nomburg

Luo De Xiu teaches Xian Tian Ba Gua.

Photo by Eric Nomburg

Luo De Xiu demonstrates a Ba Gua San Shou technique.

how I can beat you. How about I try to be very deceptive and trick you into slowing down? I need to find a way so that you aren't so much stronger than I am. This is why internal martial artists talk about the *Zhan Nian Lian Sui*, the "sticky hands." Sticking allows you to follow someone and get to a better position. Or else I get a hold of you and shake your body. That way I can break your structure and get in.

If I become stiff like a wall, you'll become more powerful than I am. Instead, if you come I will use sticky hands to reposition myself and counter-attack. We use things like sticky hands and fast movements to balance the situation, even if your opponent is bigger. This is different from the external idea of "I am stronger than you!" In the internal martial arts, they have two things, yin and yang. You don't just say, "I am soft only"—you must be strong too. Yin and yang are both used. Sometimes you may look hard but actually be soft, or vice versa.

External martial art is almost all yang. In external martial arts, I will always need more strength, more speed, more power; I will always need more than you. With internal martial arts I try to change the situation to my advantage. It's a different way of thinking. That's why we develop sticky hands—we must defend in such a way that eventually our opponent will be slowed down and become weaker, rather than focusing on making ourselves stronger than everyone else.

If you are stronger than me, I will need to use my whole body's power against you. A whole body put together is stronger than the power of one part, like an arm. But most people think in terms of who's bigger, and in that way they separate their power. External martial arts train the body in segments, one at a time With internal martial arts, you control your whole body, and bring its entire power to bear with each movement. That is the internal martial arts way of thinking.

Nei Gong

EVERY SCHOOL HAS *nei gong*, "inner work," and *wai gong*, "outer work" practices. In the internal martial arts we always talk about the body movement and structure in terms of the Yi, or "mind." Every movement must involve the Yi. If the Yi is being used, that movement is defined as internal. If I swing with hard strength and I don't care about the emotional or mental aspect, my Yi is not in use. If we do external body movement while the internal elements combine together, we say that this is internal martial art. *Nei gong* means including the internal mind, internal brain, internal focus in every movement.

After 1949, China changed the name from *nei gong* to *qi gong*, to emphasize the breathing, which is one part of the practice. Inhaling and exhaling exercises are *qi gong*, and *qi gong* is one part of *nei gong*. It's really just using the mind combined with the motion, that's all.

The key to using the mind is to combine it together with the body. How to actually do it in practice is more difficult. In Chinese they say, "Feel as if you are under water." When you are in a swimming pool, what is the feeling in your arm? Every part feels equal, heavy, like you are under pressure from all sides. If you do this you can get the feeling that something is covering your body. This is the mind.

When you move it's not only muscular; you must create a certain feeling in the body. Some teachers say, "Feel the air pressing in, feel like you are surrounded by water." Some teachers want you to feel like you are moving in oil. This is to develop a stronger mind, that's all. It's a method to get the mind into the body: practice as if you are under the water. Here you have something that you cannot use your power against. This is what you want to achieve with mind training. Every practice has a feeling in every part of the body—that's your mind being there. Then every one of your parts are very easy to control. Eventually you can change your movement quickly in response to someone's pressure. By using the mind you can easily continue and change again.

Working with the mind is an inside experience. The external body is equally important in training. However, if you are training correctly, you are training the mind and the body together. Some people want to train one move for fighting, another for *qi gong*, and so on. I don't agree. My stepping, my arm, my body—all want to approach you at once, not disjointedly. When most people learn about fighting they think, "I want to attack!" but at first the body does not respond. Train naturally, so that when the mind goes, the body instantly follows.

Books always say, "Keep your mind calm." The mind is like a wire, and the internal power and movement is the electricity that moves through it. This is why internal martial arts always emphasize the mind first. The mind controls everything. Someone might say they have a missile, maybe even a nuclear bomb. OK, but how do you launch it? That is what we want to develop. Internal martial arts people say, "I have lots of qi." OK, you may have a big bullet, but what is your gun? Your gun is your structure, the unified mind and body.

This is the concept that defines internal martial arts. You can see it in Xing Yi, Ba Gua, and Tai Ji. Forget the form, use theory. In concept, these three arts are almost the same. The emphasis is on mind, structure, and Jing. Each of these parts is very important.

Spirit

SOMETIMES PROGRESS CAN COME from changing your mentality. You think, "I want higher skill, but how can I find it?" Your teacher says, "Go up to the mountaintop and look out over the ocean." Up there on a high mountain it's only you, and you feel so small, like you are nothing. Other times you feel like, "All this is my territory!" and become very big. Then you feel small again. This is the mind changing.

If you attack, I can escape you because I become nothing. I can follow you like water. Too many people forget about this. After ten years, I think you should have had every kind of skill and power training. But still, something is lacking. The spiritual development is not complete. If your spirit can change, everything can change. Like hardware, I just change the CPU and upgrade the computer. Everything outside stays the same—just change what is inside of you.

I'm not saying that you have to do meditation or practice a religion to do the internal martial arts. Rather, every new thing you learn will change your body a little bit. If you set yourself against it, it won't work, and your progress stops right there. You must slowly ferment, the same way grapes become wine. Ideas and new understandings come along one at a time, in a lot of separate pieces. Then one day they all come together. A lot of material has to combine

Photo by Eric Nomburg

Luo De Xiu demonstrates a Ba Gua technique.

to become an idea, the pieces must all link together.

The more you change and open your mind, the stronger you are, because you become more flexible. One way of thinking is "I am stronger than you, I am the top, I can control everything." Another says, "OK, I am flexible within myself. So whatever the problem is, big or small, it's the same." You can change yourself in many ways. If you enjoy everything, you feel happy and everything around you is like your own body. I am whole, I am body and spirit, together inside. The mind becomes the body, I am spirit right here.

Integration

INTERNAL MARTIAL ARTS are about integration. You may know two hundred different martial arts, but what is the quality of your movements? It's still just movement, it doesn't matter how many forms you know. People with wisdom will use a tool properly, but a person of

Gao style Ba Gua posture. From *Swimming Body Connected Link Ba Gua Zhang* by Du Shao Tang.

lower knowledge will recognize only one function of the tool. In the same manner, internal martial arts can be used for many functions because you use the same tool. This training material is only one tool, but it has many different uses. In the external way, one move is only one move, which leads people to say, "I have two hundred techniques." For me, there is just one program; the same system can become a lot of things.

Internal martial artists prefer to say that we have two hundred different things, but one common key. If you have two hundred different martial arts techniques, you have no time to practice them all. You need to use one form for practice and include everything in it—mind, structure, movement, and qi. If you can easily do all of these within each motion, that is internal martial arts.

A lot of times, people talk about the surface, like admiring someone's clothing. But what about the inside of the body? This is not a new idea, it's in every book. How do the bones, the muscles, the brain, and the spirit interact? Don't focus on the clothes; look inside, you will find that it is very clear. The initial understanding is always difficult to find. However, once you understand, it becomes so clear. Once you enter that doorway, you gain self-confidence, and it's very easy to practice. If the program is right, like Xing Yi or Ba Gua, the book is already written. You just need to follow the process and create the structure from the outside to the inside. That is the first step.

Allen Pittman

Allen Pittman, author of three books on the internal martial arts, has spent many years practicing and teaching these styles. He began training during high school, spent a number of years learning Ba Gua and Xing Yi in Taiwan, and has dedicated his life to broadening his understanding of traditional martial, healing, and esoteric systems of knowledge from around the world.

I was fortunate to spend an afternoon with him discussing his experiences during his many travels. His perspective allows him to bring forward many of the similarities that exist among different traditions. In the process of learning different methods his dedication to his foundational arts of Xing Yi, Ba Gua, and Tai Ji was solidified. The traditions that he is a part of are preserved in their purest aspect, and he insists on passing them on exactly the way they came to him. Yet his evolution continues, as his studies lead him around the globe in pursuit of authentic teachings. This demonstrates the essential point that even as a traditional martial art is complete within itself, personal growth must never cease, and new layers of understanding emerge with investigation into fresh areas of study.

Photo by Eric Nomburg

Allen Pittman.

Allen Pittman
JULY 24, 2002

A Life's Path

THERE ARE TWO KINDS of practitioners in the martial arts. One is recreational—they do it for fun and health or to learn how to fight. The others are people who have a calling, who are responding to something deep within them. They discover martial arts and it rings a bell, it becomes an obsession and a pursuit. What it is for them is actually a life's path. They will study throughout their life; it's like a religion or a philosophy. Those people may not even be teachers— sometimes it's a very private matter to them—but you'll find that they're always studying martial arts.

For those called to the martial arts, it turns into a renaissance study. The person first starts in martial arts, maybe Japanese, maybe Indonesian, maybe Chinese, maybe Indian, maybe Celtic, maybe Western boxing, but it leads them into a kind of liberal arts study. At first they might be interested in the martial arts of China, then they'll get interested in Chinese language, then they'll get interested in Chinese religion, then they'll get interested in Chinese culture, then they go to China, and so on. The martial art as a path then leads you into other disciplines and interests, like spokes on a wheel. For that kind of person, it's a path. And they may end up doing something completely different, say translating manuscripts, or studying philosophy and religion, because of that connection to the martial arts.

That kind of practitioner usually makes a good teacher because they can relate the art to other things off the hub of the wheel. They can tell the student, "We do these movements and this is how you use it, but this is how it relates to the culture and this is why they created it." Then the study becomes three-dimensional. You get depth, and you start seeing how it relates to life.

The other kind of practitioner sounds more like, "I'm a guitar player, I work in a hospital as an occupation, I do martial arts Monday and Wednesday at seven in the evening to stay in shape and because it's neat. I can relate it a little bit to what else I do." It's part of their life's smorgasbord; they are coming at it from the perimeter of the wheel. They have a full life—spouse, family, and job. They get on the wheel of martial arts and slowly go toward the center.

Physical Education

Photo by Eric Nomburg

Allen Pittman demonstrates the Dragon Shaking Tail Ba Gua Palm change.

MARTIAL ARTS REMAIN USEFUL today because the human body hasn't changed significantly since the arts' creation. As long as we have the human body with this structure, martial arts always have relevance. We are mammals, which means we are tactile and we learn through touch. All warm-blooded animals learn by touch. In the learning protocols of a primate, all mammals wrestle in their infancy. You learn orientation, the vestibular function of the brain, where you are in space, positioning, psychological stability.

In the early childhood years all physical education comes out of crawling and wrestling. As you get older the activity takes place further and further away from your body. So you see things like boxing and basketball where you throw something away from the body. But originally it's all earth-based—grabbing and holding from the breast, all the way up to wrestling, to fighting an enemy and trying to tangle him up or hold him on the ground and strangle him.

Boxing and kicking is trying to get someone away instead of crushing him. The next step in the progression of pushing and getting away is something like baseball, where you use a stick to hit and knock a ball away, or you throw a discus or a javelin. The martial process is inherent in human development. It's a part of the physicality of educating a human body.

Human Evolution

I LOOK AT MARTIAL ARTS as a part of human evolution, part of a long history of six or eight thousand years. I think we have these impulses in our DNA. When we study a martial art we are studying our own reactions. We have a fight-or-flight nervous system centered in the lizard part of the brain.

The first thing a human being deals with is life and death, how to breathe. The doctor slaps you on the rump and you breathe, you cry—that's the first martial arts lesson. Now, there are other ways to do it: like if you are birthed in water, it doesn't start with a slap on the rump but it does start with a gasp. Swimming is closer to wrestling; the smack on the bottom is closer to boxing.

No matter the teacher, guru, style, culture, or language, these things are implicit in us, they are part of our cellular makeup. For that reason, martial arts are relevant as a form of physical and psychological education for anybody. That doesn't mean that they have to be obsessive about it, and they may not be a great teacher or master, but as part of the educational process it's very beneficial.

It also gives people insight into history, because most history is depicted or punctuated by wars. If you understand the wars and how they were fought, you understand the difficulties of the time. Because how you move is largely based on how you think. The brain patterning of a human being is largely postulated on one's habit of movement, so as you learn to move you learn to think.

You see the progression in learning to play guitar. At first you learn the fingerings, then you learn to read the music. After a while you don't think of your hands anymore, you just go into your imagination where you have a melody. Then you can do it backwards; you can write the music. But it all starts from the body.

Lineage

O NE THING THAT MAKES Chinese martial arts special is that they've preserved more than other cultures have—there's more left. But I realize that things are changing, China's changing, tradition is changing. You can find Americans today that know more about traditional Chinese martial arts than a Chinese might know.

Photo by Rick Eugeno

Hong Yi Mian
practices Pi Quan.

When I was in Taiwan, I went and I found the Ba Gua Zhang master Hong Yi Mian, and I eventually lived with him. He told me that he didn't teach any other students what he taught me—the whole system. They weren't interested and he didn't think they were up to it. The ones that were up for it were becoming hit men and debt collectors for the mafia. He said that's why he'd quit teaching.

He said, "I'll teach you, but I don't know why." And I thought, "What a weird thing to say." But that's what he said, and that's what he did. After a while he said, "We had a predestined relationship." In other words, he believed in a kind of karma, and he just had a feeling that he should teach me the whole thing. As he got to know me he trusted me more. His son was puzzled too and said to me, "I don't know why my father is teaching you, but I think he is teaching you everything."

Hong Yi Mian said, "You're going to be the one to carry the system *from me*." It's not like I'm the only one who's carrying it. I'm not making a claim of exclusivity. I'm just saying that with my teacher, I was the one he decided to have carry on the system.

That's an idea of what can happen in the pursuit of a thing across culture. If your teacher likes you, that's everything. If your teacher doesn't trust you, it doesn't matter how long you study with him. You might meet a guy who says, "I studied with Mr. Whatever for twenty-five years," but you don't know the nature of the relationship.

No matter how hard you try to teach someone, if there's no real relationship, if they don't really want it, even if you really want to give it to them, they don't really get it. And the flip side is true too. If the teacher doesn't like the student, no matter how hard they work, there's going to be this pulling away.

I'm saying this because what matters is the teacher and the student getting along. And racism enters into the equation, and belief systems enter into the equation. If they both believe in reincarnation, they might feel like they've been together before. Alternately, if someone is a very nationalistic Chinese, they might think, "Well, this person is an American, and they'll never understand this."

The more real teachers tend to avoid all the evasion and caginess and backbiting. Because if I wanted to learn carpentry I'd simply want to go find the guy that's going to teach me to make the furniture—I don't want the esoterics. But martial arts are made up of a healing side and a hurting side. You want someone who can teach you how to use it and also what the health benefits are. If you see it as a craft, a technical study, something that can be learned, then you'll be clear in your mind without getting into a lot of political ideas and a lot of abstract ideas about qi and Confucianism, and pecking order and what is a master and all of those things.

None of my teachers wore these Kung Fu uniforms, just short pants, tennis shoes, and t-shirts. But they were fighters. Some had taught at military institutes in China, and all of them were very straightforward in their lessons.

The commercial schools tend to fall into the political thing. You have to do regimentation to teach lots of people and to maintain a cash flow. It's not a bad thing. A good teacher can do all that and all the students will still actually learn.

Westerners have some very good ideals. One is that they like the guts, they want to go to the heart of the matter and get the real stuff. They don't care about all the fluff. Yankee ingenuity is all about, how does it work? Tell me how it works, then I'll do it. The Chinese way is, have faith, do it a long time, and maybe I'll tell you how it works. If you hang around long enough and practice, it pretty much ends up being the same thing. My issue is with people who never really explain it simply because they don't know.

Students and Teachers

Photo by Rick Eugeno

Hong Yi Mian practices
Hou Tian Ba Gua.

THE ONE THING A TEACHER can give a student is practical courage. You can tell them they are on the right path, you can encourage them to continue to study, you can teach them how to fight so they feel safe. Remember, though, that's not the same as how to start a fight. In essence they are supposed to give the student the confidence and ability to go on and study whatever they are interested in. If teachers would do that and get out of the student's way, students could accelerate in their development.

There are some wonderful examples of how this is supposed to work. Hong Yi Xiang studied with Zhang Zhun Feng, my grand-teacher. Papa Hong hired Zhang, who taught all three Hong brothers that were left of the five. Two had died. And after Hong was with Zhang for a while, he sent Hong Yi Xiang to Taichung to study Tai Ji with Chen Pan Ling.

Hong Yi Xiang was a good student, he's smart, he's

able, he can fight, his Xing Yi and southern Shaolin are good, so at that stage of development his teacher recommends not that he stay with him for the rest of his life, but that he go study with this other man. Obviously Zhang Zhun Feng and Chen Pan Ling were pals. So Hong Yi Xiang traveled to Taichung periodically to learn the Tai Ji form of Chen Pan Ling. Zhang himself taught Hao style Tai Chi. But he didn't teach that to Hong Yi Xiang; he sent him to Taichung. The third Hong brother learned Hao Tai Ji.

Master Zhang didn't say, "You must do the Tai Ji that I do." He sent his student to another guy to learn a totally different style. While Hong was there he studied with another man who was a master of hitting vital points. His teachers didn't just say, "Oh, I know vital points too." They said, "This other guy specializes in it, go to him." These teachers were very clear on what they knew and didn't know, and they didn't try to know everything. These were traditional boxers on Taiwan and this is what they did.

I want you to know that that really did happen, because it seems like everything negative gets press. It doesn't have to be like the police blotter—the best martial artists have mutual respect and camaraderie.

Training Softness

EXTERNAL ARTS TEND TO DEPEND upon methods that are harder on the body. For instance, their forms are not as ergonomic; they tend to test the joints more. You might hit in two different directions at once—it's a little more shocking on the spine. In the old days they depended on the sandbag work and the wooden man work—toughening the hands and so on.

The external forms usually have more acrobatics. The range of movement is different; your foot might go one way, the leg another. Their squats are a lot harder on the knees. The angles of the legs are tougher. And although they have them, they don't always use the six alignments: hand over foot, elbow over knee, shoulder over hip. That is a mark of the internal styles.

Another aspect of internal style is the understanding of qi. Qi is basically how the air and oxygen move in the body. But Shaolin has that as much as internal martial arts do. When Huang Po Nien wrote his text on Ba Gua in the forties, he said, "How can we say that Damo's art was not internal when all the Shaolin monks practiced meditation? If you meditate and do a form it is internal."

In the historical continuum the only thing that can safely be distinguished between Nei Jia and Wai Jia is the level of rigor. Those things that are called external usually have a much stronger element of hard conditioning. But they all had meditation, they all had breath work, they all had qi, they all knew body alignment, and how to hit hard and how to root. So the division might actually be useless; there might be no real difference at all.

What you might really be looking at is preferences in training protocols. Internal arts seem to prefer more ergonomic movements that are less harsh on the body, with more gradual conditioning. Start hitting the bag softly then build up with the breathing, very gradually. There's a big emphasis on tactile two-man drills, feeling, moving, fluidity. Whereas in the hard schools, you just develop a punch that will knock down a bull. And if you get hit going in, fine, but when he gets hit it's over.

Some things aren't a question of internal or external, they're a question of conditioning.

Photo by Eric Nomburg

Allen Pittman demonstrates a Ba Gua technique.

Most people would say that bag kicking and endurance training are external, but in the old days, the Xing Yi boxers used to hit 300-pound sandbags with their elbows and knees. Ba Gua is so soft, would it work against Thai boxing? Yes, if the guy trains as hard as a Thai boxer, it would. If he did his heavy bag work and he did his wooden man work and his partner practice.

The evidence is, to me, that all of these things come from a common place. It could be that at one time the Shaolin Temple was more like a university and you had classes in different things. Any art can be internal or external depending on how you train and with what emphasis.

Consciousness

WANG LAI SHEN and some of the older boxers said that art is consciousness. In other words, it's how you are. It's a game of perception. You have to understand what you are doing—that's what makes it art. It doesn't matter what form it is: Jeet Kune Do, Eskrima, Kali, Tai Ji, Zu Ran Men, Ba Gua Zhang, Celtic wrestling, or Western boxing. What matters is how well you understand what it's for and how much you train it properly. When you get inside something and study it for years, and think about breathing and psychology and see how you feel when you do it, you change and it changes. Things really shift.

People put their hands out, and I show them some Ba Gua things. Then they'll say, "Let's spar," and they'll come in and maybe I'll kick them in the head. They'll say, "Hey, you don't have that in Ba Gua!" Who said I had to use Ba Gua? Hong Yi Mian would say that it's all Ba Gua.

That's just an example. I'm not likely to do that—I'm likely to use a Ba Gua hand technique because it's safer. But it's one thing to know an art, it's another to be a person. If you're attacked you're not responsible to respond according to a certain formula. You've learned those formulas so that you have a choice.

You can use two very simple models of understanding qi in the martial arts. One—you take a deep breath and you make up your mind and you do something. That's qi. Put oxygen in your bloodstream, think clearly, concentrate, then you do it.

That's what they mean when the Japanese say *ki*—it's raw, focused, absolute will power. But when the Chinese say *qi*, it's more complex. Because what they're talking about is a change inside the human body that is electro-chemical. They talk about secretions from the kidneys and the gonads that flood into the bloodstream, including testosterone and adrenaline, coupled with extra oxygen from deep breathing.

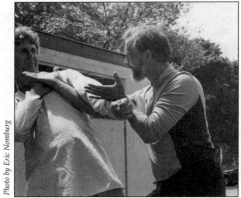

All of those chemicals are mingled together, and over time and practice, what happens apparently is that the cerebrospinal fluid changes. This gives you additional electrical current in your nervous system. You can use the energy to change your tissue and change your physiology, which makes you healthier and stronger. You end up hitting harder and you're more aware. It changes your psychology as well as your tissue.

Qi translated often means "breath." If a guy can kick hard, he probably exhales when he kicks. So he is accessing his qi already. If he learns right where to exhale, suddenly his kicking can double in power. He'll notice that he's more balanced because his mind is on his navel instead of his chest.

If he breathes right and his mind is in the

Photo by Eric Nomburg

Allen Pittman demonstrates a Ba Gua technique.

right place inside his body, he'll find that he doesn't strain, he's more balanced, he's more relaxed, and he doesn't get injured as much. What I'm saying is that these lines between internal and external are blurred. You'll find that old-timers in the external arts who maintained their health usually figured the tricks out.

You can learn from the outside going in or from the inside going out. In external styles your attention is usually projected at a target. In internal styles you often focus on the inside so you'll know if you are hurting your organs or your muscles. A lot of internal teachers would have students do forms while they feel how their joints and breathing and everything feels. They would start with the inside and learn the feeling from the form. Then when you go into application you try to keep that feeling. That's the way of going from inside to outside. But a lot of the old Shaolin guys, they've done forms a long time and guess what, they have the feeling too.

Either way you eventually have to be aware of both sides. It's a game of awareness. Eventually you have to be familiar with how you are within, and how that works out there during interaction.

Focusing the mind inside the body is found in all martial arts. Even the old-time professional strongmen had it figured out. If they breathed a certain way and had their mind in a certain place, they could pick up a heavier weight. The principle doesn't significantly change from culture to culture. The Peruvians had it, the Celts had it, the Vikings had it, and so on.

The Tan Tien is the center of gravity structurally, so if you put your mind there you're going to be more balanced, regardless of qi cultivation. If you put your intention down there, you're going to brace with your knees and you'll be more balanced automatically. I used to teach this awareness to old people in nursing homes so they wouldn't fall down and break their hips. I said, "Whenever you get dizzy, bend your knees and think of your navel." As soon as they did they would quit swaying. They didn't have to practice it for twenty years.

There are tricks, but when you do those tricks for decades it becomes something else, then it's a habit. You move differently, more like a panther than a man on stilts. Low, graceful, connected. That is an effect of using the tricks over time. The Chinese would say that's *gung fu*, skill. A man who thinks of his Tan Tien when he does his Tai Ji twice a week is one thing. A man who's thought about his Tan Tien his whole life is another thing entirely.

Chren Bu—The Whole Ball

THE CHINESE HAVE an interesting phrase, *chren bu*, which means "whole ball." It's about understanding how the whole thing works together. It's not this or that, it all works together. The strength is found when you have the *Liu He* (the six basic alignments), the breath, the will, the understanding of how it works in a fight, the health benefits, and then the long-term practice, *gung fu*. All that sown

Photos by Eric Nomburg

Allen Pittman demonstrates the Dragon Shaking Tail Ba Gua palm change.

together can make some remarkable people. That's why the old insistence was on training for long periods of time, but it wasn't meant to be blind training.

Say you do a form and for one month and all you think of is your elbows and knees. The next month all you think about is your fingertips and toe tips. The next month you think of your shoulders and hips. Then you do bag work, one month just hitting with fingertips and toes, and one month just hitting with elbows and knees, then one month shoulders and hips.

After you do that for a year, when you do your form it will be unlike anyone else's because of what you've put into it. You understand it, you've done it different ways, you've come to an understanding over time of what it can do. That's intelligent training.

For a beginner, I'd say they should train hard and regularly, and that they'll learn a lot by getting a training partner. You'll always learn twice as much if you have a training partner. You have someone to work out with on forms, weight training, calisthenics, and applications. You experiment and talk together. It's important to have a friend to work things out with. And in martial arts it's best to start with someone your size because your geometry is approximately the same. If they're two feet taller than you, then everything's off a little. As you progress it also helps to work with people that are bigger than you.

Then just basically read everything you can and experiment as much as possible. Pay attention to the teacher, but don't be bound to what the teacher says. It's very important that you have fun and experiment and read and try out different things.

Liu He

IN TERMS OF POSTURE, the most important thing is *Liu He*, the six alignments. Particularly the knees—there are a lot of mistakes made about the knees. The knees and elbows represent the will power in internal boxing. Above all else, the most important thing that a lot of young people need to do is listen to their knees. Don't try to force the knees; let them determine the angle of the feet. Then they can go into the waist and the torso. I've had many knee injuries, and people have come to me with them many times when I worked as a physical therapist. It's important to pay attention to that because a lot of teachers force the knees.

There's a culture gap there because the Asians have a patella that's twice as thick as the Caucasians. The medial tendon of the patella on an Asian person is double thickness. And it's a squatting culture. So it's part genetic, part conditioning. We have to be more careful to build up that medial tendon. Just start with a higher squat, and go lower and lower until it's butt to heels. But you always go all the way up to tighten the patella down so it doesn't get too loose.

The squat and leg extension are practiced to preserve the health of the legs, and they can be mixed with running and kicking or whatever. All the old power lifters know the squat is the king of all exercises, and that should be a cardinal rule for anyone in any physical activity. But if the patella or the kneecap gets any trouble from squatting, then one should do leg extensions to tighten it back up. That's just straightening the leg out and back with a weight on the ankle.

All health is generated out of the simple action of squatting. Babies do it naturally. It helps you with digestion, it helps your lower back stay straight and strong, and if you squat heavy weight high reps, it's man-killing work, but it's a terrific aerobic workout. It'll allow you to go backpacking and never get tired; it will give you the wind for running. There's all sorts of talk about specialized training, and this and that, but really every culture has squatting as a core exercise. The Hindu wrestlers do squats by the thousands on a daily basis without weight, doing them in rounds of five hundred, like jump rope. Eventually they don't get tired at all.

In the West we tend to do less repetitions with more weight. There's something to that because we economize time. Without weight we'd have to take a long time. But do it smart. You can use a squat cage if you need to; the real key is don't use too heavy a weight. Never try to squat a weight you can't pick up, hang on to, and maneuver.

Symbols

TRADITIONAL MARTIAL ARTS SETS are each built around a specific theme. This idea goes back a long way—in any culture there's usually a set of religious symbols. The way early people connected their ideas to the world was through symbols. So you would memorize a symbol, then when you looked at it you would remember all the teachings about that symbol.

Most ancient cultures were not literate, so they remembered through stories and symbols. And the stories and symbols were also the common language of the dances and martial arts. A lot of the old martial arts have common symbols—I don't mean recent stuff like Karate and Judo, but the older martial arts that have connections to religion and dance. The symbols are made to memorize, to be able to reproduce easily, and to use as a map of the method.

It just happens that Ba Gua Zhang uses the Ba Gua trigrams as its symbols. Those trigrams have meanings, and depending on which Ba Gua system, they have different associations. I know that there are Ba Gua teachers who say that it has nothing to do with the *Book of Changes*. Maybe their Ba Gua does not. But mine does, and I was taught that it does by my teacher.

The Gao Yi Sheng system is definitely very tied in with the *Book of Changes*. I was told distinctly which hexagram goes with each movement. The way I was taught, the *Yi Jing* is woven together with the physical art like a rug. Of course, there's sixty-four hexagrams in eight categories of phenomena: light, water, mountain, thunder, wind, fire, earth, and lake. Those categories are very shamanistic.

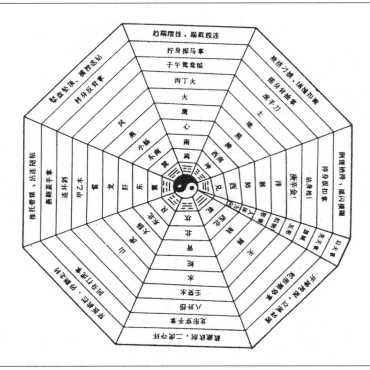

Ba Gua diagram.

Hong Yi Mian demonstrates
Hou Tian Ba Gua.

The Gao Ba Gua System

FROM A COMBATIVE PERSPECTIVE, the points you
attack correspond to the trigram that relates to
those techniques. From a survival point of view, if
you get injured on the head, you need to know what
herbs are needed and how you treat head injuries. In
the particular method of Ba Gua I learned, this was
all classified as a system, in a very logical manner. So
when Hong taught me, I learned the movements and
how to use them. He said, "You're smart—over time
you'll figure it out."

After I learned all the movements, I couldn't photograph him, so I drew figures of everything, and he liked that. Then before I left, he reproduced a chart that apparently Grandmaster Zhang had given him. It was a chart with the symbol, the house, the movements, and the hexagrams all placed in order. He gave me another which was a poem about fighting, and how to use the art. He said, "Now, you've got the system, just keep working. Another five years and you'll have a hold of it." I went back and saw him about ten years later in 1995. I told him what I had discovered, what I thought, and how I was working. He said, "Excellent, you're on the right track. I'm glad you figured it out."

Hong Yi Mian died in the year 2002. All these years I was trying and searching, and he pretty much confirmed everything I had been working on. This system is carefully connected; all these different themes are meaningful. The symbols pertain to both target and therapy, as well as the locations where you put your intention when you practice. Because when you put your attention at your head and heart, you learn to hold your neck very straight. So when you go through each house you are doing a different alignment principle. When you're done, you're doing them all.

Roots of the Martial Arts

IT'S VERY TYPICAL of revisionist thinking to say, "Well, these old guys had their fighting techniques and they wanted to make them legitimate, so they gave them philosophical names." But I think that's wrong. These people in the past did have belief systems and they were inspired. They had time too—there was no TV. Some religious practitioners lived up in the mountains. They had time to write and think and organize and work.

I always assume that they knew more about it than I do. Whenever I've doubted something in the system, after I've studied it long enough it finally becomes clear to me what it's about. I don't ever change it. If I have a question about the method or the movement of a form, I'll do it and study it; and if I study the history, eventually it will become clear why they did it that way. It's never failed me. Sometimes there will be a weird movement and I'll think, "What is that about?" Then I'll read up on the history and I'll realize that that movement was for a specific weapon that they used at that time.

For instance, the first trigram in Ba Gua is Chien, the creative; it corresponds to enlightenment. You begin with that search for insight. The first movement in Ba Gua is Kai, to Open. In Buddhism they talk about beginning on the path. The gate opens, Kai. The originators of these arts were very wise and they had great instincts. They were very much alive in their bodies. They were hunters and farmers, and they were tuned in perceptively. They listened to their dreams. In some ways they were ahead of us because they were so integrated. A lot of times they were not distracted like we are today.

That doesn't mean that they went and got in fights, it meant they wanted to live. Because it's dangerous living up in the mountains or in a rural settlement. It's tough traveling from one place to another by yourself. And people usually didn't travel by themselves because of the dangers involved. If you study a martial art knowing that it's a catalog of wisdom and you aren't in a hurry to change things so they make immediate sense, eventually you'll figure it out. My bone of contention is with people who see a form and say that won't work and then they change it. My question is, "What was it for?" Don't change it—find out what it was for originally.

The question is not, is this art better, is this art worse, is Gracie Jujitsu better than Jeet Kune Do, is Ba Gua better than Celtic wrestling? The question is, what is it for? The only real question is, what's the function of the art? Because they all developed in a context. If you understand that then the form makes sense and you can practice it intelligently. And you can teach it intelligently; you can know what the limits are because no one form answers all needs. And that's why you study different martial arts.

Nurturing

I NTERNAL MARTIAL ARTS are often associated with meditation, whether it's a sitting practice or within the martial training. In Tai Ji you practice slow movements to develop this. But the old-timers did seated meditation as well. When you do a lot of combative training you can really get wired. If you punch bags, spar, swing weapons, and lift weights an awful lot, you can get a little edgy. Anyone who's

Photos by Eric Nomburg

Allen Pittman demonstrates a Ba Gua technique.

doing regular harsh physical training needs rest time.

You start seeing Post-Traumatic Stress Disorder if people overdo it—guys who walk into a restaurant and sit down and think of all the different ways they could take out whoever's around them. What they need to do is go sit down under a tree for a while. The harder you train, the more important it is to do a little seated practice. It allows you to process. Something else that people don't realize is that when you're sitting still you are resting. But it's not the same as sleeping. Like, if you've ever gone into a bookshop and sat down with a book, and when you closed it suddenly four hours had gone by. You feel like you're in another world. Then when you leave you feel like you've had a vacation. That's what seated meditation is about. It allows you to rest and process and do something else with all your energies. So for me, if you are doing rigorous training you need a few minutes a day to read quietly or sit quietly or watch nature. For some people it's having a smoke.

It's not a formalized part of the training because some people have good instincts and they'll just go off and do it on their own. They'll get a book and go to the park. Or they'll know they need to go out to the country for a few days and play their guitar or something—mellow out.

We're not taught we can rest—we're taught that that's being unproductive, that we're losing money. But it's important to go take five or ten minutes now and then. If you're doing a lot of serious training and your nerves are really jangled, after a while you start feeling pretty beat up. You need a girlfriend, you need some chocolate ice cream, you need to go to the zoo, you need to go sit out under a tree and watch the clouds for a while. Let your nervous system recalibrate.

The Chinese originators didn't say "recalibrate the nervous system." They said, "nurture qi." When you're younger you have visions of flying through the air, rescuing damsels, smashing things, all that. As you get older, you realize that you also want to live and have a good life. You realize that when you rest you feel better. You don't like feeling like crap. Yeah, it's great to train, but you also want to feel good. It's that feeling thing again—how do you feel inside?

There's a nurturing aspect to the training, so you don't prematurely age, so you don't get used to having the crap kicked out of you. You're not supposed to get used to that. If you're hurt that means something's wrong. The idea of the martial arts is to keep you from being hurt. I realize in competitive sports like kickboxing you're going to get hurt. But if you do get hurt, go rest.

Healing Arts

MOST MARTIAL ARTS in their traditional form have a healing component. Like Okazaki Sensei—he was a Jujitsu guy with a big school, the Kodenkan. People would come to him with everything from broken arms to bruises. And here he was, this muscular Hercules-like guy, and he would say, "Oh, here," and fix it. He was a near miraculous healer. He was known as an excellent physical therapist, as well as being the holy terror of Jujitsu.

Every martial artist should learn something about massage, or they should take a paramedic course, or study naturopathy, or whatever catches their interest. Traditionally you'd end up at least learning some herbal medicine or some acupuncture points from your teacher. The wrestlers in India are some of the best massage therapists in the world. Generally the teachers are the ones who work on the students. The students learn all the nurturing techniques from the wrestling guru. So not only are they skilled wrestlers, but they work on each other.

The Hong brothers were bone-setters and doctors of herbal medicine. When I lived with Hong Yi Mian, a lot of times when I was helping his daughters make bread he'd call me over to the other side of the house to hold someone while he worked on scar tissue or something. He'd be pulling on an arm, breaking up scar tissue with his thumbs, and I'd be holding the patient, and with the flour on my hands they wouldn't slip.

He taught me his bone setting and he expected me to know it. And by the time I went to learn from him, I had already worked as a physical therapist. He was thrilled because he knew I could catch on. Even if teachers didn't learn it from their teachers, they picked it up somewhere else, because sooner or later something is going to hurt.

Ultimately, Ba Gua is not for everybody, and martial arts aren't for everybody. You're either just coming in to sample it or you're going to stick with it for a while and really learn something. It may not be for everybody, but if it is for you, you are going to learn a lot about yourself, and it's going to become a very important part of your life.

James Wing Woo

James Wing Woo has been practicing martial arts for more than seventy years, making him one of the most senior practitioners located in North America. He was born in California, but spent his youth in Canton (Guangzhou), China. On the outset of World War II he joined the U.S. Navy, finally ending up back in California. He eventually settled in Los Angeles and has been actively teaching since the early 1960s.

Mr. Woo is a relentless scholar, and his appetite for researching the martial arts led him to the doorstep of any teacher he could find throughout his youth, meeting and practicing with many famous teachers in both southern China and San Francisco. Through exhaustive study of anatomy and kinesiology, his knowledge of human movement is highly developed. And even exceeding eighty-two years of age, he is unquestionably capable as a martial artist.

We arrived to train at Mr. Woo's in January, so it was a cool morning in Hollywood, prelude to a scorching hot day. When we walked into the gym it was like stepping into a martial arts laboratory. Everything from his Daoist altar, to the dozens upon dozens of traditional weapons, to the numerous anatomy wall charts showed that his investigations into the workings of the human body have never ceased. After a workout in the Southern style basic training and an introduction to his Yang style Tai Ji Quan, we went to Mr. Woo's office to discuss martial arts. His bookshelves are crammed to overflowing with all manner of manuals and textbooks, in both English and Chinese, from detailed anatomy texts to philosophical treatises, as well as numerous rare, old, martial arts books. Over tea we talked for a long time. He told me many stories of his years in the martial arts and shared some of his insights into the true nature of Chinese gung fu. Above all, he emphasized that this isn't really about fighting. We use this art to learn about ourselves, and that study never comes to an end.

James Wing Woo
JANUARY 13, 2002

Chinese Martial Arts Culture

THE CHINESE PEOPLE have two different aspects of their culture generally, the scholastic arts and the martial arts. What happened in the past was that the scholastic arts tended to be dominant until there was a war, then the martial arts became more popular again.

In the past, martial artists were almost always illiterate. It was very rare that you found one with good martial arts and good scholastic skills. Of course, there was some cross-over; for instance moving the sword is considered a scholastic art. The bow is also considered to be among the scholastic arts. These are all arts from the beginning of time as we know it.

The Chinese martial arts have been handed down, mostly word for word, from person to person over the years. In the past, whenever people found secrets that made them become a better fighter, they would keep them to themselves. And if they did teach, they always taught only the boys (never the girls) to keep it within the family. There were a lot of things lost over the years for that reason.

When I trained in China, the teacher didn't usually teach you directly. It was the elder student that taught us; we called them "student brothers." The thing is, they usually wouldn't teach any basics. They would just put us into the horse stance, make us do a few punches, and then we'd go right into the forms practice.

James Wing Woo teaching.

The problem with that way is that if you don't have the basics practice that you do on your own to get the real fundamentals of movement, you're going to run into trouble. If all you learn is a lot of forms, you just become a good dancer. People believe they don't need to worry about it because when the teacher gets around to them, he is going to give them the secrets. But the teacher usually just drinks his tea, looks up at you, and says, "Oh yeah, you're doing all right, go ahead." When the teacher passes away, he always has a favorite student. And that's who he usually calls in before he passes away, so everybody thinks that the student got the secret. But really the teacher only said, "Hey, you take over." That's it! After that, since everybody thinks he's got the secret, the new teacher has to build up an image. I have seen a lot of bad teachers, even in China, that are like charlatans. They train a lit-

James Wing Woo, early 1960s.

tle while, then they go out and open a school, but they don't know what they're doing. At least they're giving you exercise, but that's all it is.

The hero worshipping is a big part of the martial arts environment in China these days. All the little Chinese kids going into the martial arts schools want to be Jet Li, Jackie Chan, or Sammo Hung and make millions. That's their goal, but in the past it wasn't. In the past the arts were in the family, and you had to protect the family so that nobody picked on them. The idea was not that you were learning to fight, you were learning the martial arts to keep a continuous trend going. If the father teaches, the sons will follow.

In China today, you still have people training. Some are professionals, and some are just hobbyists. I believe that the hobbyists are better off than the professionals because they don't do the things that other people want—they get to do their own thing. The hobbyists keep on moving and feeling, and keep the traditions going. When the communists took control in China, there were no martial arts allowed. After Mao died, these other bigwigs started thinking about big dollar signs, and they figured that if they rebuilt the Shaolin Monastery and put a bunch of attractions out there, people would come visit. That would be a lot of money coming in! It's on a mountain in Hunan, and down around the edge of the mountain there are all kinds of martial arts schools. The original Shaolin Monastery was burned down in 1666 and it was never rebuilt. It was only rebuilt after they found out about the American dollar!

I admire some of the modern Wu Shu people that come out of China today. In my training I did the splits, I did the jumps, and I did the tumbling. But training means more than that. Some do the "light body" training like Jackie Chan. That's where you rush right up there to the ceiling and you turn around and spin the body three times sideways. They're almost ice skaters the way they do the spins. It looks good but what use is it?

In China there are a lot of different styles. North of the river you have the Long Hand style, which is the Chang Quan or Cha Kuen. Then the Mieu Kuen and all these other different styles like Buck Tong Long, which is the Northern Mantis. Then you have the Northern Tiger, the Kun Lun Pai, and the Wo Mei Pai. Most of those northern styles gathered together within the Shaolin system.

In the past people in the north were generally taller and their arms were longer. They tended to be the bigger people. That's not true now, though; it seems like their people are shorter. The southerners used to have shorter arms and a smaller stature. That's in the past though— it seems like the world has changed. That goes to show that eventually, everything changes.

Sil Lum

MOST OF THE CHINESE EXTERNAL ARTS come from the Shaolin monastery, known as the source of the Sil Lum system. The Sil Lum system started in the fifth century A.D. when Bodhidharma came from India and traveled to many of the temples in China to introduce Buddhism. Some of these Buddhist temples were a haven for bandits and martial artists that were going to get killed by the authorities. They were outlaws, so they trained to keep themselves protected. Bodhidharma picked up things here and there during his travels. Eventually he landed at Shaolin monastery, and the legend says that he sat there gazing at the wall for nine years. Of course, that's just a legend. While he was gazing at that wall for nine years, one day he fell asleep. He got mad at himself and cut his eyelids off! When he threw them on the ground they grew up into two trees, which became the teas of China. Now, that's a lot of bull! Anybody who believes that will believe anything.

Anyway, he taught Zen Buddhism (the Chinese call it Chan) to the monks in the Shaolin monastery, but they all kept falling asleep on him. He was going on and on and on about throwing the books away and how they're going to do this and do that, and the guys all fell asleep. And so he said, "Now, wait a minute here. You guys are too weak! Let's go outside and I'll teach you something." So he taught them what we now call the Muscle Changing Classic. He also taught the Marrow Washing Classic. These were both *qi gong* movement sets.

The warm-up that we do in my gym is part of the Muscle Changing Classic. The idea is that you lock the body in place and nothing moves except one part, which then moves everything else. That's how you learn to use the body's stretching power, which has more strength than the contracting power. The contracting power is called the inner range power; the extending power is called the outer range power. In order to explode, you've got to have outer range power. Grappling uses inner power, like Judo or Jujitsu, anything that's pulling in close.

Mechanics

ONE OF THE BIGGEST PROBLEMS with people training these days is that there's just not enough emphasis on basics, on learning to move properly. Then again, you may ask, what are basics? The basics teach you to make the best use of your body that you can. Learn how the mechanics work and feel where the force comes from. Most people choke up physically because they can't seem to feel their own power unless they choke up and clench their muscles. But you don't have to choke up, you just have to move. Let the bones, joints, and muscles move freely. The bones are the structure of the body, the muscles are the power, and the joints are the agility, the ability to move.

Another thing to do is learn the mechanics of the three lever systems of the body. Identify the fulcrum, the power, and the extension. Use the three levers along with the laws of gravity and physics. All these people doing "amazing" demonstrations are using physics. The man that can't be pushed over, the man that's breaking bricks, the man that's run over by a truck—anybody can do these things.

Posture is another factor. You've got to feel the spine going straight up and down. Feel the seven cervical vertebrae go back and up, feel the lumbar vertebrae come forward and down. Then lift the whole spine up, and always keep it feeling like that. Anything that you can do to help the body get that feeling is good. You don't have to lock up your muscles to feel it.

If people want to be successful in martial arts, they have to be willing to change their habits. At first when they train they want to

Photo by Eric Nomburg

James Wing Woo teaches Wu Shu Kung Fu.

feel power. And they all want to be fast. As strange as it seems, in the beginning, the more power they get, the slower they are. When they let go of all that power the speed comes on its own.

By wanting to feel the power they clench up. Don't try to hold the arm back, let it go! It's important to feel the trunk muscles, feel the leg muscles. Most of all, put your arm out and feel your triceps engage. Use the lats and the triceps to move the arm. Learn to use the muscles for what they are supposed to be used for. Find out what the primer is and what the antagonizer is, then let the antagonizer do the primer's work, and let the primer do the antagonizing.

Chinese Martial Arts in Canton

I STARTED TAI JI QUAN with my number-five brother's godfather at his martial arts studio in Canton. I used to hang around quite a bit, and I learned the Tai Ji form there. I practiced there between the ages of eight and twelve years old. Until twelve, I didn't know the difference between *gung fu* and Tai Ji. I learned it when some kid beat the heck out of me! I thought, "Wait a minute now, what was he using?" So I ended up going to follow his teacher, where I learned Hung Gar for a while. From there I kept on moving. I was catching stuff from different places, learning here, learning there, and putting them together.

At that time the five southern Chinese styles were popular—Hung, Lao, Choy, Lay, and Mok. That was right after the coming of the Republic of China at the end of the Ching Dynasty. During the Ching Dynasty the five southern forms from Guangdong became popular in Canton. The Japanese invaded Manchuria in 1936. In 1937 they came into Shanghai, and most of the northerners from Manchuria and Shanghai fled to Canton. All the martial artists came down and there was quite a bit of martial arts going on, so you had your pick of good teachers.

The first thing you have to learn is how to watch and analyze what you've seen. Then you learn how to learn. Learning takes a lot of changing, don't hold onto any one thing and think that it's the only way.

Territorial Rights

I N CANTON WHEN I WAS TRAINING as a boy, there were a lot of fights between schools. The way it was back then, if I had a gym right here, there couldn't be any others within the next five blocks. If there was one nearby we'd go check them out. We'd ask them, "OK, how good are you?" And then the fight was on. I saw lots of these fights when I was a kid, and these guys didn't fight too well. Even if they trained well in the school, out there on the street they would fight differently—a lot of wild swings and brawling. They didn't use the techniques that they learned. They did learn to use weapons against each other though, and a lot of blood was shed.

If there was a small club without too many students, and this big club of fifty guys came at them, they'd end up saying, "OK, OK, we'll move," and that's what they did. Territorial rights were a big deal. In fact, the territory issue was the same with the Tongs of the Chinese-Americans. All the big families had family associations. The Wongs were a big family, the Woos, the Chans, and so on. When they'd go into business they'd help each other out. If a smaller family was right next door, you'd kick 'em out. So all the small ones got together and grouped into the big Tongs so that they

Photo by Eric Nomburg

James Wing Woo demonstrates a punch.

could get protection. That's how the Tongs came into being in San Francisco.

The structure of the Tong is like the structure of a government. You have the president, you have the vice-president, you have the treasurer, you have the board of members, as well as a leader for the single bachelors. Every three or four years they had an election. Before the thirties, forties, and fifties, the Tongs were pretty prominent. Now there's no use for them; there are just too many people around. They've ended up becoming gangs.

Everybody thinks these guys in the Tong train, but most of them don't practice martial arts. You see, I've gone to train at the Tong before. At that time the Tong had two teachers. One of them was Lau, and the other one was Wong—they were both famous. And they were both opium addicts. Each one opened up a school that the Tong provided, and if you were a member you could learn from them. They were skilled because they'd trained when they were younger, but they were over here in America for thirty or forty years already and they didn't keep it up. That's why I say—always be a student, you catch more of what's going on.

The Inside of the Body

THE EXTERNAL FORM of *gung fu* is about using the external muscles of the body. The internal form is about using the inside muscles of the body. People wonder how to feel the inside of the body. How do you feel the inside of your rib cage? To begin with, you have to feel the outside before you can feel the inside. Between the ribs there are muscles on the outside called the intercostal muscles. Those are the ones that hang down from the top rib to the bottom rib. Now, the muscles layered on the inside stretch upward, from the bottom going up. Feel those muscles go up. Now what do they feel like, are you feeling the inside or the outside?

Meditation helps, because you can use the mind to help you feel inside. Looking at pictures in books also helps. Get a good anatomy book and look at what each muscle does, and how best to move it. People in the past didn't have anatomy books, so they used words to remember the secrets. Phrases like "contain the chest, drop the back"—everybody in *gung fu* does that. "Contain the chest" doesn't mean to suck the chest in, though; it just means to hold it where it's at. Then draw the back up without inflating the front. Now, feel the shoulders widen, feel the elbows torque.

The head should always be up, not coming forward. One way you can get your head up is to remember this: move as if you have four eyes. Two eyes in front, and two eyes in the back of your head, looking the other way. Now, what happens to the head when you do that? It should help it to lift up straight. Every little thing helps. Little things eventually make big things. After all, there are only so many bones and so many muscles. Concentrate on the ones you want to control.

What you get out of martial arts all depends on what you're looking for. People are looking for a lot of different things. There's all kinds of trickery going on, too—people hitting five pieces of ice with their head and so on. Now what does that prove?

Jeet Kune Do

As far as Bruce Lee goes, I give him credit for bringing Chinese martial arts to the world at large. But he was a horrible martial artist! All of that Jeet Kune Do, I call it B.S. Do! I told that to him and he didn't like it, so I said, "If you don't like it, what will you do?"

I first met him when he was doing Kato in the Green Hornet series. I was called by *Black Belt* magazine to write an article about Tai Ji. I was up in their office when in came Bruce Lee. I was sitting down, and he was standing up over by the door. You know, he was only five foot five inches tall, and I looked at his shoes and they had inches of extra sole on them. The first thing he asked me was, "Do you box?" I said, "I boxed a little in the Navy." He dropped that subject really quick.

Then he said that he was going to show me Jeet Kune Do. I told him, "B.S. Do! You should stick to Wing Chun, you'd be a lot better off!" At that time he hadn't yet had the big fight with Wong Jack Man. He asked me, "Well, what do you think, are you going to demonstrate for me?" I said, "Now, wait a minute, if I get up out of this chair, only one of us is going to leave through that door, and I don't care if it's you or me. So let's not get into it." So he romped out of there.

There has always been a lot of talk about Bruce Lee's fight with

Photo by Eric Nomburg

James Wing Woo teaches Wu Shu Kung Fu.

Wong Jack Man. Five different people were there, and I heard five different stories. So what can I say? The story most likely is that Bruce Lee was waiting there at the school in Oakland, and Calvin Chin drove Wong in the car from San Francisco. It was after class and all the students were sent home already. So these five people walked in and they all sat down. Calvin Chin was the instigator. He said, "Come on, Wong, let me introduce you to Bruce Lee." Bruce Lee was standing there and Wong was stupid enough to put his hand out. As soon as he put his hand out, Pow! Bruce nailed him and put him right back against the wall. From there on I don't know how it happened. They fought for fifteen minutes, but neither one got hurt. They were making so much noise that some of the neighbors called the cops. Then they stopped it. When I talked to Wong's student, he said that he won. When I talked to Bruce Lee's friend, he said that he won.

One thing I'll say about Bruce Lee, though—after that day he found out that he wasn't so great, so he started training like a madman. He used to have a studio at the end of Chinatown here in L.A., over by the Meredith Theater. He used to use all these guys as training dummies: Chuck Norris, Bill Wallace, Mike Stone, Danny Inosanto, and this guy Wong, who's teaching now. He'd turn the record player on and used dancing to put rhythm in the kicks. They also did the Chi Sao, which he did pretty well.

Bruce Lee went back to China on a contract for fifteen thousand dollars to do a part in a Shaw Brothers movie. When he got to Hong Kong, he said, "I don't care about the money, but I want a starring role, not just a part. I want to be the star! Not only that, I'd like to write my own story. And maybe I'll direct it, too." But he couldn't have it all so they let him go. He was on his way back when he met Raymond Chow. And Raymond Chow said, "Fine, let's do one since you're here. I'll give you the same fifteen thousand dollars, and we'll go to Thailand and do *The Big Boss*." *The Big Boss* broke all the records in Hong Kong. Then the second movie broke the records. Then the third one broke the records and he started to get some clout. Luo Chit was the director of the first one; he was a gangster in Hong Kong.

Sometimes people wonder why he died, but it's not too hard to figure out. How many ways can you burn a candle? Top, bottom, and the middle. The guy had two girlfriends on the side, he was writing and planning for all these movies—you know, that's a lot to do for one person. He ended up dying at one of his girlfriend's places. People say, "Somebody hit him with Dim Mak [death touch]." No way, forget it. He'd always had those headaches.

Judo

"JUDO" GENE LeBELL is a good friend of mine, he's a rough one. There's a story about how he and Milo Savage had a fight in Utah. In the early sixties, some magazine had an article called "Judo Bum." It talked about how all these Oriental arts are nothing, about how the practitioners are a bunch of bums and so on—it tore them down. So Gene wrote a letter to the publisher asking if he could talk to the writer. They got him and the writer talking together and he told the writer, "Tell you what, you get whoever you want to fight me, and I'll represent Judo. We'll meet at Utah, we both put ten thousand dollars up, and winner takes all." In 1960 ten thousand dollars was a lot of money! Then again, you have to remember that Gene LeBell is an Eaton, and they're a very rich family. Before Gene went, he and the other guy got a hold of a middle-weight boxer, about a hundred and seventy-five pounds. At that time Gene LeBell was about a hundred and eighty pounds, short and strong.

Gene took the ten grand to Utah, and he won. When he came back he told me, "It's a good thing that guy didn't follow up on that first jab." The boxer was allowed to use those bag gloves with the metal strip in them, the gloves that you use to hit the heavy bag. And Judo only wore a gi and gi pants, no gloves, so he could grab. The guy went in there and Wham! Hit him once, nailed him back. Man, he felt that punch. LeBell said "If he had followed through, I would've been down." So he got his breath back and took a little while to run around. Then Gene took him down and choked him out and that was that.

The funny part about it was that after he came back, two weeks later somebody called me and said, "Hey, Jim, are you fighting Gene LeBell?" I said, "What are you talking about?" Then I thought for a second and I called Gene up. I said, "Hey, LeBell, want to fix this one up?" He just laughed. It's funny how things go along.

Photo courtesy of James Wing Woo

James Wing Woo demonstrates weapons practice, early 1960s.

I see him once in a while at interviews, you know. He works as a stunt man quite a bit.

Lethal Weapon

I MET JET LI on the set of *Lethal Weapon Four,* and he told me he had made twenty-two movies. He's not bad, he's a nice fellow, but he doesn't talk too much. He has his own crew and choreographer, as well as one student and his body double. The student does stand-in, and his double does his stunts. But he still does a lot of the stunts himself. He's getting a little chubby, though. I remember when he first came in 1972. At thirteen years old he was the head of the Wu Shu troop.

One thing about Jet Li is that he's studied everything. You name it and he's learned it. He maintains a school in his hometown in Hong Kong. He hires people to teach there in his name. He can afford it, you know, so he doesn't charge people; he just lets them come and train. That's why all the kids want to be Jet Li. Now, one thing about *Lethal Weapon Four,* that scene where he disarms the man and takes the gun apart with one hand—it just can't be done. I don't care who it is. It can't be done, but he looks nice doing it.

In the movie I was the only one that stayed alive; they never showed me getting killed. They planned to kill me, though. In fact, we did a scene where Danny Glover grabs a hold of me, grabs off my glasses and breaks them apart, picks me up by the crotch, and throws me in the garbage can. But he couldn't lift me. So they used a double because the double agreed to jump. They didn't like the looks of it, I guess, because they didn't end up using it. It took almost half a day to shoot that scene.

Real Power

PEOPLE TALK ABOUT how much bigger and tougher fighters are today than before. Actually, there isn't any difference; there were people like that even in the old days. In the martial arts, there's more than meets the eye. People think it's all about how big you are. So what! An elephant is big, but some guy can move it around with a little hook. The real power is when you learn to give. Yield, give, then if you have to, take over. Some of these big strong guys look like they could punch straight through you, but big arms aren't everything. Look at a big guy's leg, then look at his ankle. The ankle is tiny compared to the rest! You kick him in the ankle, then what happens?

They used to say that any man who graduates from the Shaolin Temple has to carry a red-hot thousand-pound urn! What? That's a lot of bull. I mean, it is a good legend but in the first place, if that urn were hot, how would you grab hold of it? In the second place, if it burned

Photo by Eric Nomburg

James Wing Woo teaches
Wu Shu Kung Fu.

into the arm, there would be scar tissue. There'd be no symbols, just scar tissue! But it's a nice story, like the one about the 108 wooden dummies you had to fight to get out of the temple. These kinds of legends make up a lot of the stories in the martial arts.

A lot of books talk about Daoist power. It's all in the imagination. Same goes for all the books on Dim Mak. When I was in China, I realized that that stuff was a lot of baloney. I always asked people, "Who can do it on me? I'll volunteer. Try it on me!" The old saying goes that if you can do it on someone, you can also make them come back to life and reverse the damage. But nobody could do it in the first place! I couldn't find anybody who would admit to it.

On the other hand, I have seen some things that can't be done. One guy put a mirror in front of him, then a candle right here behind it. He could shoot a punch and put the candle out. Now, I don't want to explain that. The man has such a velocity that his punch goes right through the pane of glass? Like I said, it can't be done! But, I saw it once.

You have to remember one thing, everybody works on their legend. Like my legend around here, one time I went over to the Paramount Theater to do a job. Some guy came up to me kind of sneaky-like and asked, "You, are you James Wing Woo?" I said, "Yeah." "Are you the guy who killed two hundred people?" I asked, "What are you saying!?" I have a lot of students that are actors and extras, and they always like to boast. You never know what they'll come up with next.

The Three Bigwigs of Canton

I N THE OLD DAYS IN CANTON, Ku Yee Cheong was the one that everybody talked about. He was a slim one-hundred-and-forty-pounder who could hit a stack of bricks and crack any one that you wanted cracked, or all of them. He and "Eagle Talon" Chan and a Tai Ji teacher by the name of Jang were known as the Three Bigwigs of Canton during the twenties and thirties. Ku was the head of the Jing Wu Association in Canton. Chan was the head of the Eagle Talon school. One time I saw Chan do something pretty unusual. He had a guy stand there, almost in a horse stance, and he did the splits right between his legs, and stood up in back of the guy. Can you imagine how much leg strength he had? I was amazed by the velocity of the movement and how much power he put into it. But he shook it off like nothing.

I learned some of Chan's Eagle Talon system, and I also learned some of Ku's martial arts. He taught Chan Kuen and Tam Tui. In the Jing Wu there are ten big forms that they teach. You'd go in there and have

Ku Yee Cheong.

forms classes but no real basics. You'd just go to class and follow each other. I was a kid, you know, and I would sometimes wonder, "Why isn't the teacher teaching us?" but that's how it was done in those days.

Tai Ji Quan

MY FIFTH BROTHER'S GODFATHER and his friend Choy who lived up the block both learned Yang style Tai Ji from Chen Wei Ming. Then they started teaching it all over Canton. I started at eight years old, and I think at nine years old we did a demonstration in some park—my brother and I were both there. I never learned the Chen form, but I studied the Wu form and the Sun form. I didn't like either of them so I stuck with the Yang style. I just play one position, that's it, the Yang form. It's the same form that I still practice today.

People always argue about internal or external martial arts, but it doesn't matter. They used to ask me, "How would a Gung Fu man

deal with a Karate man, or how would a Karate man deal with a Jujitsu man?" It's the man, not the style! It's how much intelligence he has and how well he's trained. And it also depends on what degree he's been trained, because nobody is on the exact same level. There's always a little something that changes the balance between two good fighters. If you're in that position, you have to learn the Chinese art of war from the book by Sun Tzu. Make use of it; it's the Chinese version of *How to Make Friends and Influence People.*

Chen Wei Ming. From *The Art of Taijiquan* by Chen Wei Ming.

Tai Ji training is not that much different from other styles, except that it's more about internal awareness and using the whole body correctly. The thing is this: it's always the legs that are doing the job. The legs or one leg is doing the job. One side of the body is doing the work. But it should be the same in Gung Fu. Except that the legs in Gung Fu use the external muscles and that's why people tend to choke up. Don't choke up, use expansion, extension, and explosion. Those are the three E's to remember.

If you talk about fighting with Tai Ji, it's always the circular motion that controls the straight movement, whereas the straight movement stops the circular motion. It's a catch-22, depending on where you are. When you say "circle," it could mean circle the wrist, circle the arm, or circle the body. When you say "straight," it could be anything that's straight.

A better way to say it is that internal movements are invisible. External motions you can see. Internal martial arts training aims to really stretch out the body on the inside. Keep the shoulders in place and just let everything move. Don't force it. Always use the legs to activate the movement. Pull and push on the inside. In the external styles, usually there is the same goal, only it's more of a muscular feeling. You lock the shoulders out, you feel your arms pump up, feel your head pull back, feel your body stretch out, and feel the lats tighten up. You also feel your abdominal muscles tighten up. Then you let go of the outside tension, keep the stretch inside, and notice what it feels like. There's a definite feeling. Both internal and external aspects have to be used.

This is why one of the laws of Tai Ji is to let the internal and external come together. That way you can use them as one. The three planes of the body—the left and right, the front and back, the top and bottom—all have to be used together. It's a hard thing to do because people have a lot of bad habits.

One time I trained with Yang Cheng Fu. It was in 1936, the same year that he died. He was teaching in the Canton City Hall. I went with Choy, who lived on the

Yang Cheng Fu. From *Essence and Applications of Taijiquan* by Yang Cheng Fu.

same block my family did and had studied with Yang. He invited me so I went, but I wasn't too impressed. It was partly because Yang was so fat and partly because everybody just did what he wanted them to. If he touched them, they would just fall back. Of course I was only a little tot then; I was just fourteen years old. They were also practicing joined hands, but I just followed the form with them. And I didn't like the way they did the form either, so that was that. It's like I say, we all have likes and dislikes, and everyone is different.

I've noticed that in Tai Ji a lot of people move their bodies too much. They're using the body to move the legs instead of letting the legs move the body. Since I was young, I've trained the legs to move the body. Take a look at a car. What moves first? The wheels do because they're on the ground. It's only common sense. I usually use this example: if you have a cart that weighs five hundred pounds, how does the horse get that five hundred pounds moving? He pushes against the ground, then he lifts up and goes. It's basic physics.

James Wing Woo teaches Tai Ji.

Daoist Martial Arts

THERE ARE THREE DAOIST FORMS of martial arts: Tai Ji, Xing Yi, and Ba Gua. I trained in Xing Yi and Ba Gua but I didn't like them. I liked Tai Ji better. Xing Yi is a little harder, more like straight Gung Fu, but it involves Daoist practices. Everything Ba Gua has, Tai Ji has too. So why practice Ba Gua?

One of the teachers that my brother's god-father hired was from Shangtung, and he taught us Xing Yi, Ba Gua, and Tai Ji. His name was Chang. His family used to be road guards —bodyguards who accompanied shipments from one city to the next. In China, martial artists would hire out on guard duty from one state to another. His family had been doing it for three generations, so he was a born fighter. He sometimes trained with a pair of marble spheres. He would throw one up and catch it with his neck, shoulder, or foot. But his main practice was either stretching or forms; no basic training.

Lien Wan

I GOT THE HELL BEAT OUT of me one time. So I made friends with the guy and asked him, "What do you train in?" He said, "I train with a teacher who's only got two students." I asked, "Can I go?" And he said, "I don't know, you have to talk to him." The teacher was a businessman by the name of Lu who told me that he had enough students already. So I had to bribe him—take him to the movies, or out to have tea cakes. After a year he said, "OK, I'll start training you."

Instead of putting wax on the floor like I do today, he poured cooking oil on the red tile floor. When you put your foot down on it, the shoe stuck to the oil and you couldn't pick that foot up. If you wanted to jump, you'd have to take all the weight of the body and lift it up just so you could move. But he could do it like he was walking normally.

He taught us a Northern system called Lien Wan. It means "repeating." It's not a system that anybody knew much about. He studied it back in the mountains when he was a young kid. If you propped up a pole on the floor, he could sweep his leg right into it and break it. But his legs were all black and I didn't want to end up like that. He would have us run through the horse stance moving drills, the box step [a square-shaped stepping pattern], and the "H" step [an H shaped stepping pattern]. I teach those patterns today to my Gung Fu students.

Another person who taught that was Wong Kit Man in San Francisco. They used to do it on a cement floor. They did the "H" pattern and the box pattern. Some people do it, some don't. But those that do

Box Step pattern. From *Secrets of Chinese Karate* by Ed Parker.

have a little bit more strength in their legs.

Without the power of the legs there's no punch. I don't care how much weight you can carry. The force has got to be coming up and going out. The mental focus is to try and learn to use the force of the bottom of the foot. Feel two pegs in the bottoms of the feet and connected to the floor. Pull and push on those pegs. Remember that you have to move them—you can't just stand still.

Not too many people emphasize the horse stance that I use. Everybody sticks their butt out. You can see it in all the books: they go down low, but they stick the butt out. I want the front half of the body pushing into the back. Use the dorsal flexion of the ankle with the toe and shin bone. And try to get the weight off the knees. That's the biggest problem with people. The knee is an instrument that's only got two meniscuses and two crucia, and they can break pretty easily. Learn to use the whole leg, not just part of the leg.

Using the Qi

QI IS ENERGY. Usually you discuss qi in terms of the prenatal qi and the postnatal qi. Prenatal qi is created when you are conceived—when you are a kid and the life first comes into you. Then there is the postnatal qi, which forms all the body: the trunk, the essentials, the organs, and so on. Prenatal qi splits into two points, the heavenly qi and the earthly qi. Heavenly qi is the breath you take in and out. Earthly qi is all the food and water that gives you the strength in your body and organs.

Photos by Eric Nomburg

James Wing Woo teaches the Six Count Salutation.

Prenatal qi is always in the body, you're born with it. In martial arts you pump the prenatal qi, keep it expanded, extended, and ready to explode. Then you use the joints to do the movements. You use the legs, through the body, to put the movements out. This is how you work with the qi.

As far as breathing is concerned, always breathe up and down the spine. Breathe in the nostrils, go down the spine, and exhale up the front. Feel the body expand on the exhale. Forget the inhale. It's like squeezing a ball with a hole in it: When you squeeze it, the air goes out, but when you release it the air goes in by itself. That way you never have to gasp for air. Just let it come in naturally.

You pump the prenatal qi by letting everything stretch out. Stretch out, extend your arm, then expand the arm. Let it expand and extend, don't freeze the ball joint. Feel the expansion, feel the tendons, feel the muscles. Give it time and it'll come, but don't contract all the time! When you contract, you become slow. When you extend, it just happens. Don't try to affect the prenatal qi, just let it move, let it change. The changes make the difference. Moving it left and right, up and down, keep it changing with the mind. Give it enough time, then you can do it. Qi is only a little part of it, you know. The body has to do it! The mind can't do it! The mind can only help and plan it. The body has to do what you want it to do, with muscle, bone, tendon, and nerves.

Sparring and Fighting

WHEN IT COMES TO SPARRING, my advice is don't do it. You build up too much respect for the other person and you don't really want to hurt him. Remember this: I want you to punch him all the way through up to your elbow. I don't want you to just hit him with a fist! And someone's going to get hurt.

Chinese martial arts aren't the same as Western boxing. The boxer goes for three-minute rounds, and then he rests. Boxers go for twelve rounds these days, not fifteen. But when you're in a fight you don't get a rest! You don't get any three-minute rounds. If you can't do it for real, you'd better go ahead and get out of here! Also, a boxer doesn't worry about anything from the belt down.

And as far as kickboxing, forget it. They're full of bull. If they're so strong and powerful, how come nobody ends up in the hospital? These kick boxers, they kick all right, but they don't know how to throw punches. And when you kick the leg out like that, you open up your treasure. Who's going to keep the treasure protected for you?

Suppose you train at a martial arts school and you work at a job to feed your family. One day you go to the school and they say, "It's time for the tournament and you are going to represent us." If you get hurt, who's going to take care of your family? Who's going to pay for that? And it can happen any time. Nobody is so good that they can't get hurt. If you're in there expecting not to be hit, forget it, don't fight.

Now, my student Leo Whang loved to go out salsa dancing. He went out with a girl one night and took her back to East L.A. where she lived. The girl handed him the key to open the door. But her boyfriend was in the house. When Leo opened the door, the guy put a two-by-four over his head! Leo just blocked it with the right arm and shot out an overhead punch. Whack! And the guy went down that way. It just happened on its own because he knew how to put out the punch.

You don't want to set your hands up and fight, or watch each other and

Photo courtesy of James Wing Woo

James Wing Woo and students, early 1960s.

dance around for ten minutes. They don't happen that way. Not real fights, anyway. So why should you do it? It doesn't make any sense!

This is not to say that you can't do techniques back and forth. I do have students do things like Chi Sau, or arm blocking like the Three Stars drill. The purpose is to get extension in the arm to get it pumped and learn how to roll the arm when you touch. Touch and roll. When you roll the bones, it takes the shock out of the impact. The blow doesn't hit as hard. If the arms clash, you're not rolling. The arms need to deflect off each other, to get the extension and roll. So when you touch somebody, you should be able deflect them away. The two-man drills still aren't fighting—they're training the arms, training the legs, training the body.

Anyways, put this down: be a professional student always. Master's degrees are not for us. Every man should be a professional student. It doesn't matter how long he has practiced. Learning is all right. Learn everything you want, you can always discard it. But don't think it's all true! Only believe half of what people say. Writers these days have

got their heads in the clouds, imagining they know everything. I don't know how many times I've re-written my book—over and over again for the last thirty years. It changes and I'm never quite satisfied.

Three Star drill. From *Secrets of Chinese Karate* by Ed Parker.

Tony Yang

Tony Yang, or Yang Shu Ton, has been based in the Midwest since coming to the United States from Taiwan in the 1980s. His school in Akron, Ohio, offers a full curriculum of traditional Chinese martial arts, including Qi Gong, Tang Lang Quan, Ba Ji Quan, Pi Gua Quan, Tai Ji Quan, and Ba Gua Zhang. His teacher Liu Yun Chiao, founder of the Wu Tang organization, was famous for his skill in the combined arts of Ba Ji and Pi Gua. Lesser known was his training in the Yin Fu style Ba Gua Quan of Gong Bao Tien, which he passed on to his students within the Wu Tang.

Tony Yang.

Mr. Yang has been a professional teacher for most of his adult life, and his dedicated students are a testimony to his efforts. Their forms are performed skillfully and powerfully. They undergo full training, including conditioning, two-person exercises, fighting, and weapons. When he performs, Mr. Yang makes it look easy, gentle, and effortless, the result of his many years of cultivation and thorough investigation of the arts. Even his performance of Ba Ji, known for its harsh stance training and hard power, looks open and relaxed while fully conforming to the style's high-speed and heavy impact attributes.

One cold winter's night in Ohio, I had the chance to talk to Mr. Yang about his martial arts training and teaching, particularly the Yin Fu style Ba Gua that he keeps particularly close to his heart. His common-sense approach to training and keen sense of humor made the discussion a truly enjoyable experience. Mr. Yang's wealth of knowledge and insight is open to any who make the effort to seek it out.

Tony Yang
DECEMBER 20, 2001

Self-Defense

IT'S COMMON FOR PEOPLE to ask me why I practice martial arts in this
age of machine guns and modern technology. One reason is that this
is our five-thousand-year-old tradition. Up until now mankind has had
to fight with the animals and with other men. People have always been
fighting. Nowadays people want to focus only on the art of it, so lots
of real fighting applications have been lost. They say, "Why train so
hard? Just use a gun, that's it." I disagree with people who try to change
it exclusively into an art, without the knowledge of how to use it.

We have to remember how to use it. It is still useful in today's
world. Even if someone threatens you with a weapon, sometimes if
you are good enough, and close enough, you will be able to win. Yes,
at a certain distance you would have to run. But if you are at close
range you can block and defend yourself; that's why they call it self-
defense. In Chinese we call it *Zu Wei Xu*. It means self-defense: not
just that you want to punch someone, but that somebody really wants
to hurt you and you want to take care of yourself.

You teach the martial arts with fighting applications to help the
student get more understanding of the correct way to move. Just like
when you first start to play Tai Ji, you wonder, "What's this movement for?" For instance, Da Hu Say from Tai Ji Quan: The original
fighting technique is to block down and punch across the body, but
the application is hidden. As the tiger comes in, you grab the tiger, *Da
Hu,* and you punch him right in the nose, *Say.* That's why it's called Da
Hu Say. Everybody says "Ah, this move is beautiful," but if they never
show you the application, how do you learn to use it?

Beyond fighting, I think the martial arts can teach what we call
Shou Yang, which is training how to take care of yourself. *Shou* means

"relaxed, learning to relax and find peace." *Yang* means "to take care of yourself." That's why when you learn the high-level skills relating to qi, if you feel bad here, or you feel bad there, you can train to strengthen that particular area. If you reach really high skill in martial arts you start to talk about *Shou Yang.*

We practice not just for application, but for our overall health. "*Shou Shen Yang Xin*" is the phrase that represents this. *Shou Shen* means "to take care of your body." *Yang Xin* means that you are very quiet, not easy to anger, relaxed. Lots of people who play martial arts get angry very easily. But among the Chinese martial artists you don't see people walking around like they're very tough or something. They tend to be quiet and relaxed.

First you have to follow the energy, which is called jing. Then you learn to change it into qi, which gives you power. Then develop your mind so that you can control your power. Once you control your power you can focus on *Shou Shen Yang Xin.* At the high level in Chinese martial arts is the stage of *Yang Xin,* very relaxed, at peace with yourself.

That level is very hard to reach. These days people have lots of distractions-computers, movies, things like that. They can't concentrate on so much stuff at once, and that's why they want to know how fast they can learn martial arts. But you can't do it that way. Martial arts are learned step by step. You can't jump ahead. Then you understand why it takes that long. If you move too fast sometimes you can't control what you develop, and you can harm yourself.

Tang Lang Quan

M Y EARLY TRAINING was in Tang Lang Quan [Praying Mantis] with Master Su Yu Zhang. If you read the history you'll see that Praying Mantis comes from Shaolin. A man named Wang Long played Long Fist, part of the Shaolin system. When he would try to compete or figure out how to use it, he always lost. One day he didn't feel good because every time he fought a certain guy he would lose. He decided to go to the mountains and relax. Up there he saw a praying mantis grab a *zun yao,* a cicada. After he saw that he thought about how the mantis' arms were very sharp and how it grabbed that cicada real tight so that it couldn't move. He took the praying mantis home with him and fought with it using a blade of grass. That's how he created the hundred and four hand movements that he put into his Shaolin form.

Within the Praying Mantis system you see all kinds of different attacks. Some things look like Ba Gua, others look like Shaolin or Tai Ji. He put in moves from many styles and mixed them up. Praying Mantis is only three or four hundred years old but has become very famous in northern China. It's also very dangerous—that's why in Taiwan they don't teach it in high school or junior high. It's very fast and very powerful with lots of groin kicks and strikes to your eyes,

Photo by Andy Lianto

Tony Yang demonstrates Praying Mantis.

chopping your throat—they all use that, so they can only teach it to college students or older. If they tried at the high school level somebody might get hurt bad. Twenty years ago when I first came, not too many people knew of it in the United States.

Martial Arts Are All the Same

AT THE TIME THESE ARTS WERE CREATED, there wasn't a separation between internal and external style. Martial arts are martial arts—they're all the same. At a certain point they decided to try and classify styles as internal and external because it's easier for competition. If he plays slow and you play fast, you can't compete together. Praying Mantis is called external but it has the *qi gong* exercises, it has the breathing exercises, it has all the different exercises. They grab and hit, just like Ba Gua. If you do the tree or post training, it's exactly the same except that it's done faster, more straightforward, no turning, you just go back and forth on a straight line. If you see any kind of Praying Mantis form, they don't go around and around in a circle, they just go straight out and back: one, two, three, four, that's it. I think this is more in line with the Northern Long Fist styles.

When I was learning, we never talked about what's internal or external. These are all just martial arts. Some people might say Ba Ji is external. No, Ba Ji training is different; you must breathe in and out eight times in every posture. Just like in Tai Ji, you breathe in and breathe out in a rhythm. But instead of one movement to one breath, Ba Ji requires eight breaths per movement. Ba Ji still has the *qi gong* training exercises within it. You need that in any kind of martial art: you have the form, which is the outside, then you go inside of it.

If on the first day you come I teach you about breathing, it will take you a long time to develop. If I teach you the kicking and punching to build up the muscle and tendon so that the outside becomes stronger, then later you can go to the inside. Once you make the inside strong, then focus on the outside again and you will have more power. The best way is to practice in a cycle, inside, outside, inside, outside. That way the inside and outside all come together.

Every system has internal and external training. For example, our system, Wu Tang, has specific post training for Ba Gua, Ba Ji, and Praying Mantis. I have the posts at my house in the back yard and can use them to train any kind of movement. Any style can use post training. It makes your skin and muscle harder; your whole body gets stronger. But you should wait until you are able to hold all your Ba Ji stances first—that's where you develop the internal. Then the strength inside can start coming out, and you will get more power that way. Once your insides are stronger, when you work the outside and you hit the post you won't get hurt anymore. If you have lots of qi inside, you can fall or get hit pretty hard without getting hurt. Ba Gua post training uses nine poles. Ba Ji and Praying Mantis use three to emphasize the triangle or straight line. Every system has different training methods.

In the big picture, all martial arts should have the external and the internal within them. In this regard, all styles are the same. Just like in Chen's Tai Ji— the form comes from the Tai Zu Chang Quan. Originally it was used to teach the army to be powerful and strong. Later on they made changes and added breathing and *qi gong,* then they called it Chen's Tai Ji. Chen's Tai Ji is done both fast and slow, just like we play Ba Ji. Xing Yi too, alternating slow and fast. I don't know whether this is true for the southern styles, but I know that among northern styles, internal and external are all the same.

The outside movements work the inside of the body. When you lift the arms in the Ba Gua Eight Mother Palms form, you are lifting the internal organs. You can feel it in the chest when you pick the heart up. You need to exercise this area: you lift it up, you turn and come down. You don't want your heart to pump really hard. You need to relax and do the kind of exercise that's not going to hurt you. The internal way is to gently squeeze and relax, squeeze and relax. That's why it takes a long time to learn the internal styles like Tai Ji or Ba Gua—it may take ten years.

Conditioning

CHINESE MARTIAL ARTS CONDITIONING is hard training—you're jumping, you go down in low stances, lots of kicking, lots of different training drills. The walking around the circle is like running if you go fast. If you are jogging, there's nothing in your way, you just run. When we train, it's like running but you have a post in front of you just like an enemy. You have to block so it's not just running. Your body movement has to be precise, like a boxer. They train body movement using a heavy bag. We do the same thing but we use the post.

Ba Gua has weight training as well. You can hold an iron ring or a sandbag, wear a weighted vest that wraps around the waist, or do other simple stuff like holding a brick during your practice. Anybody can grab two bricks—most all houses in China have brick construction. In Ba Ji you can wear metal plates on the body; that's a form of weight training as well. Grandmaster Liu wore different weights for three to five years at a time without taking them off. If you are lifting regular weights you hold them up for a minute then you put them down. With this training they lay all the weight on and never take it off. They eat with it, they sleep with it, they play with it, it's always there. This training has to be step by step, though; you can't just do everything at once or it can hurt you. Train step by step and you'll get better and better.

Photo by Andy Lianto

Tony Yang demonstrates Ba Ji's Collapsing Palm technique "Ta Zhang."

Just like Eagle Claw training, if you grab somebody and your fingers aren't strong enough, why did you grab him? When you grab somebody you have to make sure to hurt him. Make sure he's lost power, draw him out then move. In Eagle Claw training we would fill jars with sand little by little and carry them to build finger strength. We had probably ten or twelve different exercises. Your fingers get strong and your grab gets very hard.

The Kidney Energy

B A GUA PRACTICE begins with the Xiao Kai Men form to open up the kidney's energy. This relates to Chinese medicine, which studies the five elements: Water, Fire, Wood, Metal, and Dirt. Although there are five, every one of them is dependent on water, just like your body. Your body is around eighty percent water, but if this water isn't exposed to fire and heated up, then nothing can move. The kidneys contain what we call the Jing energy. Between the kidneys we must form a gate so this energy can flow freely.

It all begins as a fetus in the womb. At this stage you breathe through the umbilical cord. Your vitality comes through this cord into the Life Door, what we call the *Ming Men*. After birth, when the cord is cut, this supply is stopped. At this time the newborn must breathe air through his mouth and nose. If you watch a newborn baby breathe, he still breathes down at the belly button. He never breathes up in the chest, and he always breathes very deeply. Around two years old or so, he starts getting thoughts in his head: "Oh, I want this, I want that." He starts thinking, and that's when he

Photo by Andy Lianto

Tony Yang demonstrates Chen's Tai Ji.

starts to close down more and more as the years go by.

When we play Ba Gua we want to go back to how we were when we were young. For this we must open the gate between the kidneys. Any kind of martial art can help you do this, but the Ba Gua Xiao Kai Men training makes it go faster. After you play it for half an hour, you are sweating everywhere. That's the water of the body being stirred with fire. The doors inside you have been closed for a long time; to open them you need steam. You want to boil the water inside. Once the steam comes out you're open.

That's why every time we play, we finish with the horse stance. You've already walked around doing all kinds of twists, so you've started a fire. When you do horse stance that heat starts coming up. You can feel it—your back gets hot, your chest, your knees, your feet, your hands. When you first start, maybe only your back, maybe only your knees, but that's OK, the rest will come in time. That's why it's very important to open the gate between the kidneys.

When you make the steam come up, you are filling the body with energy. You can use it for fighting, but health comes first. Make sure your heat is balanced. If there's too much fire, you need water to cool you down. For fighting, you can use your concentration to bring heat anywhere you want in your body—that's the qi—but you have to train your mind to do this. If you want to punch somebody, you start thinking of your hand getting bigger and bigger, and the qi starts coming. Your hand becomes like a sledgehammer. People who have developed a lot of qi can be very powerful; if someone tries to punch them it's not going to hurt. Their body becomes like a balloon.

Jing, Qi, Shen

GRANDMASTER LIU used to emphasize the idea of *Jing, Qi, Shen.* Jing, Qi, Shen is very important in the martial arts. Jing is the energy, Qi is the breathing, and Shen is the mind. If you don't have your mind focused, it doesn't matter how good you are—you are like a robot going through the motions.

To develop the mind in Chinese martial arts you have to learn to focus. When you punch, wherever your hands go your mind goes there too. When you focus your mind you become quiet, more relaxed. Just like when you put on music that you really like, you think about the melody and you become very relaxed. That's the way you play the forms—it's just like music, that's why we call it art. If you play fast and sudden, it's over and done quickly. That feels like a firecracker. It looks good but inside you don't have anything. It's better if you play alternating fast and slow, fast and relaxed, like music, up and down so you have a sense of feeling it. This helps make you more quiet and relaxed.

The Jing, Qi, and Shen have to be trained together. But you have to start with the jing. Jing supplies your power from the kidneys. Once you can play the jing then concentrate on the Wei Qi. If you practice that then the internal qi can come out.

It's your mind that controls it. So if you feel like your heart is beating fast, you need to breathe, bring the qi down, relax. When you think about it, your qi will move to wherever you need it to go. This can help you relax and start healing. That's what we call internal healing. But the fighting's different—when you are fighting you want the heart's power to come out. The heart is symbolized by the fire element, and fire always expands outward. That's why when you punch with an uppercut, the other hand covers down over the heart. If you punch down, that emphasizes the water element, as water tends to go downward.

The first thing to understand is that qi in martial arts refers to the air you are breathing. If you don't have air, you die. Secondly, qi is your power. When you breathe in you save power; when you breathe out you deliver power. Your power follows this flow. Very simply put, qi is just breathing. It depends on how deep you breathe. You can generate more power if you breathe deep, but lots of people breathe into their upper chest. You're not relaxed if you breathe with the chest alone. Try to just relax and breathe deep into the Tan Tien.

If you want qi, you've got it inside of you. If you don't want it, you'll never know it's there. You can't see qi, but you breathe it! To use it you have to train the inside of your body. Follow a teacher and learn how to train it properly. Everybody knows the breathing and *qi gong* exercises—there are thousands and thousands of different methods. It's also important that you breathe in and out of the Tan Tien. But you don't want to talk about it too much at the beginning; people don't understand it.

Developing the qi gives you power and makes your mind stronger. Just sit and see how many times you can breathe while thinking about it. Breathe in, breathe out. When I started my master told me to breathe in and breathe out. I began to breathe but right away I started thinking about things: "My girlfriend is waiting for me!" My heart was beating fast, you know, stuff like that—I couldn't relax. If you can do two or three breaths while concentrating, that's good when you are just starting. Later on you will build it up a lot until you are very relaxed. Just like when you play Tai Ji, about halfway through the form you start to breathe faster, and you start to think about something. You started out very quiet, then halfway through you started thinking too much. You have to build more concentration so you can finish the whole thing in a relaxed state.

Liu Yun Qiao

THE FIRST TIME I met Grandmaster Liu, Master Su took me there, and I just watched the guys do different stuff. At that time Master Su learned there, too. He said, "Do you want to try it?" I said, "Yeah, sure." I liked it so I joined the Wu Tang school. To start Grandmaster Liu taught me Xiao Ba Ji. It helped me a lot, not just making my legs stronger, but my body started getting very healthy too. We trained every day in Ba Ji. It wasn't very hard to learn; it has very simple, easy movements. The hardest part was the legs—there were lots of stances. Xiao Ba Ji emphasizes horse stances.

If you didn't try to hold the horse stance for three minutes or more, he would never teach you more than that. If you stayed and tried hard and he liked you, he would teach you very slowly. I probably spent three years on the Xiao Ba Ji form alone. He would never say what more he had. If you started to progress and learn more and more, you could begin to see the extent of his system. But the old masters would never tell you much. Grandmaster Liu never said, "Oh, I have this form, and I have this form." I just learned the stuff and shut up, that's it. If you became good enough, he would teach you more—that's the old-fashioned way.

We didn't ask questions, we were too afraid of him. If he wanted to teach me a form, I learned one. If he wanted to teach me two, I learned two. I just kept practicing. At that time I had already practiced Praying Mantis for a long time, but the Ba Ji was new to me. I started to like it because it made my Praying Mantis stronger and more powerful.

Grandmaster Liu hardly ever did the applications in class. If you asked him, he would show you a couple of moves, but if he hurt you one time you didn't want to ask again! One of his favorites we call Ming Hu Ying Pa Shan. It means Tiger Climbs to the Mountain. It's all straightforward, straight punches and elbows. If you saw Grandmaster Liu do a demonstration, you saw Ming Hu Ying Pa Shan, and number five, Shou Yu Lan Chuei,

Photo courtesy of Tony Yang

Tony Yang with his teacher Liu Yun Qiao.

which is two punches and then one across the side, like a cross. Even though it's a strike, when you do it in slow motion you can see the twisting of the arm, which is very powerful. He trained lots of secret service officers in Taiwan, Vietnam, Malaysia, Singapore, and Indonesia. He taught the president's bodyguards for a number of countries. They would come to Taipei to learn and return to their home country.

Ba Ji was originally taught only to the king's bodyguards. The bodyguard and teacher of the last emperor (Pu Yi) was Grandmaster Liu's gung fu brother, Huo Deng Dun. Throughout time all the Chinese kings learned martial arts, because they had to defend themselves in an emergency. They had bodyguards, but if somebody got through them to attack, the king would have to do something himself. They needed a good master to teach them. During the late Ching Dynasty, all these teachers were Ba Gua masters. Right now in Taiwan and China, Ba Ji is popular. Every secret service officer trains in the Ba Ji system.

Ba Gua Quan

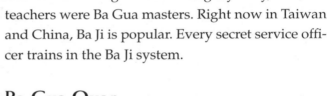

IN REGARD TO BA GUA, you can call it both Ba Gua Zhang and Ba Gua Quan. Ba Gua Quan is correct because Ba Gua teaches the use of the fist. In the Ba Gua Fist form, the whole set uses the fist. Ba Gua Zhang is also correct because there is the Ba Gua Palm form. There are a number of different forms in the Wu Tang Ba Gua system: Ba Gua Tight Hand, Ba Gua Lian Huan Zhang, Ba Gua Leg, Ba Gua Fist, and the Ba Gua Combination Fist. More people say Ba Gua Zhang because everybody sees the internal practice, where someone is playing the circle and never using the fist in it, only the hand. The original name was Ba Gua Quan because they didn't just use the

Yin Fu.

open hand; sometimes they used the fists, too. And if you have two weapons, that's also using the fists!

Most styles of Ba Gua contain similar elements. I think the post training is what makes our style unique. In the movies the heroes go up on top of the posts for a fight, but the real training is done standing at the base, working against the post. This is a very important part of the Ba Gua system because Ba Gua has a lot of close-range fighting, right at the body where your opponent is very close and you are practically touching. So that's why when you want to train to fight up close, you have to get a post there in front of you, where your opponent would be. If you don't have it, you don't have it! If you train only using your hands, you'll never make it. You have to use a post just like a boxer needs a punching bag.

In the Yin Fu style you practice with nine posts. At the basic level you have to do the walking while performing Guen Zhang Zhen Guo, the arm-twisting exercises, using the posts. There is a lot of Zhang—palm training—like Quan Zhang, or An Zhang. It depends on where your strike goes, as there are different palm positions to hit with. For this type of training you have to use a post or you won't have any power! You won't be able to hurt anybody! If you just practice the hand forms alone, a strong opponent will stop you from using your techniques.

You can play a set form or single movements among the posts. Usually we make a combination on the spot, or else just play single palm movements, whatever you need to work on. We do lots of Guen Zhang Zhen Guo, lots of arm-circling movements. In a real situation where someone tries to grab you, no way can they hold on if you circle the arm correctly.

Tony Yang demonstrates Ba Gua.

If you use the circular walking he can't follow you, either. If some-body grabs you and pulls very fast, you just walk the circle and they open up right away.

What makes Ba Gua different from other martial arts is the circle walking. Lots of people go straight forward, but Ba Gua is about walk-ing in a circle. So when the attack comes straight into you, you are already walking. He thinks you are one place, but you are already somewhere else. If you walk faster than he can track, you are always making him confused. We train this a lot for fighting.

Walk the circle until you see the hole in his defense. It works well because you are used to it from playing Ba Gua. You've trained to go back and forth and in a circle, so you don't get dizzy. But the other guy has never played Ba Gua. He's confused because he has to make a small circle as you make a larger one outside. As soon as your move comes, he's wide open because when he kicks and punches you have already moved to the outside. That's why they call sometimes call it Ba Gua Yu Shen Zhang, because it's like swimming on land.

Our Ba Gua system contains lots of different kicks: heel kicking, side kicking, outside and inside kicking, and tornado kicking. Yin Fu style has a saying, "Shu Shan Liang Yi." *Liang Yi* means "two kid-neys." *Shu Shan* means "four elephant trunks," referring to the two arms and the two legs. The Yin Fu Ba Gua training philosophy is guided by the idea of Shu Shan Liang Yi Ba Gua. The Xiao Kai Men form initially strengthens Liang Yi. The Ba Gua Combination Fist, Ba Gua Hand, and Ba Gua Leg forms strengthen the outside of the body. Then with Ba Gua Nei Zhang Eight Mother Palms, you go back inside the body. Four forms train the inside, four forms train the outside. We start with Liang Yi to make sure the kidneys become strong. Then develop your arms and your legs. Then go back inside again.

When you first start training in Ba Gua, you should just let go and play in a free and relaxed manner. Later on as you get better you start to do stances, you turn the body back and forth, and do the breathing exercises. At first you do the walking and arm-turning while breathing freely—that's as far as you can understand initially. When we train, we always start with the basics—just breathe freely. Then later as the student gets into it we show him breathing and that kind of stuff. Martial arts breathing is more deep, relaxed, and slow.

You focus on the breath when you play slow. Sometimes you play fast and you can't think about it. When you want to get the body to heat up, you should train Ba Gua fast. Then slow it down again, and every time you turn you breathe in and breathe out very slowly. Your movements follow the breathing. When my hands go out I breathe out, when they come back in I breathe in.

The advanced stage is more difficult. You still have to work on breathing but I focus more on the feet and Tang Ni Bu, which is the "mud slide step." When you play Ba Gua, as you walk the circle you can think about where your qi is going at any time. Every time you twist the body before you turn you can stop and breathe, in and out three times before you return to the circle. In, out, in, out, three times, that will make a big difference in your training. It makes you sweat more. First you tighten up the area around your kidney, then relax it. Tighten it again, then relax it again. In every single movement you have to think about the breathing while focusing on your hand when you are walking.

At a certain point you begin to feel heat come right to your chest. It's like you are in the steam room, the body gets so hot. Qi is all over the place. It's very fast in coming, but it takes a long time to get good, especially in Ba Gua.

The Five Elements

THE KIDNEYS ARE VERY IMPORTANT, especially in wintertime when the kidneys are naturally very weak. So that's when we have to train them. Spring is the time to train the liver. In summer train the heart—everybody knows that the heart is paired with fire. In fall train the lungs. Using all five elements you can put your health together. The kidneys help every other internal organ because everyone and everything needs water. So you can play anything during each of the four seasons, but the kidneys are very important and remain central to your training.

You break the elements apart when you want to hurt someone. Fighting is dangerous. Think of the elements of water and fire. I punch you downward, this is water; then I come right up with an uppercut, this is fire. That can hurt you really bad because as I take your mind to one place, the second hit comes up where you don't have a defense. For fighting strength Ba Gua uses the heart, the lungs, the organs and the internal power. It's not that you put your mind in your heart when you do that—just let it go free. But when you train, make sure your heart energy is strengthened, then you can use it.

In Western boxing, it happens too but they don't talk about it. They use an uppercut and the other hand naturally covers down. You can feel that they use the heart power, but they don't talk about it this way. They say that they just use the waist. Every time you throw an uppercut your other hand drops downward, covering the chest. This is because your heart qi is coming out. Your heart is weak when its power is coming up, so you have to make sure you protect it.

Jie Mai and Dian Xue

O UR SYSTEM OF PI GUA strikes with *Jie Mai*, which means "to chop" something. This stops the blood flow for a second so you feel numb in that place. It's not a hard strike; you just touch it on the spot. When I chop that area you can't move your arm very well, so I can hit you much more easily.

Dian Xue is different, it means "to point," like touching a point. Ba Gua uses Dian Xue, but few people train this any more. In Ba Gua you learn to use the Dian Xue Zhen, the Ba Gua needle. I have one in the office. It's a small metal bar with a ring in the middle. Put the ring onto the middle finger, so that it can swivel back and forth. The bar should be as long as your hand. At one time the King's bodyguards used them because you weren't allowed to bring weapons into the

Photos courtesy of Tony Yang

Tony Yang demonstrates Ba Gua Deerhorn Knives from the Tight Hand form.

King's presence or he might decide to cut your head off. If somebody swings a weapon you can block it easily with the needle in the palm of your hand, then go into him. Because the ring is loosely fitted you can throw it as well.

Concealed weapons are one of Ba Gua's specialties. That way the King can't see it, because you can't have weapons in the royal palace, but the guards still needed to ensure the King's safety.

Grandmaster Liu taught us a form using one Dian Xue needle in each hand. The Ba Gua Tight Hand form is used to train the Deerhorn Knives and the Hook Swords. The Ba Gua Combination Hand is used to train the Dian Xue Zhen. Ba Gua Combination Fist trains the Pa Gua Bi, the Judge's Pen. Dong Hai Quan, the Ba Gua originator, said that every form can be done with weapons in each hand. Everything's done in pairs—two swords, two deerhorn knives, or two Pa Gua Bi's.

Dong Hai Quan was very good at double weapons as well as throwing. One story is that one day while he was smoking opium a very loud bird was making a racket outside. He threw his pipe and killed it with one shot.

Xu Xue

It's not necessary to learn acupuncture for martial arts, but my teacher did tell me the locations of *Xu Xue,* the death points. If your life is in danger you might have to strike one of these points on your opponent's body. You must learn how to punch, where the points are, and at what time they are vulnerable. Everybody has four different death points. Sometimes you hear how somebody punched someone not very hard, but he killed the guy anyway. He just hit him accidentally at the right time in the right place. There are four points with different times when they are open to attack. Picture your blood moving through you like a snake. As a snake has a head, the blood has an area where it is centered at any given time. In the afternoon, the blood's "head" should go to the heart.

All the old masters knew enough medicine to be able to fix themselves. They knew all that kind of stuff. They knew where they didn't feel right, and where they felt good. But they didn't become doctors to fix everybody else. They didn't have the time to do that, they were already teaching martial arts! So they taught their students how to fix themselves. I was there when Grandmaster Liu fell down once, and his knee became very swollen. The next day we went to practice and everything was back to normal. He was walking pretty well. I asked, "How did you do that?" He said, "I fixed myself, don't worry about it." All the masters knew that. You should know that too if you play martial arts.

Ba Ji Quan's Eight Alignments

THE BA JI SYSTEM requires that you make sure that all parts of your body are kept in the right place. The head, shoulder, elbow, hand, the *Wei Yi* (which means the tailbone), as well as the *kua*, knee, and foot are all in the correct position. Inside you must keep all the organs in the right place, too. If your shoulder is lifted up, you are picking up your internal organs with it. That's why we say *Shan Ten Shwei Zhou*, "the shoulder has to drop." Because when the shoulder drops, everything inside relaxes. If you pick up your shoulder on one side, your liver and gallbladder are lifted. If you pick up the other side, your heart gets lifted. It's not comfortable. When you feel that you are not comfortable inside, it means that something is

Tony Yang demonstrates Ba Gua.

wrong with you at one of the eight different places. In Ba Gua it's the same thing: you have to make sure the eight different places are relaxed and comfortable.

Wai San He and Nei San He

THE SIX OUTSIDE HARMONIES are called *Wai San He,* and the six inside harmonies are called *Nei San He.* They apply to different things, depending on what you're talking about. In terms of the sword: your eyes, your sword, and your hand have to be together. The internal body is looked at in terms of the five elements, and the ideas of Wai San He and Nei San He are usually more concerned with weapons.

In sword training you have to make Wai San He and Nei San He combine together, just like when you punch. You have to make sure

Photo by Andy Lianto

that your eyes, your hand, and your foot act at the same time. Same with the elbow, the knee, and your eyes— they have to be moving at the same time. Your shoulder, your hip, and your eyes—all three have to be together. Everything goes at once. You can't just have two go together while you look the other way. You wouldn't know if you hit him or not! If you strike here while you look away, maybe your mind goes away too, and you're not concentrating. You have to focus on where you are going, where your hands are, where your feet are. You should be there, and your eyes should be looking there. Which means your mind is there.

Tony Yang practices Kun Wu/Ba Ji Sword as taught to Liu Yun Qiao by warlord and older Ba Ji Kung Fu brother Zhang Xiang.

East and West

WHETHER THEY ARE CHINESE OR WESTERN, I teach all students the same. I just make sure you want it, and if you do, you can come and get it. But you have to take the time to do it correctly. For instance, Praying Mantis and Ba Ji have the stances—make sure these basics are done right. Horse stance is the most important stance. We call it the "Long Life Stance." This practice can heal you. All the stances, but particularly the horse stance, done the right way will heal your body anywhere you are hurt.

I've noticed that lots of the American students are really enthusiastic about martial arts. In Taiwan I taught at a college, and they play because they just happen to go to that school, but they always put more importance on book learning. Over there if you aren't good with the books your parents will get mad at you. The martial arts are always secondary. When people asked me, "What kind of teacher are you?" and I said, "I teach martial arts," they looked down on me. It's not very popular to teach martial arts professionally. Some students want to learn because they might teach it later. But ninety percent do it just to be healthy themselves—they don't want to fight. Because they have a good job coming when they graduate college.

It's harder for American kids to learn martial arts because after they're eighteen they have to go to work to support themselves. In Taiwan I didn't work while I was training. My Mom supported me. I just learned martial arts and that was it. Where I come from if you really want to do it, your parents pay for you to learn. Here the kids have to go to work and get money to come here and practice. I feel very good here because the students try very hard to learn, so I have to make sure they learn good martial arts skills the right way.

I first came to Ohio because I'd never seen the snow. In Taiwan there is no snow unless you go up to the mountains to see it. But I never had the money to pay the fees, or get a car up the mountain.

When I first came here I saw the snow and I liked it. Here the four seasons are very clear. Plus, it's a lot easier to learn English. If I had gone to Los Angeles or New York, all the Chinese people speak Chinese! So I stayed to learn how to speak English, and after that I got married, and since my wife's American I'm stuck here! But I like it here a lot; the people are all very nice.

Persistence

I TEACH A LOT OF OLDER PEOPLE at the hospital. On the day I teach they have lots of energy, but the next day it goes down again. They don't practice every day so they fall back. That's why in martial arts you have to keep at it continually. If you were young when you started, when you're in your nineties you still have to practice. If you stop and you want to practice again and get back into good shape, you've got to go back to the beginning. Just like when you stop for a couple of weeks, and you start again, you're sore all over. That's why day by day, every day, you have to keep doing it.

My training schedule begins with Ba Gua in the morning. It gives me more energy, helps my internal organs, and makes me stronger. At night I train Ba Ji very hard. It makes me tired so it's easier to get to sleep. If you train Ba Gua at night it can make it hard for you to sleep. You can have too much energy if you play it the right way. The morning is the best time for breathing, Ba Gua, Tai Ji, and other internal practices so you can go to work with lots of energy, feeling very happy. Lots of people do the Xiao Kai Men form every morning.

Tony Yang and Richard Yang practice a Ba Ji two-person application.

Ba Gua and Ba Ji both have internal and external elements, but Ba Gua is more internal. It contributes more to your internal health. It gives you lots of energy inside, which can then come out. Play Ba Gua ten times, just the straight-line form, slow and relaxed. Then after you finish, hold horse stance for two minutes and that's it. When you go to work you'll have a lot of energy. Then at night play Da Chung, the big spear, play anything that builds stronger muscles. Train hard at night, get tired, and go to bed.

Chung Wen Fu Wu

I N THE OLD DAYS there was a phrase, "*Chung Wen Fu Wu.*" It means that the poor people study the books, and the rich people play the martial arts. The poor study so they can take the examinations and raise their station in society, whereas the rich can afford to hire good masters to teach them. If you look at the background of the famous masters, they were all rich people. How could the average person afford to hire a teacher like Gong Bao Tien? Gong Bao Tien smoked opium, and that costs lots of money. Only rich people would have the gold and gifts necessary to hire him. One of his students was a general. He would catch criminals and pay for his lessons with the money and goods he confiscated. That's how they got the old masters to teach the good stuff. If your master isn't real happy, what's he going to teach you? Their attitude was, "Don't waste my time!" Masters like Sun Chow, Ni Sun, "Da Qiang" Li Shu Wen, the big spear master—if you don't have lots of money, don't even think about it! He was a big shot, he taught the generals Li and Zhang. They paid big money for him.

Now my master, Liu Yun Qiao, his family wasn't rich, but his father was able to hire Li Shu Wen as a teacher. His father was the mayor of their town so he had some money, and he gave Li a place to stay and hired a cook for him. Liu's father said, "You don't have to do anything, just teach my son martial arts, and I'll give you five pounds of gold."

When we teach traditional martial arts these days, it's not about the money. We teach because we love the martial arts and we want to pass it on. I could make more money in the restaurant business, but I don't want my stuff to get lost. That's why I have to pass it on for everybody that likes it. In the old days a master would try you out and if you were no good, he'd kick you out. Because they didn't need the money! They didn't need you for anything. But now the traditional masters want their arts to survive. They have to teach anybody, everybody. Once you open the doors of a school, you have to make sure people come in so you can make enough money to pay the bills. Right now in America it's very hard. I know lots of friends, masters that can't make much money.

That's why they have good martial arts in China and Taiwan. People hire you and say, "Come teach my son, I'll give you a lot of money."

That way he can defend himself and he can have a healthy, strong body—this is something that they want. Chinese martial arts are the result of five thousand years of development, and the martial arts themselves are like gold. The Chinese people like to keep this tradition alive.

Photo by Andy Lianto

Tony Yang demonstrates Chen's Tai Ji.

Zhao Da Yuan

My meeting with Mr. Zhao took place during one of his yearly seminars in San Francisco. After many years of training in a gamut of Chinese fighting styles, Mr. Zhao became a disciple of the famous Ba Gua Zhang master Li Zi Ming. He appears in the landmark translation of Li's book, Eight Diagram Palm, *demonstrating the forms of the Liang Zhen Pu style. His book on* chin na, *the controlling techniques of Ba Gua, was also very well received in the West. Since that time many practitioners have sought out Mr. Zhao's instruction in the complete traditional art of Ba Gua Zhang. Mr. Zhao's seminars cover many aspects of the style and include forms, weapons, and fighting instruction for his senior students. I was able to attend a class on the Ji Ben Gong, or basic training, of his Ba Gua. We learned the stepping methods, characteristic body shapes, and twisting exercises, as well as some of the foundational fighting tactics of the art.*

When I had the opportunity to attack Mr. Zhao, he lightly deflected me and moved to the side while retaliating with a palm strike to the face. I was impressed with his speed and timing, and particularly with the fact that I hardly felt his deflection before I was at his mercy. With a gregarious smile he proceeded to show me a few more angles of possible deflection and the various techniques that would come off of them. After watching him demonstrate his chin na *skills on some of his long-term students I could see that his playful, kindly attitude didn't prevent him from unleashing a multitude of very effective locks, throws, and pins with great enthusiasm.*

Mr. Zhao puts his emphasis on the character-building possibilities of the Chinese martial arts. Without this key aspect, he feels that all fighting techniques are pointless. A style that teaches only how to harm others is no more than barbarism and cannot be truly counted among the traditional Chinese Wu Shu.

My interview with Mr. Zhao was ably translated by San Francisco martial arts expert Bryant Fong. His careful translation made all of Mr. Zhao's answers very clear.

Zhao Da Yuan
OCTOBER 28, 2002

Beyond Techniques

O UR PRIMARY PURPOSE for learning Wu Shu, or Chinese martial
arts, is not to go out and fight. The first thing is to improve our
health and decrease internal resistance. Then we study philosophy,
anatomy, and medicine. Through the martial arts practice we learn
how to be harmonious in society, how to be a useful person, and how
to interact respectfully with others. And of course we can participate in
activities with others like martial arts competitions and performances.
Then, at the end, we can talk about how to use it for combat. Real Wu
Shu has to have all of those components. Wu Shu is a bridge to philosophy, a bridge to society, a bridge to medi-
cine. It also creates a way of meeting people—
you get a lot of good friends out of it.

You cannot look at martial arts as being just
punching and kicking techniques. It's a kind
of cultural art, and if you limit it only to technique it has no use. Chinese martial arts contain the most essential parts of Chinese culture
—especially Ba Gua Zhang, because Ba Gua is
derived from one of the cultural treasures of
China, the *Yi Jing* [Book of Changes]. The *Yi
Jing* of course is from the Daoist religion. It is
used to create the basic techniques of the style.
Through centuries of examining nature, Chinese thinkers came to the conclusion that things
in the universe interact based on the theories
of the *Yi Jing*. Human movement is based on
that theory, too.

Zhao Da Yuan and his student Bryant
Fong.

Wu Shu is the art of not fighting, not an art of fighting. The character "Wu Shu" in Chinese is made up of two words, "stop" and "fighting," therefore it means "stop warfare method." People in the west think that Wu Shu is only for fighting, but that's not the true purpose of martial arts. All different aspects of Chinese life are included in the study of Wu Shu. When you are studying Chinese martial arts you are supposed to be studying five different things at once: philosophy, culture, medicine, physiology and fighting techniques.

Philosophy and culture includes how we lead our lives, how we write calligraphy, and our history. If you understand the name and background of a movement it shows you part of the history of the Chinese people; it gives a description of the movement in literary terms. When you study martial arts you also study the cultural meaning—it's not just the straight translation of a movement's mechanical description. For instance, the name of one Ba Gua move from the Sixty-four Linking Palms form which looks like an elbow strike is about the Daoist deity Guan Gong lifting up a weapon.

The practice of Chinese martial arts also has to follow the theory of Chinese medicine; you can't go against that. Part of the practice is for health, to nurture your qi, your energy, and to heal yourself. Not only for sickness but also if you get cut or injured, you must learn how to heal the body.

Another aspect involves investigating the natural way that the body moves. You have to learn anatomy and understand the biomechanics, and understand all the aspects of how the body is put together. For instance, at first when you are driving your car, you need to understand how to operate it. It's the same thing when you are fighting somebody: you need to understand what a human body is capable of. Just as you learn which things might wear out in a car so that you can be aware of them and repair them, as a human being you have to know your weaknesses and your strengths.

The last category is fighting techniques, the art of how to attack and defend. If you are just going to do the fighting, a gun is much more effective. If you want to achieve that purpose only, you don't need to study Chinese martial arts.

Finding a Teacher

SINCE NINE YEARS OLD when I began practicing martial arts, I've learned from many different teachers. I've practiced Mi Zhong, the "Lost Track" style, Shaolin Lo Han, Tang Lang, Tong Bei, Ba Ji, Cha Quan, Tai Ji, and Xing Yi. The very last style I learned was Ba Gua Zhang. When you seek out a teacher at first it depends on what method of training you like. Decide if you prefer to practice slow or fast.

The other factor is whether you meet a skilled teacher, which is very special. If you meet a teacher who treats people well, whose technique is very good, and whose theoretical explanations are succinct, you should follow that person. I didn't learn Ba Gua because I thought it was better than Xing Yi or Shaolin or any of the rest—it's because of my teacher. I learned Ba Gua because the teacher could explain the theory and the application. Most importantly, he was a very good person and he treated people well.

It's the teacher that makes the difference. No one can say what style is better—they're all good. For instance, if you see someone doing Xing Yi and you say, "Oh that's not very good," you cannot say that Xing Yi is no good. It's the person doing it that's not very good. It's how you practice it that matters; it's up to your ability.

If the style wasn't any good, it wouldn't have been preserved. Time will decide what's good and what's not. So people shouldn't say, "I will learn this style because this one's better," or "This style has some secret that this one doesn't." It's only a matter of how well you understand it, and whether the person teaching you can really explain it, so that you can bring out what that method is really about.

Wu De

I F YOU LEARN JUST TECHNIQUE, then you're not really learning Wu Shu. The philosophy and how you are supposed to live your life are much more important. That's why when we learn Wu Shu, the first thing we learn is *Wu De*, meaning "ethics." Without ethics, your technique cannot be very good. You might be able to punch really hard and jump really high, but if you're a terrible person and your relationship to the world at large isn't good, how can you say your martial arts are any good?

The purpose of martial arts is to teach you to actually be a good person, and with good technique you are able to interact with the people of the world. When you need it you have it to use; when you don't need it you can use other methods to deal with people. Martial arts isn't merely a matter of physical technique but mental training, cultural training, all of those things that make a complete art.

Li Zi Ming.

One of the problems with Wu Shu as we're propagating it throughout the world is that our method of spreading it has faults. In past times, my Ba Gua teacher Li Zi Ming and others like Wu Tu Nan of Wu style Tai Ji had a very advanced cultural understanding of literature, art, and philosophy. In modern times too often we associate Wu Shu with what we see in competitions or fighting. All we see is that small aspect of it. Especially modern Wu Shu athletes—many of them spend all their time learning techniques but spend no time studying culture and philosophy. That even goes for many of the teachers in the United States now. The main thing that many Wu Shu athletes know is the way it is supposed to be done physically. There is no mental development.

Most people who study Wu Shu these days think, "How am I going to win a tournament, how am I going to be the best?" But with that attitude you can't say that you've studied Chinese Wu Shu. All you've learned are a few techniques. Without the rest of it, it really means nothing, it's just an exercise. If you're talking about real Wu Shu, you have to study all aspects of how you're supposed to lead your life.

Divisions

CHINESE MARTIAL ARTS have many ways to distinguish and define themselves in different categories. Internal and external is a concept that was not developed until after the Ching Dynasty when people started saying that the Buddhist styles are external and the Daoist styles are internal. So there were religious reasons for separating the two arts—their traditions are different.

In the past the main way to divide martial arts was between north and south. That was created not on the basis of some scientific explanation of why they are different; rather, it was convenient to separate them that way. There's also another way to separate Chinese martial arts: Buddhist arts from India and Daoist arts from China. However, recent studies have found that Zhang San Feng, the so-called Daoist monk who founded the internal martial arts, was actually a Shaolin monk. He also influenced Da Mo with his writings and thought, which Da Mo later included in his teachings.

You can't divide it between Shaolin and Daoist, because over time they've thoroughly interacted with each other. During the Republic there was a writer named Tang Hao who specialized in the history of Chinese martial arts. He decided that those ways of dividing it according to religion were inaccurate. In his writings he said that we could separate it into internal and external arts, but it's not that all internal styles are Daoist from Wudang, or all external methods are from Shaolin—it's not divided that simply.

Tang Hao proposed yet another way to categorize them. He decided that external martial arts are the ones that develop the external body's muscles through exercises and weight lifting—things that increase your physical strength. This is one way of increasing the body's health. Whereas internal arts practice should circulate your qi, increase your life, and heal your body.

But you can't say, for instance, that Praying Mantis doesn't have internal practices, after all, they talk about qi and how to control it. But they're external practice is completely different from Tai Ji. External styles are aimed at exercising your outside body. And through that you increase your qi. Whereas internal methods use development of the qi to strengthen the body.

Internal moves from qi to form, and external moves from form to qi. Tang Hao decided that this would be the best way to explain the difference. So you have to be careful about what you think internal and external are. Their method of reaching the same goal is different. You can't think that since you're practicing Choy Lay Fut or Hong Gar there's no internal—this isn't true. The emphasis is just a little bit different. If you think because you do Tai Ji there are no external elements and you don't need strength, that's not real either. You need to develop the body as much as the qi.

A lot of people say that Wudang martial arts include Tai Ji, Xing Yi, and Ba Gua. But that's an inaccurate description because none of them came from Wudang mountain; they all developed somewhere else.

Basic Skills of Internal Martial Arts

I F YOU WANT TO PRACTICE internal martial arts, the first thing you need to do is learn how to circulate your qi and improve your health. To do that you'll have to spend a lot of time learning the basic internal arts techniques—that means walking the circle for Ba Gua and standing for Tai Ji. First you need a healthy body that's in good enough shape to learn. You need to have a body that's able to do a lot of activity, so you develop strength, speed, internal strength, flexibility, and liveliness.

Until your body is healthy and able to accomplish many types of physical activity, you aren't even ready to learn internal arts. One thing the Chinese say is that in order to do internal martial arts you have to be able to do external first. So when doing your exercise you have to increase your conditioning. If you're very strong but you get tired quickly, the strength is useless. It's the same as having a little boat and putting a large cannon on it: when it fires, you capsize the boat. The first thing you need to do is take care of your own health and make the body strong. Then you can talk about learning martial arts.

If you're older you can't do external styles because your body can't take the tough conditioning and movement, so you have to go a different way in order to achieve the same result. That's why older people practice the internal arts—it's somewhat easier on their bodies.

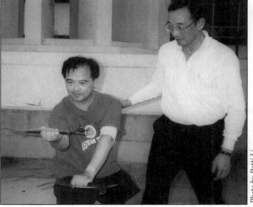

Many external martial artists when they get older begin to realize that they need to develop their internal body to preserve their health. But they have a good place to start from because they already have strong physical ability and they can learn it very rapidly. Many of them as they age begin practicing Tai Ji. Once you've been a Wu Shu athlete, you should eventually move on to Tai Ji.

Master Zhao teaching Crescent Moon axes.

Tien Ren Hu Yi

WHEN YOU REALLY PRACTICE Ba Gua circle walking, you don't think about anything in particular. But to get to that point you have to understand that I and the Universe, nature and I are one. See yourself as if you were the Earth turning around the Sun. First the Earth moves around the Sun, but it also turns on its own axis. Since the Earth is doing that, I follow along with it. In other words, as nature is going in a certain way, I am going in the same way. If nature is the Earth going around the Sun, I am also doing the same kind of thing; my motion is matching that of the universe. Heaven and Earth are harmonious. They are combined into one.

There is a phrase, *"Tien Ren Hu Yi."* It means that Heaven and Man are combined into one. Ba Gua movement follows cosmic movement. Atoms spin that way, planets spin that way, galaxies go that way, even our molecules go that way, so why should your movement not be the same? Are you going to go opposite of that?

Ba Gua fighting philosophy is exactly the same as cosmic law. For instance, if we are in combat, how do I deflect your attack? First of all, when we're fighting I'm not going to collide with you, I'm not going to stand in the way, I'm not going to block it and hit you back. Instead I redirect the attack, I rotate. When you want to come toward me I will let you go by; when you want to retreat I will go with you. It's not like you punch me, I block you and hit back—that's not harmonious. If you come forward I redirect you, or I just avoid you, because I never want to clash with you. I don't oppose you—I allow you to do what you want to do. The idea in Shaolin style is that if you punch me, I block it then hit you back. Ba Gua is different. When you try to hit me I'm not there.

The Poems of Ba Gua Zhang

TRADITIONALLY, THE NAME of each move goes into a poem, and if you understand the poem you understand the technique. The poem has a story that goes with it; that's why if you learn real Wu Shu you have to learn all of that.

I'll give you one example. The first move in the Deerhorn Knives form is called White Carp Plays in the Waves. When you do the movement it's supposed to look like waves going up and down. So if you have no idea what the story is that goes with it and you simply translate it, you might say that it's just a pretty name. But no, your movement is supposed to emulate the wave hitting the beach and bouncing up into the air then coming back down. When you do your movement you have to make it look like that. You need to feel like you're moving in the same way—this image is really important.

One of the reasons for having names within the forms is to describe the form, or *Xing*. The *Xing* is the form, *Yi* is the mind's intent, and *Shen* is the spirit. For instance, the name "White Carp Plays in the Waves"—even the first word has many different meanings. Just that one character describes different movements. The form of the writing itself communicates the essence of the movement. The next thing to discover is its literal meaning—not just the shape of the character, but the actual meaning as well.

Its meaning is that the move should be done like a fish swimming in the ocean, then jumping out of the water. It describes the movement and how your power is supposed to be transmitted. The wave hits and comes up suddenly. It also describes the spirit in which you do the movement. Your movement begins like that and then the wave is falling and the fish jumps out of the water. That's White Carp Plays in the Waves, just one name of one movement.

When you've mastered the form, the understanding of it and the spirit within it, you've internalized it and you perform it like that naturally. You go from form to no form. When you learn it you count the moves out, one, two, three, but when you have mastered it, you no longer have a form. So from form you go to no form, *Bu Xing.* Like the Daoist concept of *Wu Wei,* it becomes automatic.

You cannot see spirit. There's a saying in Xing Yi that once you've mastered the five elements there are no elements. At the highest level you cannot tell what is going to come next. In Ba Gua they say that form has no form, technique has no technique. When you have technique, yet there is no technique, then you can have big success. When you have no form, when form and essence have become the same thing, then you can say that you've mastered martial arts.

Ba Gua Zhang's Weapons Practice

I T IS SAID that the weapon is an extension of your arm. It includes its own history, culture, and technique, just like the unarmed forms.

Photo by Patti Li

Sifu Fong and Master Zhao walking the Ba Gua with Crescent Moon axes.

Only instead of using my body to deal with you, I use an external instrument to deal with you.

For instance, if I want to learn to use a *dao*, or broadsword, the first thing I need to know is how it can be used, and which side is sharp. Every weapon you pick up has a different use. If you haven't studied the technique of a particular weapon, when you pick it up you won't know what to do with it.

The purpose of learning a weapon is not to use it to fight. It's to try and understand its usage, what's special about it, and all the techniques that go with it. For instance, I can support a broadsword with my hand and not cut myself; with a straight sword, or *jian*, you can't do that or you'd cut yourself. Straight sword doesn't have that technique.

Holding a weapon gives you additional options, so you have more techniques than you would have empty-handed. Learning to use a weapon would also help you understand your empty-hand techniques. It's an extension of your arm, so a weapon presents other ways in which your arm can actually move. Think about it this way, too: if both hands are active, because you have to use both hands moving one or more weapons, it's good for your mental development. It teaches your mind to concentrate and coordinate various movements.

Scientific Exploration of Qi

THROUGH EXPERIMENTS IN CHINA scientists have begun to use the scientific method to study qi. There are two ways of investigating it. They've used Kirlian photography to photograph the body, and they've found that you have an aura around you. This aura is related to your physical condition. Since we can see it with technology, we can now examine it with pin-point accuracy.

Scientists now also have an instrument that measures the resistance of your skin. In some places the resistance of the skin changes so you can actually mark and follow where various points are. Interestingly,

Ba Gua diagram.

the latest research shows that where the acupuncture points are, the resistance of the skin drops, which can be mapped. The points when connected correspond to the meridian system of Chinese medicine.

This tells us that when you act, your mind coordinates with your body. It has to move energy in order to move your body. So the connection between your mind and the different parts of your body causes energy to flow. They've found that the practice of moving this energy in your body is able to increase your longevity and improve your health.

Since qi has something to do with your mind, the state of your mind has something to do with the state of your health. There's a lot of literature, even in Western medicine, that is now coming to the conclusion that the mind/body connection is related to the condition of your health.

A human being is made up of a number of different elements. First is your genetics. The next thing is what you eat. You convert that into your energy and your body's growth. What you are eating is very important to what kind of qi you have overall. The things that you eat are converted into energy, and the energy helps you feel a certain way. What you eat is what you are. So it's very important that you eat correctly; otherwise you don't energize your body properly.

Your form, *Xing,* is determined from your essence. Your form is made up of your bones, your organs, your DNA, and then you add things like food to it. All those things make you up and affect your qi flow, your energy. Your body also interacts with the environment. For instance, if you don't get sunshine then your body doesn't work properly. If you don't eat, the same thing happens. Many different things make up the body's qi.

The Chinese divide qi into many different types. There's the guardian qi that surrounds and protects your body, there's the qi in your kidneys that determines your longevity, and there's the qi that goes through your meridians. All of these different types of qi have to be fed by your respiration, your eating, your exercise, and your interaction with the outside universe.

You're born with a certain energy, the original *jing* which the body transforms into the original qi, but it's through food and interaction with the outer environment that you increase the energy inside your body. That's why we exercise, that's why we eat—to increase our qi. Your work throughout your life is to increase this energy through interaction with the universe, through exercise, through practicing Tai Ji, Qi Gong, Xing Yi, and Ba Gua. This is to increase the ability of your body to work in society. So those two things, what's within you and without you, come together to make qi.

Chinese martial arts developed in ancient times, but we're beginning to see that what we understood back then often fits quite well with modern science. In the past the ancients determined the types of energy that flow through the body and extrapolated that this is how the organs work. With modern science we begin to understand the body more thoroughly; we begin to understand that there are molecules, atoms, there's DNA, and different chemical reactions in the body. However, our basic living experience of the human body is the same as the ancients understood it.

You can't use qi to hurt someone else. All qi does is improve the health of your own body, making you stronger so you can be more efficient with your technique. Shooting out your qi is completely impossible. Qi can only make your bones and body stronger, so that your technique can be connected together faster through your training and tactics. You can fire up all your nerves at once, and everything is faster. Using qi what you train is your speed, your strength, your mind connection.

Some people say, "Oh, I can project energy and hurt you." No, your body cannot do that. The only thing I hit you with is my bone and my muscle. Qi has nothing to do with it, except that it strengthens my bones and increases my flexibility and efficiency, so that my strike can utilize the maximum potential of my body. However, I cannot give you qi. There's a lot of misunderstanding in the martial arts world over what is qi. It's not a mystical thing—it's very scientific and based on real results.

You Shou

MASTER LI ZI MING never boasted about his fighting skill. However, when he did demonstrate, his ability was extraordinary. One of his favorite techniques was called *You Shou*, or the "Asking Hand." Asking Hand means I give you a hand and you try to answer, and the answer is that you get whacked. In other words, I extend my hand, you do something, and I do something back to you. This technique is based on my understanding of how you will react to what I do. I base my movement on the fact that I know what you will do, and when you do that I apply my technique. It's a trap!

One hundred percent of the technique is forcing you to do what I know you're going to do. As I advance, I know you're going to do something, and as soon as you do it I apply my technique. This is based on my understanding of your psychology and reactions. I can change if you try to escape, so you can never get away from me. I'm always one step ahead of you. While you are thinking about the first technique I have already thought about the second technique.

Another part of You Shou is the idea that "if you don't come I ask you to come." And you come based on what I require you to do. When you die you won't even know how you died. That's what Master Li was most famous for. That is Wu Shu at its highest level—it's what you should strive to achieve. So it's not one technique, it's beyond technique. I invite you to come. When you come, you come because I require you to do whatever it is you do. Then when I reply, you won't even know what happened to you—it'll be too late.

If you apply a technique and then I apply a technique, and so on, that's not real Wu Shu. It is the type that doesn't cooperate. It's not harmonious, it's reactionary. Real Wu Shu means that I lead you to do what I want you to do, then you follow me. That brings us back to the beginning of our discussion: The full study of Wu Shu must include the philosophy, physiology, medicine, and science. When we talk about Wu Shu we should talk about the complete study. Wu Shu is not about hitting and blocking and punching.

Practice for most people means you have fun, you're able to interact with others, you get some exercise, and make yourself healthy. However, if you are talking about the real study of Wu Shu, to become a Wu Shu master, this is what you have to do. Unless you bring all of these aspects together, all you know is a bunch of techniques and that doesn't mean anything.

Appendix
Albert Liu

Since his arrival in San Francisco from Shanghai, Albert Liu has limited his teaching to a small informal group. Although well-known for his landmark translation of Sun Lu Tang's famous Xing Yi Quan Xue, *Mr. Liu has always kept a low profile in the martial arts world. I sought him out to hear some of his insights into the history and practice of one of his martial arts,* Liu He Ba Fa, *also known as* Water Boxing.

I first found his class practicing the Water Set on a windy afternoon in downtown San Francisco. The form seems to combine the flowing nature of a Tai Ji Quan form with many classical Chinese fighting techniques. In addi-

tion to giving intense instruction in the postural requirements of the form, Mr. Liu is quick to demonstrate its martial functions. After a fascinating conversation about martial arts history and culture, a field in which he is exceedingly well versed, Mr. Liu agreed to write a short introduction to the history of Liu He Ba Fa for the readers of this book.

Photo by Eric Nomburg

Albert Liu demonstrates Liu He Ba Fa.

A Brief Survey on the Origin and Development of the Water Set

By Albert Liu, June 19, 2002

Martial arts are one of our most precious inheritances from ancient China. Many events relating to martial arts are recorded throughout Chinese history. This began in the time of the later Chun-Qiu period of the Zhou Dynasty (1122–255 B.C.) when Kong-Zi (Confucius 551–479 B.C.) proposed that archery be put into the Six Arts. In the dynasty of West Han (206 B.C.–A.D. 23), about one hundred years B.C., Si Ma-qian wrote the famous book *Shi-Ji* (Historical Records), in which were included biographies of many chivalrous persons with martial arts skills. In the dynasty of Sa Guo (The Three Kingdoms, A.D. 221–265), the famous doctor Hua Tuo (died in A.D. 208) invented a special physical exercise called Wu Qing Xi (The Motions of Five Kinds of Animals). In the dynasty of Northern Wei (A.D. 386–535), the famous monk Da-Mo (Bodhidharma, the Buddhist missionary who came to China from India in the year A.D. 526) invented the martial arts set called Five Boxing. This Five Boxing exercise forms the first typical complete set for physical training located in the historical records and thus became a precedent in martial arts history.

In the Liang Dynasty (A.D. 502–556), during the Epoch of Division Between North and South, there was a special martial arts school founded by Han Gong-Yue. This special martial art was inherited and promoted by Chen Ling-Xi, who was from South China. The practice of this school was characterized by attaching importance to the movement of internal strength in accordance with outer performance. This is the origination of the category "Internal Training" and the initiation of the so-called school of Internal Martial Arts. Chen Ling-Xi collected what he had learned from his practice into a book called *Ming-Shui Ji*. In the Song Dynasty (A.D. 960–1278), Chen Bi was the famous inheritor of this special martial arts school. He gave this special set the name of Xiao Jiu-Tian (Small Nine Heaven), which basically includes fifteen movements. He left two writings: "Yong Gong Wu Zhi" (Five Inclinations of Practice) and "Si-Xing Gui-Yuan Ge" (The Restoration of the Four Properties).

In the Tan Dynasty (A.D. 618–907), a Taoist called Xu Xuan-Ping from South China learned a special martial arts form from Yu Huan-Zi and called it Sa-Shi-Qi. Sa-Shi-Qi means "thirty-seven," because it has thirty-seven stances. The outstanding poet and historian of the Tan Dynasty Li Bai (A.D. 701–762) was familiar with him. The set Sa-Shi-Qi is nearly the same as Chen Ling-Xi's Siao Jiu-Tian. This special school was later transferred to Song Yuan-Qiao in the Ming Dynasty (A.D. 1368–1644). He left his writings: "Song Shi Tai-Ji Gong Yuan-Liu Zhi-Pai Lung" (The Origin and Branches of the Song Style Tai-Ji Practice) and "Ba-zi Ge" (Eight Words Song).

Albert Liu demonstrates Liu He Ba Fa.

In the same Tan Dynasty, there was another person called Li Dao-Zi, also from South China, who was versed in a special martial arts form which he named "Xian-Tian Fen," meaning "A Priori" or the Prenatal Way. This special school was transferred to Yu Qing-Hui and Yu Yi-Chen in the Song Dynasty (A.D. 960–1206) Later this school was inherited by Yu Lian-Zhou and Yu Dai-Yen in the Ming Dynasty (A.D. 1368–1644). This is another branch of inheritance.

There was yet another branch of similar martial arts forms in the Tan Dynasty, the representative of which was Hu Jing-Zi. He named his own form "Hou-Tian Fa," which means "A Posteriori," or the Postnatal Way. It was inherited by Song Zhong-Shu and transferred afterwards to Ying Li-Hen in the Ming Dynasty. The similarity of the two branches "A Priori" and "A Posteriori" lies in paying attention to the transmission of internal qi while practicing the forms training.

A prominent martial arts master named Chen-Bo was born at the end of the Tan Dynasty (A.D. 618–907). He lived through the Five Dynasties (A.D. 907–960) and died during the Song Dynasty (A.D. 960–1206). He lived more than one hundred years, from about A.D. 880 to 989. He had various names, including the alternative name of Tu-nan. However, he liked to call himself Xiao-Yao Zi. Xiao-Yao means to be leisurely, free and unfettered. He was a friend of the famous philosophers of the time: Chen Hao, Chen Yi, and Zhu Xi. He was devoted to the practice and research of Tai-Ji theory and wrote a book called *Tai-Ji Tu Shuo* (The Theory of the Tai-Ji Diagram). He summarized the principles from his research and practice and titled it "Liu-He Ba-Fa." Because it is as natural as flowing water during its performance, his descendents gave it the beautiful name of "The Water Set." When the second emperor of the Song Dynasty, Song Tai-Zong, called Chen-Bo in to the palace to have an interview, he was about one hundred years old already. The emperor asked him many questions. He answered clearly and fluently.

Photo by Eric Nomburg

The emperor asked him to stay at the palace as an instructor and advisor, but Chen-Bo graciously declined. The emperor could not but send him back to the mountains after giving him the imperial nominated name of Xi-Yi. *Xi* means "strange and precious," *Yi* means "old and healthy." So he was a strange and precious senior.

Among master Chen-Bo's disciples, two are

Albert Liu demonstrates Liu He Ba Fa.

rather famous and noted in the records. One is called Jia De-Shen. He had the Taoist name Fire Dragon. The other was called Li Dong-Feng. Both of them inherited master Chen-Bo's knowledge and the essence of this set and transferred it to later generations. Among a new generation, almost four hundred years later, there was a person who received and developed this precious set and promoted its resurgence with his own special form. This person was called Zhan Sa-Feng.

After verification according to different historical materials, Zhan Sa-Feng, with the original name Zhan Jun-Bao and the Taoist name Yu-Xu Zi, is now known to be of the Song Dynasty. He was indifferent to fame and wealth and had no interest in the official career given by the authorities. After declining an official position and dispatching his property to his clan, he traveled around the country.

He stayed at Hua Mountain in northwestern China for several years to deepen his own self-training. Afterwards, he left Hua Mountain and lived on Wu-Dan Mountain in central China, leading a hermit's life.

Zhan Sa-Feng was versed in Shao-Lin Gong-Fu from a young age. After contacting the internal Gong-Fu transmitted from the line of Li Dong-Feng and Jia De-Shen, he changed his ways and turned to internal cultivation. He concluded four principles about his own system: First, control motion with repose. Second, conquer hardness with softness. Third, surmount swiftness with uniformity. Fourth, overcome the many with the few. Thus Zhan Sa-Feng composed a complete internal Gong-Fu system. Because this internal Gong-Fu was explained with ancient Tai-Ji principles, it is called Tai-Ji Gong-Fu by the people.

At the beginning of the Ming Dynasty there were various persons inheriting the arts from different branches of esoteric Gong-Fu ancestors. Among them were Song Yuan-Qiao from the Xu Xuan-Ping line, Yu Lian-Zhou and Yu Dai-Yen from the Li Dao-Zi line, and Ying Li-Hen from the Hu Jing-Zi line. These persons had been at Wu-Dan Mountain to meet each other and promote their research and training.

The most important inheritor of the Ming Dynasty was Wan Zong-Yue in the middle of the fifteenth century. Tai-Gu County in Shan Xi Province was his hometown. He learned Tai-Ji Gong-Fu from a Taoist in the Jing-Tai Taoist Temple at Bao-Ji County in northwest China. This Taoist was a disciple of Zhan Sa-Feng. Wan Zong-Yue left the famous article "Tai-Ji Quan Lun" (Thesis of the Tai-Ji Boxing). He had two important inheritors who were active in the succession of the internal martial arts. One was Chen Zhou-Tong, who was from southeast China and spread the Tai-Ji Gong-Fu in southern China. The other was Jian Fa, who was from northern China and spread the Tai-Ji Gong-Fu in the northern regions.

Between the fourth and the sixth decade of the sixteenth century, Zhan Sun-Xi was the most prominent practitioner. He had only a few students. Among these students, Yi Jing-Quan was the foremost. He

Photo by Eric Nomburg

Albert Liu demonstrates Liu He Ba Fa.

had more students, and Dan Si-Nan was the most famous one among them. Dan Si-Nan handed down his Tai-Ji Gong-Fu to Wan Zheng-Nan, who became the most eminent one in the early part of the seventeenth century. After his death, the famous historian of the Ming Dynasty, Huang Zong-Xi (A.D. 1601–1695) wrote an epitaph to memorialize Wan Zheng-Nan called "Wan Zheng-Nan Mu Zhi Ming" (The Epitaph of Wan Zheng-Nan). Wan Zheng-Nan's prominent disciple Huang Bai-Jia, the son of Huang Zong-Xi, inherited Wan Zheng-Nan's Gong-Fu and left behind his writing, "Nei-Jia Quan Fa" (Internal Boxing).

In the middle of the eighteenth century, Gan Feng-Chi inherited this Tai-Ji Gong-Fu through Huang Bai-Jia and became the most distinguished of his time. From Chen Zhou-Tong to Gan Feng-Chi, all came from the south of China. So they are generally called the southern branch. Others who came from northern China also inherited this Tai-Ji Gong-Fu. Most of them were Taoists. They always concealed their own names and shut themselves off from society. Even up to the middle of the twentieth century the Taoists in the Jing-Tai Taoist Temple at Bao-Ji County could perform Tai-Ji Quan.

Photo by Eric Nomburg

Albert Liu demonstrates Liu He Ba Fa.

The Bai-Yun Taoist Temple in Beijing has existed since the twelfth century. It is said that Zhan Sa-Feng once lived there. In the twenties of the twentieth century, one of the Taoists in this temple named Hu Yu-Xi was a Tai-Ji Quan master in Beijing. Hu Yu-Xi said that all the Taoists of the Bai-Yun Taoist Temple practiced Tai-Ji Quan as their routine exercises along with their religious courses. This is a tradition handed down since the Ming Dynasty. From the Taoists in Jing-Tai Taoist Temple during the fifteenth century to the Taoists in the Bai-Yun

Temple in the twentieth century, all of these belong to the northern branch of Tai-Ji Gong-Fu development. However, it is hard to find a clear line of inheritance between generations of the northern branch. This is because most of the Taoists lived a hermit life separated from the common people and each generation held their training set as a special treasure which should be kept secret.

Qi Ji-Guan (1528–1587), a famous general of the Ming Dynasty in the middle of the sixteenth century, noted the essential Thirty-two Styles of martial arts in his writing *Ji-Xiao Xing-Shu* (The New Book of Ji-Xiao) based on his experience of Gong-Fu practice among his army and the people.

In the age of "Wan Li" (1573–1620) during the Ming Dynasty, the Tai-Ji style of Gong-Fu was introduced to the Zhao-Bao town of Wen County in He-Nan Province. This introducer was Jian Fa. Jian Fa was born in the year 1574, a native of the Zhao-Bao town. He liked to play martial arts from the time he was a boy. In the last decade of the sixteenth century, Wan Zong-Yue went to Zhen-Zhou County in He-Nan Province to do some business. When he was on his way through Zhao-Bao town, he saw the young man Jian Fa playing martial arts, which gave him a very nice impression. After Jian Fa's hearty petition, Wan Zong-Yue brought him to Shan-Xi Province to teach him. Because of old age, Wan Zong-Yue let his daughter do the teaching work instead of himself and he did the corrections. Seven years later, Jian Fa came back to Zhao-Bao town, and Tai-Ji Quan thus rooted there and was called Zhao-Bao style afterwards. Among the foremost students of Jian Fa, one from his hometown was named Xing Xi-Huai, and another one came from Chen-Jian-Guo Town named Chen Wan-Ting. Xing Xi-Huai handed down his Gong-Fu to Zhan Chu-Chen, who transferred it to Chen Jing-Buo and Wan Bao-Qing. Their inheritor was Zhan Zong-Yu, who transferred it to Zhan Yan. Among the students of Zhan Yan, Zhan Ying-Chan and Chen Qing-Ping were the foremost.

Chen Wan-Ting, born in the year 1600, was a native of Chen-Jia-

Guo Town of Wen County in He-Nan Province. He absorbed the movements of the Thirty-two Styles handed down by Qi Ji-Guan and also learned the Tai-Ji Gong-Fu from Jian Fa. This is the predecessor of the current Chen Style Tai-Ji Quan. Chen Chan-Xing (1771–1853), a descendent of Chen Wan-Ting, inherited what Chen Wan-Ting had handed down and became a coach in his home area.

Ma Yung-Sheng, born at Liao-Chen County in Shan-Dong Province, learned the Tai-Ji Gong-Fu from Zhan Yan while Zhan Yan taught his Gong-Fu in Shan-Dong Province. Afterwards, Ma Yung-Sheng invented his own style, called Ba-Gua Tai-Ji Quan.

In the nineteenth century, internal Gong-Fu was practiced by different persons with different stances, movements, and usages. In the long run they all formed their own special styles and sets. Thus the internal Gong-Fu was developed into different branches, the important three being Tai-Ji, Xing-Yi, and Ba-Gua. At the end of the nineteenth century and the beginning of the twentieth century, the Tai-Ji branch was again subdivided into different styles, in which the prominent ones are Zhao-Bao style, Chen style, Yang style, Wu style, Wu' style, Sun style, and Ba-Gua Tai-Ji style.

In the year 1896 there was a nine-year-old boy named Wu Yi-Hui. His father was a rich government officer who associated with various prominent friends. One of those friends called Yan Guo-Xing was a player of the secret Water Set. Wu Yi-Hui's father ordered him to learn this set from master Yan at home. Two years later, in 1897, his father's friend introduced another person, called Chen Guan-Di, who was also a master of this secret set but from a different branch; this man also taught Wu Yi-Hui at home. Master Chen Guan-Di had learned this secret set from two persons. One was a monk called Da-Yuan, the other was a Taoist called Li-Chan. The boy Wu Yi-Hui learned this special set from both masters at home for about ten years.

In the year 1905 Wu Yi-Hui was nineteen years old. He passed the entrance examination at the Bao-Ding Military Officer Institute. At that time my father was nominated as an instructor at this institute, and the master Sun Luo-Tan, who is the inventor of Sun style Tai-Ji, was an officer in the army. They recognized each other's skill in the martial arts.

In the year 1936 master Wu Yi-Hui (1887–1961) came from northeast China to Nanjing, the capital of China at that time, and was engaged by the Nanjing Central Martial Arts Academy as the Dean of Studies. Thus he became a colleague of the famous masters Zhan Zhi-Jian and Wu Jun-Shan, who were the originators and organizers of the Nanjing Central Martial Arts Academy. It is master Wu Yi-Hui who made this secret Water Set known to the public and began to teach it after this special legacy was hidden away from most people for over a thousand years.

At that time, there was a private martial arts organization in Shanghai called the Jing-Wu Athletic Association. Invited by this association, master Wu Yi-Hui came to Shanghai to impart this set that he also taught in the Central Martial Arts Academy in Nanjing. Master Wu Yi-Hui raised many students. Among them Li Dao-Li and Lian Zi-Peng were out of the common. After the Chinese-Japanese war, Lian Zi-Peng moved to Hong-Kong and Li Dao-Li stayed in Shanghai. I learned this classical set from master Li Dao-Li in the seventies. I also learned to play the Rod Set from him.

Photo by Eric Nomburg

Albert Liu demonstrates Liu He Ba Fa.

The principles of this Water Set include six fundamental combinations and eight special ways. They are as follows:

Six Fundamental Combinations: LIU-HE

The coincidence between body and heart.

The coincidence between heart and mind.

The coincidence between mind and Qi.

The coincidence between Qi and spirit.

The coincidence between spirit and motion.

The coincidence between motion and emptiness.

Eight Special Ways: BA-FA

Qi:	Run Qi to concentrate spirit.
Bone:	Hide strength inside bone.
Form:	Naturalize the imitations.
Harmony:	Holistic movement.
Suspension:	Raise up the Du channel.
Agility:	Round continuation.
Empty:	Spirit in empty.
Changing:	Out of tracing.

The alternative name "Water Set" comes from the characteristic resemblance between the movements of this set and flowing water. This mutual resemblance may be noted as follows:

Running forever without stop.

Melting together without separation.

Slowing, whirling, speeding, and rushing.

Inside and outside matching each other.

Penetrating stones by drops.

Spreading throughout the sky and covering the earth.

The specialties of the Water Set include the following four points:

Hardness and softness mutually compensate.

Void and solid mutually compensate.

Slowness and swiftness mutually compensate.

Activities and tranquility mutually compensate.

The functions of the Water Set can be concluded as the following four effects:

Strengthen body and maintain health.

Remove illness and prolong life.

Protect from harm and defend from attack.

Develop internal Qi and foster true energy.

Photo by Eric Nomburg

Albert Liu demonstrates Liu He Ba Fa.

北方元陵七烝壬
癸亥子水其神元
武.其色皂.
旗心黑邊白爲金
生水不可用黃犯
土剋水.

Illustration from *New Book on Records of the Army* by Qi Ji-Guan.

Please see
http://www.humboldt.edu/~jd02/neijiaquan
for more information.